THE
FUTURE
NOW

THE
FUTURE
NOW

HOW TO USE PREDICTION IN YOUR LIFE

DEREK & JULIA PARKER

Mitchell Beazley

For Lori and Fraser Reid
with love

Executive editor   *James Hughes*
Senior art editor   *Paul Wilkinson*
Editors   *Julia Gorton, Nigel Rodgers*
Art editor   *Rupert Chappell*
Picture research   *Pat Hodgeson*
Production   *Ted Timberlake*

Edited and designed by Mitchell Beazley International Ltd
Artists House
14-15 Manette St
London W1V 5LB

Typeset by Litho Link Limited, Welshpool, Powys, Wales
Origination by South Sea International, Hong Kong
Printed by Graficromo, S.A., Cordoba, Spain

British Library Cataloguing in Publication Data

Parker, Derek, *1932–*
The Future Now: how to use prediction
in your life.
1. Fortune-telling – Manuals
I. Title   II. Parker, Julia, *1932–*
133.3'24'028

ISBN 0–85533–721–4

Contents

Foreword

To know "what the future holds" has been one of the perennial desires of humanity, whether in a stone age cave or the booth of the gypsy at a fairground today. To have some idea of what is likely to happen in a few hours' or days' time is not just desirable – it is essential. A hunter predicts where and when he will find game; a traveller sets out to catch a particular train or flight; a stockbroker foresees a rise in a chosen investment. All are attempts to foretell the future.

Predictions may be right or wrong – the train may be delayed, the game fail to materialize, the stockbroker lose rather than gain. Such failures may be due to some unexpected element disrupting the patterns on which prediction is based – or to some other failure, perhaps in the predictive technique. Prediction has always been a chancy business – in the literal sense too, for today we can look at many of the most ancient methods of prediction in the light of modern theories of chance or probability, mathematically based, to calculate what will *probably* happen. Some scientists maintain that all prediction is based, consciously or not, on the complex Theory of Probability. Others suspect that there is some mystery involved – that time, for instance, is qualitatively far more difficult to explain than we may, or even can, think; that we do not simply progress in a straight line from birth to death, but that time, the fourth dimension, is much odder than we can tell. Possibly some people somehow are able to "break the rules" and actually look into the future.

This may not be as improbable as it seems, even to the most rational of us. The first and essential thing is to suspend disbelief – even if possible to get into the mood *for* belief. This should not prove too difficult. Many things in the world are, at first glance, unbelievable. There is no reason to suppose that we know everything – or even most things – about the real nature of the universe, and time is certainly one of the most mysterious phenomena of the universe as we think we know it.

Time's many dimensions

We tend to think of ourselves as travelling through life rather as we would drive along a road through a landscape, but in a car with a much restricted view – we can look neither directly behind nor ahead. At any one moment, we remember the road we have passed over (though we cannot actually see it any more) and we can see the scenery which lies in "the present" on either side of us; what lies ahead is hidden.

But some of us seem in some way able to leave our "vehicle" and soar to a point from which we can see not only the landscape on each side, but the road winding far away behind us and stretching ahead into the distant future. Here we can see a sharp turn for which we must slow down, there a vehicle we must overtake; behind a hedge is someone waiting to mug us, and in the far distance is the precipice where the road stops for us – and where we shall either fall or take off into the freedom of the air, according to our view of what happens after death. Even then, time, whatever we mean by it, continues – for other people, perhaps for ourselves.

If we are trapped in the present, totally unable to look either forwards or backwards (except in history), then this book is pointless. But the evidence seems to indicate that time is an *artificial* concept created by man for his own convenience – that we are not locked into a capsule travelling on a straight line from birth to death, unable to look before or after. Even scientists, since the general acceptance of Einstein's Theories of Relativity, allow that space, like time, is not absolute and fixed, but relative and changeable, according to the beholder.

Possibly everyone has the ability to take off in this way, to enter a fifth dimension and see the future for themselves. This book explores that possibility, attempts to put it in proportion, and suggests many ways to test it.

Props for predictors

Probably the most common manner of glimpsing the future is in dreams. Many of us have had dreams where we seemed to receive a message about what would happen in a few days' or months' time. But we have little or no control over our dreams. Professional "seers" – as we describe everyone who attempts to foresee the future, though some will dislike the term – often depend on "props" of one kind or another. A gypsy woman of dubious intent with her crystal ball is probably the most obvious of this type of seer, which obscures the fact that not only has this sort of "scrying" a very long history, but that the crystal ball is no more than a means to an end. This is true of most of the other "props" used by fortune-tellers.

These props may have an objective aspect, as in astrology. However, the oil floating on the surface of a bowl of water, tea leaves in a cup, or runes that are cast on the ground, are regarded by many practitioners as merely providing the image to focus a sixth sense. Cards or stones are not in themselves messages from beyond the Fourth Dimension but merely the "trigger" enabling the predictor to slip the bonds of the present.

We can only guess how this happens. It has been suggested that time could resemble a spiral, each of its turns operating on a special wavelength; by tuning into higher or lower wavelengths or vibrations we can

Palmists would agree. Attitudes to all types of prediction are discussed in turn in this book. "Scientific" forecasting – such as meteorology or psephology (forecasting election results) – is based on statistically tested methods, which may be more or less accurate. The more facts available, the greater the accuracy of the forecast; but a freak storm can upset the best weather forecasts, and pollsters have been proved wrong frequently. Prediction by what might be called personal inspiration is equally uncertain, although it can frequently prove correct.

The purpose of this book

In this book we examine most of the ways in which humanity has attempted to lift the veil of time and

These Mayan glyphs (right) from Yaxchilan have calendrical meaning but do not represent a 365-day calendar – another example of the relativity of notions of time.

7

"jump" to another turn or time. As with external means to help achieve the right mood for meditation or control the pulse, some form of "prop" is often needed to help power the lift-off into another dimension of time.

Seers – who claim to be able somehow to stand outside time – have frequently used objects or sounds merely to help them focus on the future; palmists or astrologers, by contrast, use much more complex "scientific" methods of prediction, based on textbook interpretations of symbols, lines or angles. Most contemporary astrologers would claim that, while there is an art to interpreting a birth chart, the chart itself, with the positions of the planets for the time and place of birth, represents certain characteristics, not unlike the weather chart produced by a meteorologist.

peer behind it. Some of these are as popular now as ever – astrology and the *I Ching* for example, and to a lesser degree palmistry, card-reading and the Tarot. Others, while less popular, still have their adherents – casting the runes, studying crystals or even tea leaves.

We shall look at all of these equally dispassionately. While some, such as astrology, depend on a set of rules often thousands of years old, others, like the Tarot, depend also on the skill and knowledge of the interpreter, while yet others, such as crystal divining, depend to a great degree on intuition.

We attempt to give enough information to enable the reader to try and test each means of prediction. Some are easier than others. Astrology, even at Sun-sign level, demands some study, though anyone who reads pp. 93-127 carefully should be able to write his or her Sun-sign prediction within a few hours of opening the section. On the other hand, anyone can immediately ask questions of the dice, without prior knowledge or expertise.

But *should* we try to glimpse the future, even if we can? And just how useful is such knowledge? It may be of less use in dictating exactly what path to take in life than in giving us a clearer vision of the choices available. Then we can decide more easily whether to take the rougher or smoother path, so the divinatory technique helps us in the same way that weather forecasts help gardeners. The study of our biorhythms (see pp. 186-189), a well-researched modern aid to living endorsed by a number of insurance companies, has the same aim as many less widely accepted means of divination – to make life easier.

Precisely accurate prediction of future events is, on present evidence, so rare as to seem almost impossible. But few will find themselves able to argue convincingly that, occasionally, we do not seem able to catch fleeting, frustratingly incomplete glimpses of what lies ahead.

If we consider it, this is reassuring. Although life might be impossible if we could not to some extent predict the future, it would be intolerable – and terrifying – if we could do so totally.

This book provides the necessary information to enable everyone reading it to conduct their own experiments with time, to try to leap its boundaries. It reveals how, over 4,000 or 5,000 years, various people have tackled the problem of the uncertainty of the future. Some have devised means which apply to every possible alternative; the great Chinese textbook the *I Ching* does this, and has been found by many generations of readers to be an enormous help in organizing their lives. Others have worked out complex systems of interpreting physical data – astrology is a case in point, taking the planets as tools. Others have devised ways of interpreting the lines of the palms of hands or handwriting itself, others have studied the implications of symbols in dreams. Yet others – who perhaps need to be the most talented of all – have used for their imaginative theories about the future some very odd starting points – crystal balls, oil floating on the surface of water, cloud shapes (aeromancy) birds pecking corn from letters of the alphabet (alectryomancy), chance meetings with animals (apatomancy), onion sprouts (cromniomancy) and even the sound of rose petals slapping against the hand (phyllorhodomancy).

The one thing essential when investigating these and other predictive techiques suggested is the suspension of disbelief. It has been shown repeatedly that whatever the means used to demonstrate any occult practice, including attempts to look into the future, they never work well in the presence of a total disbeliever. This has bedevilled many scientifically formal attempts to test theories and practices in futurology.

Cynics argue this simply means that practitioners are unable to deceive the more critical members of their audiences. But there is really no need to accept this explanation, for the negative effect has been measured in cases where no sleight-of-hand could possibly have been involved. So it is especially important to be in a positive frame of mind before beginning any of the experiments described here. It is also important to relax. Many convincing displays of "magic" come from unsophisticated or primitive tribes, where the destructive tensions of the modern world are absent.

Every bookshop has shelves full of "prediction" books, some more authentic than others; as with political parties, each tends to put itself forward as the most reliable and accurate. We make no such claims. We simply offer the first complete survey of known and tried means of prediction, and invite the reader to try them.

The History of Prediction

The Mystery of Time

Einstein's theory of Relativity juggles with accepted notions of time. It challenges the common-sense concept of a linear succession of moments by showing that time is affected by speed, slowing down as the speed of light is approached. Our time-space universe is expanding, with galaxies flying apart yet remaining constant to each other like the spots on an inflating balloon. These revelations have forced us to redefine our sense of time – past, present and future.

Thought of simply, time seems to be a straightforward proposition – indeed, it seems self-evidently and inescapably straight. It appears to stretch before and behind us like a piece of string. On this one-dimensional length, various "knots" mark the important events in both our own personal lives – where the string stretches back to our birth, or at least to our earliest memories – and historical time. (For the latter, we in the west are accustomed to dating from the birth of Christ but there are many other systems of dating or calendars.) Important events, such as the Battle of Hastings (1066) or the Declaration of Independence (1776) are big knots in public life, as marriages or births are in private life. This linear view of time seems such clear common sense that any attempt to get round it – by trying to go backward or forward in time – has seemed impossible.

Each of us has his or her own piece of string; we hold the present piece in our hands at the moment, we know it stretches forward into the future and, at some unknown stage, will fall from our hands. To try to look at time otherwise has seemed to fly against both common sense and science.

But the linear concept of time is no longer supported by science. Even the calendar, with its annual repetition of the months and seasons, suggests there are alternative ways of looking at time. Other cultures have had very different concepts of time, and modern physics, since Einstein's Theories of Relativity, now appears to undermine rather than to underpin a strictly linear view.

But this should not alarm us overmuch. We need to remember that linear time was invented for our own convenience. Like those brave first voyagers who sailed across the Atlantic in search of lands not even known certainly to exist, half fearing to fall off the map, we should accept that time is perhaps not linear but circular and two-directional. What we have made we can discard if we wish – and the regular recurrence of the seasons reminds us that nature follows a nonlinear progression.

Many other cultures have never had fully linear time. The Hindus have a cyclical notion of time, with continually recurring yugas. The four yugas last for immensely long periods, each one shorter than the one before, and each ending with a massive extinction. We are presently passing through the fourth, or Kali, Yuga– the most destructive of the four. On a different level, the Fijian and Samoan islanders base their calendars on the cycle of the palolo worm, which each year sloughs off part of its body in the sea before reconstituting itself – a reminder that biological rhythms are cyclical.

Of course, for everyday purposes, the linear concept of time holds good, for how else are we going to measure a day as we move physically through it except by timing appointments, events and occasion in sequential form. And the same applies to days and years. By the same token we treat the earth as flat for most purposes, although we know it is round. The "roundness" of time is equally not apparent to us.

In fact, the linear concept of time was unknown not only to many primitive peoples but also to the first civilized Europeans – the ancient Greeks. Although the Greeks had a system of dating from the first Olympic Games (in 776 BC), they seldom bothered to use it. The Athenians, for example, used to refer to the year when a certain individual was archon (the annually appointed head of state). Each tiny Greek state had its own system of dating by these means. They were not particulary concerned with the precise hour of the day, lacking clocks and relying on the position of the sun. The reason for this vagueness was not least because many Greek philosophers believed time was circular or cyclical, repeating itself endlessly, as the natural seasons did.

Time and Christianity

What began to change western concepts of time, even before the advent of precise timepieces, was Christianity itself. This postulated a definitive once-and-for-all intrusion of God into time, in the person of Christ,

This Aztec magical calendar (*above*) is governed both by Western concepts of linear time and by the Aztec's own particular ideas of time running in catastrophic cycles – always fuelled by human sacrifice.

that ended all theories of cycles and led to a belief in time actually going somewhere. When this was added the increasing sophistication of timepieces – first waterclocks or hourglasses, then increasingly accurate mechanical clocks – time began to press closer on western man. (The ancient world appears to have used only very simple sundials and water clocks to measure time.)

The truth, however is that time does not necessarily pass in a straight line from an invisible A to an unforeseeable Z, nor does time pass at the same speed under all circumstances. Our instincts tell us this, of course: remember Touchstone's words in Shakespeare's *As You Like It* – time passes extremely slowly for a lover on the way to his mistress, but excessively quickly for a man on the way to the gallows. Compare the long, leisurely days of childhood with the brief frenetic working days of adult life.

It may be argued that our timepieces tell us otherwise – surely they confirm that each day passes at precisely the same speed? But no, the most sophisticated atomic clocks tell us otherwise: if we send one of them into the stratosphere to circle the globe at many times the speed of sound, we find when we bring it back to earth that it has measured a perceptibly different period of time than its brother which has remained on the ground.

Moreover, it is possible to conceive of circumstances in which time does not appear to pass at all. For we measure time normally by such obvious signs of motion and change as the changing of the seasons. Imagine, however, a piece of perishable matter frozen at the lowest possible temperature – approaching absolute zero. Even after a thousand years, it will show no signs of biological decay though it will have aged. Its twin, exposed to the elements, would long have disappeared. So our concept of time passing can easily be seen to be relative.

Newton and classical physics

Most people still work with, and live under, the common sense assumption that time is not only linear but absolute and fixed. This view of time derives from Isaac Newton (1642-1727), the great British scientist whose laws of physical motion dominated the whole world view of the west for over two centuries and are known as classical physics. According to Newton, "absolute, true and mathematical time, of itself and from its own nature, flows equably without relation to anything external". And the same held true for space.

These absolutes seemed to be written into the nature of the universe itself. It was therefore impossible to imagine – talking scientifically – that anyone could catch a glimpse of event C before events A and B had occurred, making any kind of divination unthinkable. But at the end of the 19th century these absolute uncertainties began to unravel. First, in 1883, two American scientists, Michelson and Morley, disproved the existence of the "ether" – a phenomenon that had been thought to permeate space and which 19th century scientists felt could be used as a reference frame for measuring Newton's Absolute Space. Using the best instruments available, Michelson and Morley failed to find any trace of this ether.

Enter Einstein

This led Albert Einstein (1879-1955), who had been wrestling with such problems, to formulate his Special Theory of Relativity in 1905. This declared to a stunned world that there is no such thing as an absolute frame of reference. Out went the Newtonian concepts of both Time and Space; in their place, Einstein proffered a four-dimensional spacetime continuum in which the only constant or absolute is the speed of light. Three-dimensional space and one-dimensional time need to be continuously readjusted to take account of the speed an observer is travelling relative to another observer.

An ancient Egyptian horoscope *(right)* from a tomb at Athribis; all the animals of the zodiac can be seen in colourful forms. Egyptian astrology was derived from Babylonian and Greek systems and given a local flavour from 200 BC onwards, Egypt was under the rule of Greek Kings at the time, and Alexandria the intellectual centre of the ancient world.

The Delphic oracle *(above)* was consulted on matters of great importance – by powerful and wealthy individuals and by city states. The Pythian priestess was reputedly a young girl who used to squat or sit on a tripod from which rose intoxicating fumes. Thus drugged, she would prophesy – in verse and normally very ambiguously.

All this might seem rather removed from our approach to precognition, but Einstein followed with his General Theory of Relativity in 1916 which is much more relevant. This proposed that space – and time along with it – is curved, being affected by the mass of objects. In one extension of this theory, therefore, both time and space are curved round on themselves in an enclosed sphere. In Einstein's words, "this separation between past, present and future has the value of mere illusion." If the greatest scientist of the century can so dismiss the traditional compartmentalizing of time, predictors need no longer feel bashful at challenging a "common sense" view of time based on outdated and inadequate science.

A famous example of Einstein's laws in action is the 25-year-old man who travels in a spaceship for 10 years at half the speed of light. (As the speed of light is 186,279 miles per second, this voyage is not likely in the near future.) After he has been travelling for five years by his reckoning, he returns home – to discover that 10 years have gone by on earth while his own body has only aged five years, so time has indeed proved relative. Another example, closer to home, is that if five men in different places record the precise moment when they see the flashing of a light, their timepieces will show minutely different times. Radio waves travel at nearly the speed of light and a radio message from London to Sydney will arrive about one twentieth of a second later – quite big enough a difference to be measured. Yet in London and Sydney the conversation will seem simultaneous. Such findings make a nonsense of the traditional linear idea of time.

Quantum mechanics

The Theory of Relativity shows us that there are different kinds of time. Quantum mechanics, based on the Quantum Theory (devised by Max Planck at the beginning of the 20th century), shakes up our traditional notions still further, showing that it is possible, at least in one known case, for a body to move backward in time. At first Einstein was unhappy about this, saying "it is impossible to send wire messages into the past." Later, he came to accept this might just be possible – for subatomic particles.

13

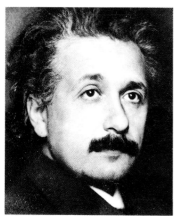

Albert Einstein *(above)*
soon after winning the
Nobel Prize for Physics in
1921. Einstein overturned
traditional concepts of time
and space with his Theories
of Relativity.

Quantum mechanics studies the basic material of the universe, the atom with its nucleus and electrons, and tells us that after the apparently random collisions continually occurring between atomic particles, some of them rebound into their own past to collide again with other particles, before returning to the present. All our experience of life suggests that this is impossible, but it nonetheless happens; physicists, led by the American Richard P. Feynman, insist on it, though the scientific and mathematical proof is very involved.

Supposing that we accept this fact, the implications for futurologists are profound – for if it were possible to study an atomic particle at the moment when it was rebounding into its past, it would in theory be possible to foretell its future. Moreover, if matter, however infinitesimal in size, can travel from present to past and back again, does it require so enormous an effort to propose that it may be possible that man's mind may be capable of the same feat? May we not suppose that we too, or certain of us, are able under certain conditions to teach our minds to break free of the constriction of time as we know it?

The dreams of J. W. Dunne

Einstein's two Theories of Relativity – the Special Theory of Relativity of 1905 and the General Theory of 1916 – were (and remain) in all but the most simplified and summary forms forbidding enough to be outside the full comprehension of the general reader. A book published only a few years after them had a much greater popular circulation, and was the first to suggest that time as most people knew it was a chameleon. This was J. W. Dunne's *An Experiment with Time*. His book, which many scientists derided at the time, was based on an experience many people have; he dreamed dreams which appeared to foretell the future. Dunne was anything but a dreamer or mystic. He had been a successful army officer for many years, fighting both in the Boer War (1899-1902) and the First World War, flying some of the first military aircraft; in short, a typical army officer – except for his ideas about time.

When he first noticed this phenomenon, he dreamed in advance of events which occurred only shortly after he woke up. Later, he dreamed of events he afterwards saw reported in the newspapers. He felt very strongly that this had nothing to do with anything supernatural or clairvoyant – in the traditional sense of those terms, anyway. He felt instead that his own internal sense of time was somehow out of register with "reality"; but that rather than being unnatural, this told him something about the true nature of time.

Dunne's conclusions

The simplest of his conclusions is obvious enough: if he was indeed receiving information from the future, however it was received, then the future must exist in terms as real as the present. (It might be suggested that the past also exists in much the same way; indeed, if the future exists, then for those living in it the present which we inhabit is, for them, the past!)

Dunne – like so many people who glimpse or seem to glimpse the future – was irritated by the fact that detailed foreknowledge was denied him. This vision he had of the future was often vague, sometimes distorted, and never, ever, complete. In fact, his "previsions" were usually mixed up with garbled bits of memories. In attempting to explain this he constructed his own theory of time, which was complex and basically faulty; his rationalizations do not hold water, and this severely damaged the effect of his work as far as scientists were concerned. But for a considerable number of readers his book described a phenomenon they recognized and had themselves experienced. A conclusion that they could accept was that time (as we have shown) is not linear, nor does it proceed at a measured pace, like a moving pavement upon which we step at birth, to fall off at death. It is rather a plane with no real division between past and present or present and future.

Three-dimensional time

Other twentieth century men who did not have Dunne's "practical" experience of what seems very like mental time travel, have produced their own theories. The Russian P.D. Ouspensky, for instance proposed that, like space, time had three dimensions. (These three dimensions of time are equivalent to the fourth, fifth and sixth dimensions of space – an extension of Einstein's ideas.) There must be a kind of time, he said, which remains forever *now*: the now which is immovable and embraces all time, which could be described as eternal. But then, he suggested, there is yet another dimension: a time which is part of our own particular *now*, but which offers us a hundred possibilities or directions in which to move towards the future. And a second after we have made our decision and taken our move, another *now* presents us with another hundred possibilities.

The stars above Stonehenge *(below)* blazed out their light millions of years ago. What the Druids – and whoever built the monument 4000 years ago – were looking at therefore, was ancient starlight – messages from the past.

15

We all recognise the truth of that proposition – but it led Ouspensky in a direction in which few would want to follow him, for he concluded that time was eternally repetitive, that every known pattern of life occurred and recurred, so that every man and woman ever born is continually reliving life, again, and again, and again. This would not have much attraction – except perhaps to believers in reincarnation.

The idea of the eternal *now*, however, remains to some extent convincing. If we imagine ourselves on a distant star, 1,000 light years away, and could contrive a telescope strong enough to be able to see events on earth, we would at this moment be able to examine life in Britain before the Norman conquest of 1066. It would be difficult to convince ourselves that the peasant we saw driving his sheep in from the downs in AD 988 was not living in a *now*, though different from our own, just as the star we see exploding in the night sky is exploding *now* for us, though its own *now* in fact occurred thousands of years ago.

Varieties of time

All these ideas were seized on by the writer J. B. Priestley, who not only examined various conceptions of time in his plays, but was preoccupied with them for most of his life. In his book *Man and Time*, he was one of the first popular writers to dismiss our conventional notion of time as something invented merely for convenience, to "explain" change, and then set out his conception of Time One, involving our everyday notion of measured time, Time Two, a time of infinite possibilities, and Time Three, a time subservient to our will.

More recently, Colin Wilson (in *The Occult*) and Lyall Watson (in *Supernature*) have advanced their own theories of time, which in general confirm the view that time is, as it were, everywhere and always: that all

Halley's comet terrified Normans and Saxons alike when it appeared in 1066 – the year of the Norman conquest of England, shown (*above*) in the Bayeux tapestry. More peaceful and more promising was the star which traditionally guided the Magi to Bethlehem (*above right*), depicted in a mosaic at Ravenna. What neither the oriental kings or the Norman invaders realized, of course, was that they were looking deep into the past when they gazed up into heaven. That is a very modern recognition.

time is omnipresent. When we say that we are "here" and "now" we may be expressing two conceptions which are infinitely limited, neither word really conveying anything much at all in terms of ultimate reality. (Where after all is "here" except in strictly geographical terms, and when after all is "now" except in terms of our material invention, the clock?)

Before we suggest, then, that the laws of physics make it impossible for us to "see into the future", let us pause and remember. These very laws have been transformed by Einstein and his successors. Although most people still live and think as though the old "classical" absolutes of space and time governed the universe, physicists have advanced far towards "dematerializing" matter. Some now see the universe more as a giant "thought" than a vast machine, dissolving the fixed barriers between matter and mind or spirit.

Time and the mystics

Such an approach recalls the perennial teachings or utterances of religious mystics through the ages and throughout the world, almost irrespective of their particular faiths. Buddhists, Hindus, Taoists, Sufis and others seem to echo the more radical western mystics who maintain that both past and future are somehow eternally present. This links up with the mystic's concept of the dissolution of the individual ego in God – deeper waters than most of us would care to enter.

Closer to our human experience may be the feeling of timelessness that a genuinely great work of art – Bach's music, for example, or Michelangelo's sculpture – arouses. In these masterpieces, does not the

16

A 15th century edition of Dante's Inferno *(above)* shows Virgil pointing out the terrible fate of men whose heads have been turned back to front – the punishment awaiting those in the next world who attempt to foresee the future in this one. For some Christians, such prediction challenged God's omnipotence.

past somehow still live in a way that defies the passage of time? Arguably, the "now" of aesthetic perception is the same "now" that the contemporaries of Bach or Michelangelo experienced.

Many poets have considered the question, none with more insight than T. S. Eliot in *Burnt Norton*, a section of his *Four Quartets*:

> *Time present and time past*
> *Are both perhaps present in time future,*
> *And time future contained in time past . . .*
> *Time past and time future*
> *What might have been and what has been*
> *Point to one end, which is always present.*

It seems most likely that the poets, mystics and philosophers are right: that the idea of a finite, linear time is too limited to be accurate. If this is so, then the boundaries crumble, and we can think of reaching out to grasp the future.

Prediction Past and Present

Found in all civilizations, periods of history and areas of the world, the arts of prediction are as old as mankind itself. Cave paintings from France suggest that 15,000 years ago the shaman's prophetic powers were used for the benefit of the community in a fashion little different from the methods of his Siberian descendants in the 19th century. Today, the immense popularity of astrology reveals a preoccupation with individual destiny that reflects our modern Western society. Altogether, the history of prediction expresses the hopes and fears of humanity in a unique way.

Man's earliest attempts to foretell the future date from long before recorded history, and one can only guess at the earliest means used – but they would probably have been similar to those used by certain primitive tribes within living memory. These include clairvoyance (second sight) and dream messages (oneiromancy), the casting of lots (sortilege) by marks on the earth (geomancy), looking into fire (pyromancy) and the use of omens and oracles of various kinds.

Although many peoples assumed that adults could receive the power to foretell the future, among others an exceptional child was recognized as having special powers which could be cultivated and fine-tuned until it became a professional diviner. Children were supposed to have sharper powers of precognition, including the intuitive "sixth sense". The diviner would usually choose the means which could help to foretell events – in Papua and Zambia a carved figure of some sort would act as a medium between the diviner and the message. In Tahiti a calabash or gourd of water acted in much the same way as a crystal ball. Elsewhere a pendulum of some kind or a simple branch from a tree would be used.

These aids provided – and today, provide – a means of focusing the diviner's thoughts or instincts; in themselves they have nothing to do with what is predicted – they are merely suggestive. But as civilizations developed and grew more complex, more systematic methods of prediction were created. Priests or magicians in Babylonia, for example, fused astronomy and mathematics before 1000BC to create astrological tables which influenced the Greeks when they came to develop their astrological systems; and they in turn influenced the Arabs and the Hindus later. Quite separately, the Mayan and other Meso-American priesthoods also worked out complicated mathematical patterns and tables. These systems are empirical to the extent that the means of prediction are based on precise observations made over the millennia. The underlying assumptions are, of course, anything but empirical.

Priests and prophets

Some of the most ancient architectural constructions in the world (Stonehenge in England is one obvious example), are thought to have incorporated systems for astronomical prediction in their designs. Another predictive method involved the use of smaller stones, or even sticks, (xylomancy) thrown onto the ground by a diviner. The resulting pattern was studied (much as the patterns of tealeaves were later studied) because it was believed to embody the shape of the future in a decipherable form.

It was often assumed that diviners interpreted in this way messages from the gods; and eventually the priesthoods of various religions became associated with prediction – by studying all sorts of apparently random patterns. A priest or magician – the terms were for a long time synonymous – claimed to foretell the future simply by referring to textbooks which laid down the rules for prediction. These rules were highly secret. If they had been commonly known the priesthood would have lost its mystery; this is why so many predictive techniques have been lost – the secret was too well kept!

The Bible is a rich source of knowledge of the early history of the subject, and Moses is perhaps the earliest magician-priest of whom we have a detailed account. He received messages about the future through manifestation (the burning bush), voices from the air, divination and materialization, among other means. But there are many references in the Old Testament to the activities of diviners or soothsayers. Some were public, such as the prophet Jeremiah's foretelling (about 600BC) of the fall of Jerusalem, for instance; others private – in the Book of Numbers, for example, men suspecting their wives of adultery are given a careful explanation of the means (involving barley meal and dust) by which they can see if their suspicions are true. The priests of the Sumerians and Babylonians are described as experts in the interpretation of marks on the livers of sacrificed animals as a means of prophesy (hepatoscopy).

Priest and predictor, this 18th century Siberian shaman *(right)* from Kamatchka fulfilled both roles. Shamans claimed to have prophetic dreams, which may often have been drug-induced trances.

20

By the time Egyptian, Greek, Chinese and Roman civilizations were fully developed, predictive techniques had become highly sophisticated. The Greeks elaborated ancient Babylonian techniques of astrology, which spread to Rome. In China, methods of divination evolved based on the throwing of yarrow sticks – a process that developed into the complex commentaries of the *I Ching* (see p. 132). Alongside this xylomancy, the ancient Chinese developed scapulomancy – the reading of cracks formed in the shoulder blades of sacrificed animals which had been heated in fires. A similar process was applied to the undershell of tortoises – the plastron – tortoises being sacred creatures.

Greeks and Romans

By the 5th century BC, the Greeks had refined the theory of Destiny: as Aeschylus put it, "Events and their causes are divinely ordered, and the next is controlled by the last." Natural objects and animals were all used in prediction: if a horse stepped from its stable in the morning placing its right hoof first, the day was fortunate; if a tossed stone fell one way up, it indicated one thing – if another, something else. Men's and women's bodies also sent signals to their owners – and to onlookers. In Greece, a sneeze was particularly auspicious.

All these signs and portents were highly regarded: after the assassination of Julius Caesar many stories were put about – including not only the famous one of the soothsayer Spurinna's message: "Beware the Ides of March", but also the report that Caesar's horses were seen to shed tears, that Calpurnia had dreamed of her husband's death, and that the door of her bedroom had been thrown open when she awoke, by no human hand.

There were, of course, many impostors – the most famous of whom was probably Alexander of Abonuteichus, who in the 2nd century AD made a fortune from charlatanism. But most diviners worked seriously and honestly, and the great Greek philosophers usually accepted the validity of astrology, among many other forms of divination. Plato, for example, wrote that the gift of prophecy lay beyond human reason, and was akin to the

A Chinese astrologer
(above) with his client,
surrounded by the 12
animals of the Chinese
zodiac. The Chinese had
their own, completely
original system of astrology,
which owed nothing to
Babylon or Greece.

state of being in love.

The Greek historian Herodotus (480-425BC) records omens and oracles – describing among other things the famous oracle at Delphi, lying above the gorge of Pleistus below Mount Parnassus. It was said to have been built by Apollo himself, following his killing of the earth dragon Python. The priestess of his oracle, known as Pythia, sat on a tripod above a rocky cleft from which rose intoxicating vapours.

Those consulting the oracle had to bring a gift of cakes and sacrifice a goat or a sheep, before putting a question. The answer came back as a confused series of sounds, the result of a drug-induced trance, which was then interpreted by the priests.

From the few accounts that have come down to us, the priests' pronouncements seem to have been deliberately ambiguous. For example, Croesus, king of Lydia, sent to Delphi to ask if he should go to war with his neighbour, the Persian empire. "If Croesus crosses the river Halys, he will destroy a mighty empire" came the reply. Encouraged, Croesus went to war – and lost. But the validity of the oracle's prediction was not questioned – Croesus had destroyed his own mighty empire. It can be argued that no means of prediction has yet succeeded in being particular, and that the oracle, like many diviners before and since, was regarding the future "through a glass, darkly".

Throughout the greatest Greek period – from about 550BC for two centuries – the Delphic oracle played a vital role in Greek affairs. Later, it fell increasingly under the sway of rulers or states who used it for their political ends. Yet as late as the fourth century AD the Emperor Julian the Apostate – the last pagan emperor, who ruled 361-2 – send to the oracle, but got in reply nothing but moans about its fled glories. The two other major Greek oracles, at Dodona and Olympia, declined in importance at about the same time – perhaps because astrology was beginning to take its place as the most trustworthy means of prediction.

Although the idea of divination was from time to time attacked, belief that it was possible to foretell the future was firmly held during the Roman empire. Priests continued to examine the entrails of sacrificed sheep or calves, for instance – arguing that these would be prepared by the gods so

21

that they told the right story. This method, known as haruspicy, was for long the commonest method of divination in the ancient Mediterranean and the Near East, used by Greeks, Persians, Romans and Etruscans alike. In Italy, Etruscan priests continued to be used as *haruspices* right up to the end of paganism in the 4th century.

The organ that concerned diviners especially was the liver, regarded as the most vital organ of the body, its silvery surface seeming – when fresh-killed – to be a "mirror" in which the future could be discerned. Models were made of the liver – one of the oldest is a Babylonian clay model dating to 2000BC – to teach the priests how to divine from living organs. Particular attention was given to any parts, such as the lobes, which might be missing or deformed. Vast care was needed to avoid damaging it when excising it from the sacrificed animal.

The 12 figures of the western zodiac *(below)*, here circling round the sun, have long symbolized the most complete system of prediction. This illustration dates from the ninth century.

22

The Egyptian goddess Nut *(above right)* is shown surrounded by the emblems of the zodiac. Egypt was very receptive to the Babylonian astrology which the Greeks systematized about 200BC.

Astrology

In Greece, but to a much greater extent in Rome and throughout her empire, astrology gradually replaced haruspicy as the most widely accepted means of prediction. Probably older than any known religion or philosophical system, we find traces of it as soon as man began to make marks on stone, bone or wood. The earliest extant horoscope known is on a tablet from the Seleucid era in Syria (c. 200BC), but prehistoric bones have been found bearing marks indicating the phases of the moon. Predictions were certainly made during the 1st dynasty of Babylon (18th-16th centuries BC).

Astrology began in Babylonia, where a calendar was devised, and there too the zodiac as we know it began to take form. By the 8th century BC, books about astrology were already in existence there, and the theory was sympathetically treated by many authors – for example, Hippocrates, the father of medicine.

The Roman empire was steeped in astrology: most emperors employed astrologers; Thrasyllus, Tiberius' confidant, was among the most powerful astrologers in history, because of his great influence on the moody emperor. This he had gained in a way that had nearly cost him his life. Tiberius, in exile on the island of Rhodes, long before becoming emperor, grew tired of Thrasyllus' constant reassurances that all would one day be well. Walking on the cliffs he threatened to have the ever-optimistic astrologer thrown off them unless he produced some concrete evidence of a coming change in fortune. Thrasyllus pointed to a sail visible on the horizon, claiming it carried good news. He was in luck, or very accurate in his predictions, for the ship *did* bring good news – that of Tiberius' recall to Rome and supreme power.

Later, Apollonius of Tyana, greatest of ancient seers, correctly predicted an imperial future for Vespasian, when the latter was a mere infantry commander, and then went on to predict the exact hour of the death of Vespasian's son, the emperor Domitian in AD96. Such knowledge could be politically dangerous, and therefore many emperors forbade the casting of their horoscopes – testimony to the power of their belief in astrology. But ordinary people employed astrologers to help them with their day to day problems – as they were to do until the end of the 17th century.

The druids in Britain and Gaul also appear to have been astrologers – or at least, so it seems from the few sources surviving. The extant fragments of a monumental calendar inscription from Coligny in central France testify to the Gaul's calendrical knowledge, but this was lost when the Romans suppressed druidism.

There is a debate among historians as to whether the rules by which an astrologer interprets a horoscope – or chart showing the positions of the Sun, Moon and planets for a particular moment – arose as the result of observations or were the result of an increasingly complex system of symbolism. Whichever may be the case, the most successful astrologers – though they have often modified past theories and sometimes evolved their own – have never worked by guess and by God, but with reference to a body of knowledge freely available, tried and tested – and brought up-to-date after the discovery of the "modern" planets.

Christianity

It has been suggested that the growth of Christianity dealt prediction a blow; but this was not the case – mistranslations of the Bible have falsified the evidence against astrology. We have mentioned the predictive techniques used in the Old Testament: with the New Testament we come to the person some might consider the greatest magician and predictor of all – Christ himself, whose history was foretold before his birth, in Joseph's dream.

Jesus not only clearly had the strongest psychic powers, but was himself a diviner (he foretold, after all, his own arrest and execution as well as the destruction of Jerusalem by the Romans nearly 40 years later). The early fathers of the Church also sometimes approved of divination – Justin Martyr c.AD150 asserted that the pagan prophetesses known as sibyls "spake many great things with justice and with truth". (This may have been because certain Sybilline utterances seemed to predict the birth of Christ).

It seems that the Church began to express opposition to divination only when the still-strong powers of the oracles began to appear as alternative sources of divine knowledge to the Christian Church and its teachings. But members of the Church still engaged in prophesy – and in stranger events, as when Bishop St Ambrose of Milan went into a trance for four hours before his astonished congregation. Later, he explained that he had been at the funeral in Tours, France, of his friend and colleague St Martin (which indeed had taken place at that very hour 450 miles away). The great theologian St Augustine (354-430) was violently dismissive of astrol-

The Roman emperor Tiberius *(above)* who ruled AD14-37, relied heavily on his own astrologer Thrasyllus, who predicted his eventual rise to power long before it happened. Astrology was very popular in the Roman empire.

23

ogy (his rebuttal is still standard Catholic dogma) but he agreed that dreams could convey useful information.

Sometimes, for reasons of personality rather than talent, certain names leap off the page of any history of the occult or the paranormal. Nostradamus the French seer (1503-66) still has the power to interest us – whatever view is taken of his innumerable prophesies, he was an extraordinary and influential prophet.

Nostrodamus

He was born in 1503 at St Rémy, France, and received orthodox training as a physician. He studied astrology and published some almanacs, but none have survived. What we do know is that in 1555 he suddenly began to publish prophesies in the form of verses – quatrains – which, he said, would be fulfilled during the coming centuries. His fame took him, as astrologer and sage, to the royal court of Henry II; it was increased when he appeared to have foreseen Henry's death in 1559.

Critics suggest – and it is difficult not to agree – that Nostradamus' words are so oblique, his verses so obscure, that one can find in them passages capable of referring to almost any human situation. But there is no denying that he seems often to hit the mark – for instance predicting to the very year the outbreak of the French Revolution and the execution of Louis XVI and Marie-Antoinette. Other quatrains seem to refer, more or less obviously, to such events as the Great Fire of London (which again Nostradamus apparently dated precisely), the fall of King Charles I of England, the rise of Napoleon, and of Hitler.

How Nostradamus produced his prophetic verses is anyone's guess; he was not a notable astrologer, and does not seem to have used astrology to produce his predictions. We can suggest that he used clairvoyance – the

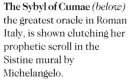

The Sybyl of Cumae *(below)* the greatest oracle in Roman Italy, is shown clutching her prophetic scroll in the Sistine mural by Michelangelo.

24

same means used by that great English diviner, John Dee.

Dr John Dee (1527-1608) was an astrologer who was of considerable service to Queen Elizabeth I – but who was also an extraordinary man in other ways: he built up one of the best libraries in Europe, was a geographer who advised many of the great Elizabethan adventurers on planning their voyages to the New World, and a fine mathematician and astronomer. He believed that a great store of knowledge was available to anyone who could tap a "sixth sense", and to do so studied the Kaballah. This was a Jewish magical theory concerned with alchemy (the transformation of base metal into gold, or the discovery of the elixir of life). It had been taken up by many philosophers, notably Paracelsus (1493-1541), who also worked on the interpretation of dreams and on the foretelling of future events "by the magic power of the imagination".

It was this power that Dr Dee attempted to harness, using various

The execution of Louis XVI in 1793 *(right)* was very obscurely predicted by the most famous seer of all – Nostradamus, who was court astrologer in the 16th century. Nostradamus relied mainly on scrying – peering into a crystal ball.

means – for instance his famous "magic mirror", now in the British Museum – as well as various crystals through which he believed he could get in touch with the angel Uriel, spirit of light, and certain other entities. He is credited with having predicted the death of Mary Tudor in 1558, the execution of Mary Queen of Scots in 1587, and the defeat of the Spanish Armada in the following year. In his later years he fell from royal favour.

With the emergence of the age of reason in the 17th century, astrology suffered a decline, at least in educated circles. However, it has always had its supporters, and in recent years the statistical researches of the French author Michel Gauquelin has provided new evidence in its favour. Gauquelin was able to analyse the birth dates of many thousands of subjects in France, where the exact time of birth is noted on the official records, and he found a statistically significant correlation between the subjects' rising planet at birth and their eventual choice of profession. Similar results have been obtained by Cooper and Smithers of Bradford University, and van Deusen in the USA.

Crystallomancy

Crystal-gazing has been derided for so long that it may seem unworthy of serious consideration, and yet it is as viable a means of concentrating the mind as any other, and has a long lineage in numerous cultures all over the world. Sometimes known as crystallomancy or scrying, the technique is basically the same even when other substances are used in place of the crystal, such as clear water, polished black stone, a mirror, or even a sword blade. The diviner or seer concentrates on the crystal until he (or she) enters a kind of trance, during which his unconscious conveys the messages for which he is searching. It has often been claimed that the diviner actually sees pictures in the crystal – sometimes of events taking place hundreds of miles away. More often, however, the flaws in the crystal, or the movements of the water, convey an image which the diviner then interprets as best he may.

The crystal-ball method of scrying may have fallen somewhat into disfavour, but it would be wrong to suppose that it was only successful in early times: the London-based Society for Psychical Research has on record many recent and apparently successful experiments, both in Europe and America, which cannot easily be discounted. In 1944, Jeane Dixon, a well-known American scryer, advised the film star Carole Lombard against travelling by air not long before she was killed in a 'plane crash. She also forecast the assassination of Mahatma Gandhi in 1948, those of Robert Kennedy and Martin Luther King in 1968; and the suicide of Marilyn Monroe in 1962. In 1952 she "saw a vision" of a blue-eyed Democrat president being assassinated in office, and put this on record in a magazine published on May 13, 1956 – seven years before President John F. Kennedy's killing. On the day of that event – but before it took place – she "saw" the White House covered in black drapes.

Of course, attempts on the lives of US presidents have not been uncommon, but too many elements in Ms Dixon's prediction were accurate for it to be easy to dismiss. But she has not always been accurate – she predicted a major war against China, which did not occur.

It is the business of clairvoyants, however they may work, to "foretell the future" with some accuracy. For whatever reason, temperamental or intellectual, many people will wish to dismiss this as impossible. Whatever the outcome of each single prediction, there have been too many successful cases for them all to be lightly dismissed.

Crystal balls have been used for prediction in all parts of the world. This one *(right)* belonged to the Dowager Empress Tz'u-hsi of China, who ruled for nearly 50 years until her death in 1905.

The Kabbala's Tree of Life *(right).* The Tarot, one of the greatest predictive techniques, may be partly derived from Kabbalistic magic.

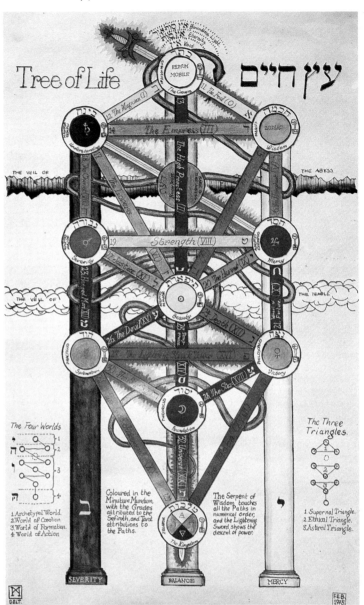

Tree of Life עץ חיים

Dr John Dee (1527-1608) *(above)* was Elizabeth I's astrologer. He was also a geographer, scholar, alchemist and diviner who used a polished black stone to "scry".

27

But many techniques have also been developed, and are described in the second section of this book, which do not so much predict the future as present it to the enquirer – showing you, to coin a phrase, "the future now", so that you can prepare yourself for possible eventualities and make decisions which might otherwise be more difficult.

The *I Ching*

Among the most interesting of these is the *I Ching* or "Book of Changes", which seems to have emerged during the Chou dynasty of China in the twelfth century BC. At the core of the book is a series of divided and undivided lines gathered into eight trigrams and 64 hexagrams (see p. 133). By casting yarrow sticks or coins, the enquirer is referred to one of the hexagrams which, when its attendant verse is consulted, reveals the truth of a situation or a question.

The *I Ching* was used for centuries in China, but has only recently been used in the West. Since its arrival it has had phenomenal success, and together with the Tarot (see p.46) it is perhaps the most common means of divination used by ordinary people. Some scientists who have studied it have suggested that it has a viability based on psychokinesis.

Two men are responsible for the popularity of the *I Ching* in the West: Richard Wilhelm and C. G. Jung. Wilhelm worked on the system during the early years of this century with the help of a Chinese sage, Lau Nai Suan, and published his own translation, with a commentary. This is still in print, and remains the fullest and most valuable of all the texts on the subject. The great Swiss psychologist Jung (1875-1961) met Wilhelm in 1923, became interested in the subject, and "would sit for hours on the ground beneath a hundred-year-old pear tree, the *I Ching* beside me, practising the technique by referring the resultant oracles to one another in an interplay of questions and answers."

Time and again Jung encountered amazing "coincidences" relating the book's replies to the questions asked, and became convinced that, not only for himself but also for his patients, significant numbers of answers were useful.

Wilhelm's view of the oracle, shared by Jung, was that it works on our unconscious – that part of our personality of which we are not aware, but which influences us and reveals to us our own wishes. If we ask the *I Ching* whether Mr or Ms X is our true love, we shall certainly not be told "yes" or "no"; what we will be offered is a series of questions which, if we follow them up, will reveal to us the true nature of our feelings about the man or woman concerned. So we will, while not learning "what the future holds", perhaps be enabled to *make* the future conform to our inmost convictions. As Wilhelm put it, it offers us a view of our lives which enables us to shape them and make them whole.

The Tarot cards

The Tarot, like the *I Ching*, offers a series of symbols on which the seer and querant (or questioner) are invited to meditate; and it also suggests specific images which may or may not become manifest in "real life". A

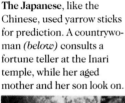

The Japanese, like the Chinese, used yarrow sticks for prediction. A countrywoman *(below)* consults a fortune teller at the Inari temple, while her aged mother and her son look on.

man or woman of the colouring suggested by the cards may or may not appear; all one can say is that it is astonishing how often chance – or synchronicity, to use Jung's word – does surprise us, and the cards turn out to be extremely accurate.

The origin of the Tarot pack is obscure. There are recognizably Egyptian elements in the pictorial symbols on some of the cards, but it can almost certainly be asserted that it does not derive from the ancient Egyptian Book of Thoth.

As far as can be discovered, the earliest Tarot cards appeared in Renaissance Italy, and were derived from playing-cards, the earliest surviving packs of which are dated about 1390. These seem to have come into Europe from the Middle East, and were possibly invented some centuries earlier in China. Three Tarot packs, used by the Visconti-Sforza family in Milan in 1445, survive today and are similar to many modern packs, although they have an extra suit of trump cards to the 52 court and pip cards we all know. There are many different kinds of Tarot cards: the

Sagittarius, the archer, whether depicted in a 16th century Turkish treatise on astrology *(above)* or in a calendar from a 15th century French Book of Hours *(right)* always has the same significance and meaning.

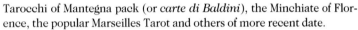

Tarocchi of Mantegna pack (or *carte di Baldini*), the Minchiate of Florence, the popular Marseilles Tarot and others of more recent date.

There is no reason to suppose that Tarot packs were not first simply an extension of ordinary playing cards used in gaming. But they so clearly present a picture of human society (see p. 47) that they were soon used – like their plainer conventional cousins – for attempted prediction, and hence all sorts of theories developed as to the origin of the pictures shown on some of them: some claimed that these had their roots in lost Egyptian libraries, others went to the Kaballah or to Indian myth. Whatever the truth, Tarot cards have now been used for divination for many centuries, and often with great success. Care is needed to learn not only the precise associations of the individual cards, but their relationships to each other; the reader must take the matter seriously if intuition – a vital attribute in this and similar systems – is to work properly.

Numerology

The Tarot cards, the dice, even to some extent astrology, all have connections with numerology. The mystery of mathematics occupied great minds throughout early civilizations – arguments about the numerical significance of the designs of many Egyptian temples and pyramids are familiar if eccentric. Mathematical knowledge was essential for priests to predict the rise and fall of the Nile, for religious festivals and the calendar. From these it was easy to become obsessed with the magic of numbers. The great Greek mathematician Pythagoras (fl. c. 532BC) claimed that "all things are numbers", that "number is the ruler of forms and ideas, and is the cause of gods and demons". He had an enormous influence on the

history of philosophy.

It seems likely that the Greeks borrowed their beliefs about the sacred characters of certain numbers from the Babylonians, who reserved certain numbers to certain gods – 15 represented Ishtar, for instance; 20, Shamash. The sacred number of Babylonia was 12,960,000, which was related to many areas of life, particularly to birth: a child born after 216 or 270 days in the womb was particularly fortunate, since both figures are divisors of the larger number.

Among many ancient people, 3, 4, 5, 7, 70 and 100 were sacred; 3 was a specially mystic number – the "perfect" number 2, plus 1. In many religions the number 1 represented the supreme god – including the Jewish and Christian religion: "The Lord our God is One," said Moses. The Muslims agree: "Say God is One," instructs the Koran. The number 2 is the perfect number, a sign of duality. While it has often been derided, the most rational thinkers have never succeeded in demolishing the superstition which relates certain numbers to fortunate or unfortunate events: some of them are relatively modern, like the association of the number 13 with unlucky events which is one of the strongest superstitions in the mind of western man. So we commemorate such events as the Lord's Supper (at which of course thirteen people were present).

Although numbers may no longer be considered "magical", some people (gamblers in particular) certainly regard them superstitiously, and their often mysterious nature is still being explored by philosophers.

Physiognomy

Studying abstract things – whether they are numbers, patterns of broken and unbroken lines, or symbols on playing-cards – can concentrate the mind on the abstract notion of the future; but every living creature also has concrete evidence of the passing of time within its own body. Our own bodies age and change unmistakably and so it is not surprising that we have tended not only to look to parts of it for signs of our future, but for signs of character, too.

The study of a man's or woman's future as shown in their bodies is one which has gone on for many centuries, and has taken various forms – from what appears to be a purely instinctive reaction to one based on rules as strict as those for astrology. All of these can be said to be concerned with prediction and futurology. If it is true that signs on the hand of a person of fifteen indicate a particular cast of mind, then we can expect to perceive that cast of mind influencing that person's future life; though he or she may fight against "fate" and make efforts to combat his or her natural inclination.

Tarot symbolism appears in many guises: two cards from the late 19th century Etteilla pack *(above)* contrast with a deck *(right)* used by Mlle le Normand, the clairvoyant.

30

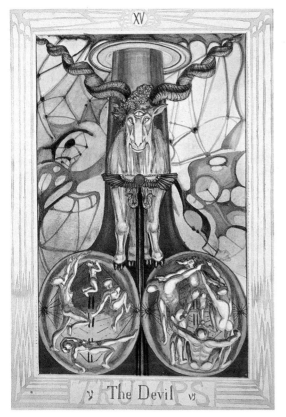

XV

ꝶ The Devil ꝸ

TRUMPS

31

Tarot cards designed for Aleister Crowley, the notorious magician, by Freda Harris. As a diabolist, the Devil, *(above)* must have appealed to him especially; the trump card *(above right)* has links to Mercury as magus.

At all events, the association between appearance and character, though now intellectually disreputable, has been studied for at least 2,000 years. Plutarch pointed out in the first century AD that Alcibiades, the Athenian general, was marked for greatness by his physical appearance; and from that time to the present day there are innumerable allusions to the belief that a person's appearance enables one to read his or her character.

The Greek philosopher Aristotle (384-322BC) was the first to establish a science of physiognomy – "the discovery of the disposition of the mind by the lineaments of the body," as Francis Bacon (1561-1626), the English philosopher and scientist defined it. He laid down rules for the study of character and appearance, suggesting what elements denoted wisdom or stupidity, dignity or impudence, what could be discovered by studying the various parts of the male and female body – also the type of voice and the style of movement (comparing men to lions, women to leopards!)

Aristotle concentrated on character; later, and especially in medieval times, other writers turned to the predictive element of physiognomy, and a flood of books translated at that time from Eastern languages enriched the subject through the work of writers like Ali bin Ragel, Rhazes and Averroes. Some famous medieval writers – among them the Dominican Abertus Magnus (1193-1280) and the astrologer Michael Scott (1175-1234) – devoted long works to physiognomy. The 16th century brought a glut of books by a variety of writers, including – for the first time – some English scholars, who published anonymously such works as *On the Art of Foretelling Future Events by Inspection of the Hand* (1504). Serious study continued until the end of the 17th century, but then – perhaps because of increasing familiarity with anatomy – interest began to decline. A final gesture was the posthumous publication in 1804 of *Essays on Physiognomy*, by a Zurich clergyman, J. K. Lavater (1741-1801), who spent his entire life studying how men's appearance seemed to reveal

John Caspar Lavater (1741-1801) was a Swiss clergyman who spent his life propounding his theory of physiognomy. This claimed that character could be determined by physical appearance – and hence so could a person's future.

32

their characters – and supported his theories with 600 illustrations. This work did the subject no service, however, for it was more an anthology of personal opinion than anything else.

A more modern and serious approach to physiognomy is shown in the work of the Scottish anatomist Sir Charles Bell (1774-1842) on the outward physical signs of inward emotion as conveyed by the facial muscles, published in his *Essay on the Anatomy of the Expression*. Work has gone on spasmodically since on the connection between expression and emotion. It is, of course, obvious that there is such a connection – people who normally smile a lot will have laughter lines on their face which will be missing from those who smile little. However, there is a great difference between this and Aristotle's contention that someone with a slender, hooked nose will be "noble but grasping", or someone with a snub nose will have "luxurious habits".

Franz Joseph Gall

Phrenology, which has the same basis as physiognomy, concentrates on the conformation of the head, and is of much more recent origin. The German anatomist and physiologist Franz Joseph Gall (1758-1828) first advanced in 1796 the theory that since the talents and dispositions of men were dependent upon the functions of the brain, they might be inferred from the exterior of the skull, which would show a bump where the portion of the brain beneath was particularly developed.

Gall spent a lifetime elaborating his theory, visiting schools, prisons and asylums, and studying many individual clients. Performing a great

Early 19th century caricatures *(right)*, ridiculing Lavater's physiognomical theory.

33

number of post-mortems, he claimed to have proved that the brain did indeed show the same conformation as the skull which contained it.

Despite the doubts of science and the disapproval of the Church (Gall was eventually, in 1802, prohibited from lecturing in Vienna because of the "danger" his theory allegedly offered to religion) phrenology, or the study of the shape of the skull, caught on first in Germany, then in the rest of Europe. Gall settled in Paris and was widely consulted; a colleague, Dr Johann Gaspar Spurzheim (1776-1832) took the gospel to England and then to America. But phrenology was a short-lived craze, disputed by psychologists and scientists. In 1906 a British scientist, Pearson, published a study of 5,000 schoolchildren and university students which proved conclusively that there was no relation between skull conformation and character; and finally phrenology sank almost without trace, its only remnants being those intriguing and decorative china heads marked with the indicative areas of the skull.

The difficulty about physiognomy is that when we consider someone's appearance, most of us are unavoidably impelled into forming judgements as a result of our observation of their tone of voice, their gestures, even their clothes; we shy away from instinctively condemning them without any basis in reason or experience, so we latch on to the shape of their hands or the expression of their eyes to support our dislike. And so, although the long association of certain physical traits with character has been thoroughly tested by scientists and found wanting, there are still few of us who do not make snap judgements in the way Aristotle did.

Palmistry

One branch of physiognomy still popular and difficult to dismiss is the study of the hand, which has a history longer than that of the study of any other part of the body – it is said to have been practised first in China 3,000 years before Christ. Palmistry was much used in China until the Communist revolution (and it would be surprising if it were no longer practised there still, though no doubt discreetly); it is certainly still common throughout India and the Middle East; it became widely practised in ancient Greece and Rome, Aristotle being the first westerner to mention it. It was attacked during medieval times as a threat to free-will, its history being almost as long and complex as that of astrology. In much the same way a system of rules has been empirically developed which leaves no room for speculation on the part of the palmist, and is as strict as that which denotes the meaning of certain angular relationships between planets.

Laymen who have not looked into the subject probably have no idea of its complexity. Some authors of textbooks of palmistry categorize no less than 80 different shapes and outlines of hands, for instance, and comment in detail on the dryness or moisture, the softness or hardness of the skin and other features, before going on to consider the marks on the palm and fingers – over a hundred of which are described in more than a hundred formal textbooks – let alone the many popular works on the subject published in this century.

There have been some remarkable palmists whose records, both as delineators of character and as predictors of the future, are well attested. "Cheiro" remains perhaps still the best known. His real name was Louis Hamon, and he was born in Ireland in 1858. He was a considerable traveller and explorer, a war correspondent and a writer for the early film industry; but it was as a palmist, under his pseudonym, that he was best known.

A phrenologist's shop *(below)* with its 35,000 testimonials, shows that phrenology continued to flourish well into this century, despite medical dismissal.

34

He set up business in London after allegedly studying palmistry in India, and became famous – or notorious – in a very short time.

One result of his fame is that many people kept careful records of his predictions. It is well attested, for instance, that after the first night of Oscar Wilde's *A Woman of No Importance* the playwright went to a party at which guests put their hands through a curtain for Cheiro to examine. Taking Wilde's, the palmist said that the left (denoting hereditary tendencies) was "the hand of a king", while the right (indicating individual development) was that of "a king who will send himself into exile". Wilde asked "at what date", and Cheiro replied "a few years from now, at about your fortieth year". Wilde was 40 when he was committed to Reading

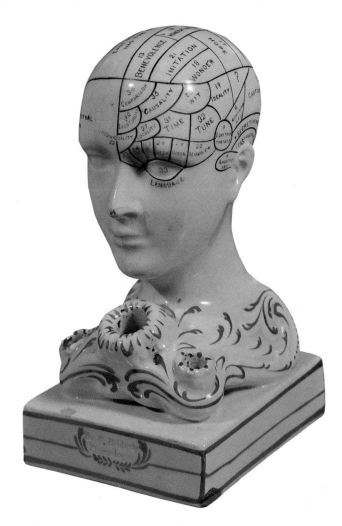

A fine china bust *(right)*, a legacy of the phrenology era, shows where the importantly indicative lumps of the skull could be found.

35

Gaol, and lived abroad after his release.

Cheiro had other remarkable successes, the most sensational perhaps being his accurate prediction that the soldier Lord Kitchener would die at sea – not a very likely prediction, but one which proved true (Kitchener was on a ship to Russia that was torpedoed in 1916), and within the time-span the palmist suggested.

Today, palmistry continues to be practised, and seems sometimes to be extremely accurate, not only in the delineation of character but in the prediction of trends in future life. There are a few scientific studies which relate to the matter, including those made of the links between abnormal palm-prints and some forty diseases, published in the 1960s.

Graphology

If the shape and lines of the hand tells something of a person's character, so too does the handwriting of an individual. Graphology has in recent years had a more "respectable" following than most other techniques in this area. The subject has been studied for many centuries: as early as the second century AD the Roman biographer Suetonius Tranquillus noted some of the peculiarities in the handwriting of Augustus Caesar; in China studies of the correlation between handwriting and personality were published in the eleventh century.

With the spread of literacy in Europe the subject became increasingly interesting, and by 1622 Camillo Baldi was claiming that "it is obvious that all persons write in their own way" and that "traits of character can be recognized in any handwriting". It was Baldo in fact who began to rationalize handwriting analysis; and his theories were developed by a number of French scholars, headed by the Abbé Michon (1806-81) – who actually coined the word "graphology" – and including Cardinal Regnier, Archbishop of Cambrai, and Crepieux Jamin.

Their claim was that the various elements of a person's handwriting could be matched to specific personality traits. They did not approve of rival claims that all that was necessary was to use a piece of handwriting simply as a starting-point for a clairvoyant or instinctive "reading", and at-

A cartoon by Rowlandson of 1815 *(right)* typifies the mockery frequently directed at the predictive arts. Despite such ridicule, evidence has continued to accrue in support of their claims.

36

tempted to lay down empirical rules similar to those which govern astrology or palmistry. They looked back, where they could, to their predecessors in eleventh-century China, and their theories were taken up by a wide range of contemporaries – including many writers and philosophers (Goethe, Lavater, Madame de Stael, Edgar Allan Poe and Robert Browning, among others). These Romantics were thrilled by the thought that handwriting gave an insight into character.

It was supposed that the character of a person unmistakably transferred itself to paper through the handwriting, which could not but be the product not only of the psychological nature (in, for instance, the placing of words upon a page, or the size of the writing) but of physiological factors (in the weight given to the pen, the tautness or looseness of the grip). Gradually, the theory was elaborated, and every element was examined.

No one could claim, of course, that one person's handwriting is completely indistinguishable from another's; the cleverest forger's work can now be scientifically identified. But the graphologist goes further than the scientist in suggesting that each element of the handwriting has a different meaning: they compare the slanting of letters, "closed" o's with "open" ones, and so on, and when the elements are all brought together it is said that there is a significant relationship with personality. It must be admitted however that sometimes their claims are based on very obvious and arguably false suggestions – that large writing denotes pride and ambition, for instance, rather than, maybe, simple short-sightedness.

There have been various developments within the field of graphology. The philosopher Ludwig Klages, for instance, studied the rhythm of handwriting and its relationship to the overall balance of a personality; Max Pulver looked at the symbolism of handwriting in much the same way in which Jung examined dreams; the scientist O. Bobertag set up tests to examine the claims of graphologists, and found them to be 85 per cent accurate in matching samples of handwriting to specific personalities.

Graphology has been used by the police, by teachers and vocational guidance advisers, in the study of insanity and in the diagnosis of medical conditions as well as in counselling. Many employers now use graphologists to test the handwriting of job applicants for any character defects. Scientific studies have revealed the possibility of diagnosing certain ailments (liver, heart and gastro-intestinal diseases, cancer, tuberculosis and psychiatric illness) and, it is claimed, "accident-proneness". These studies have shown that there are significant differences between the writing of "normal" people and epileptics, schizophrenics and manic-depressives. Graphology differs from other disciplines in that experts do not claim to be able to predict events; but they do claim to connect writing to character is such a way that, for instance, a change in its nature could well indicate a change in the character or nature of the person concerned. And they do claim to be able to see major trends in such people's lives.

One of the most interesting – and puzzling – of all apparent means of looking into the future is that of dreams. In the long history of dream interpretation, the "messages" man received in his dreams were at first regarded as supernatural. The ancient Egyptians believed that they were

Cheiro, the great palmist, predicted that Lord Kitchener *(right)* would die at sea – an odd fate for a soldier. But Kitchener's ship to Russia was in fact torpedoed in 1916 and he was drowned.

BRITONS

"WANTS YOU"

JOIN YOUR COUNTRY'S ARMY!

GOD SAVE THE KING

Reproduced by permission of LONDON OPINION

messages from the gods; for example, an Egyptian called Thothmes dreamed that the Sun-god Ra told him he would become Pharoah, as indeed happened. The Greeks too treated them as divine messages (Plutarch called them the oldest oracle); the early Christians often took the same line (there are many examples in the Old Testament such as Jacob's dream of the ladder let down from heaven). But the idea that a dream could show one the future is also an ancient one, and is found in the earliest books interpreting dream symbols. 15th century dream books attempted to teach dreamers techniques that would encourage prophetic dreams (for example, if one ate a salted herring before going to sleep one would dream of a future partner!).

In this century, the psychologist Jung examined apparently prophetic dreams. He did not believe that they always foretold the future – but that when one was asleep one somehow became capable of projecting one's thoughts forward into the future, sometimes with great freedom, and occasionally striking truth. J. W. Dunne had more specifically predictive dreams, recorded in his *An Experiment with Time* (see p.14). The British writer J. B. Priestley (who wrote several plays on the theme of time) recorded a great many predictive dreams sent to him by readers. Many of them are trivial, but remarkable. One, for instance, involved a BBC engineer who, when he was a student, dreamed that a sparrow-hawk perched on his right shoulder. Two hours later the landlord of his lodgings came into his room with a stuffed sparrow hawk he was about to throw on the fire, and one of his fellow-students took it, came up behind him, and "dug its claws into the shoulder of my jacket with sufficient force to enable it to remain standing on my shoulder". He felt the bird's claws dig into his flesh, as he had felt in his dream.

This kind of experience is in a sense more impressive than the many dreams of great national events such as earthquakes or assassinations; these are in the nature of things, and with every person on earth dreaming four or five dreams each night it would be truly extraordinary if someone had not dreamed of, say the suicide of Marilyn Monroe or the assassination of President Kennedy. (This does not make any less remarkable, however such detailed "visions" as those of Jeane Dixon – which she did not, in fact, receive in dreams).

The number of people having "prophetic dreams" of one sort or another is considerable: a survey taken in the 1960s suggests that they amount to over 80 per cent of the population. Many of them fall into the category of *déjà vu* – as when people recognize places they have formerly seen in dreams. In some cases they seem to involve time-travel into the past: the British comedian Roy Hudd, visiting for the first time the home of the great music hall artist Dan Leno, recognized it from his dreams – with the additional detail of furnishings which had long since vanished.

If one recognizes that prophetic dreams exist (and the evidence is copious and often convincing) it brings one sharply up against the problem of the nature of time and predestination. The German philosopher Arthur Schopenhauer (1788-1860), who experienced them, believed that they implied predestination, and many people fear this to be true, which results in their being terrified when they dream for instance of accidents in which they are involved. On the other hand there are examples of men and women avoiding accidents because they have "foreseen" them in dreams – getting off aircraft which have subsequently crashed, or being ready to rescue children falling into dangers foreseen in sleep.

Well established, too, is another form of "predictive" dream which is intensely useful and in fact scientifically explicable: our bodies can often signal in dreams the symptoms of an illness long before such symptoms are sufficiently strong to be recognized by doctors. There is one well-supported case of a doctor – a London surgeon – who dreamed of a malignant

C. G. Jung, (1875-1961) the great Swiss psychologist (above) was particularly interested in the *I Ching*, the great Chinese oracle, which he consulted both for his patients and himself. His theories underpin many aspects of prediction.

Jacob's dream *(right)* in which Jacob saw angels descending a ladder let down from heaven, is perhaps the most famous of all predictive dreams in the Bible.

39

tumour on the back of a patient. Faced the following day with the signs of a tumour in such a position he decided to operate despite the fact that it appeared benign. It was later shown to be malignant, and the patient would probably have died without the operation.

The claims of seers or predictors probably now meet with less scepticism or outright rejection from the varied medical, psychological, mathematical or allied scientific worlds than at any time in the last 150 years. Too many uncertainties now face previously confident scientists in their own researches for them to dismiss such claims altogether. Perhaps if all predictions were cloaked in language as ambivalent as that of the Delphic Oracle, predictors would almost always prove to be right. But even without such infallibility, astronomers, palmists and cartomancers can claim to throw uncanny light on the characters of the individuals who come to them for guidance. And, as a Greek philosopher, Heraclitus, long ago said, "Character is destiny".

Science of Prediction

The occult world – and with it the predictive sciences – retreated before the rationalism of the Age of Enlightenment. At the same time, revealed religion came under increasing attack as being incompatible with science, with the idea of God being reduced to that of a distant "clockmaker" who had created the universe and then set it to run on inviolable mechanical principles. Ironically, in this century, it has been great scientists like Albert Einstein who have undermined the earlier rational view of the Universe.

From the 18th century onwards, attacks on unconventional medicine, astrology, clairvoyance and the divinatory arts became more and more insistent. To admit to an interest in them was to invite at best laughter and at worst contempt, or even suspicion. Ironically, it was the work of certain scientists – most notably Albert Einstein – and of one of the greatest practitioners of the new art of psychology, C. G. Jung, that was to help create a new and more serious interest in parapsychology, extra-sensory perception (ESP) and psychokinesis (PK), and through them to try to illuminate the nature of precognition and prediction.

On one level, many predictive processes have been based on the fact that because something has happened regularly in the past, it is more than likely to happen again. The simplest example is perhaps the daily sunrise. Because we wake every morning to this phenomenon, we regard it as exceptionally unlikely that it will not happen tomorrow. In a universe of strange events, it is quite possible that some giant calamity may prevent it; but we are so sure of the event that we take it for granted.

We use our reliance on what might be called "normal repetition" in every area of our daily life: we expect all sorts of things because our expectation has in the past been satisfied. The coffee will be in its place on the shelf tomorrow because that is where it usually is; the television news will begin at a particular hour this evening because that is when it usually begins.

What might be called scientific prediction depends entirely on this same expectation that patterns will be repeated: the English meteorological service uses the largest computer in Europe to forecast the weather, in the confident assumption that sufficient information, fed into it, will enable it to predict the pattern of meteorological events on the basis of past experience, where such events have followed a similar pattern.

Some things, of course, are far more uncertain than others: if we toss a coin and it falls head-up, we can really make no firm assumption about how it will fall when we toss it a second time. It is this uncertainty which is at the heart of the gambling instinct.

Gamblers toy with the idea that they *can* predict the fall of the coin. They are often wrong.

In the late 18th century the mathematician Pierre-Simon Laplace (1749-1827) thought a great deal about chance and our experience of it, and in 1795 published his Theory of Probability. Taking the example of the tossed coin, he pointed out that (provided the coin is not weighted) when we call heads, we have one chance in two of being right; if we attempt to predict, in the same manner, which way up a six-sided die is cast, we have one chance in six of being right. So the probability of an outcome can be defined as the ratio of the number of correct predictions to the number of possible ones.

This is not a scientific theory, because it depends on our conviction that each result is equally possible. We all know that that is untrue. If it were, when we tossed a coin one hundred times it would come down 50 times with the head uppermost and 50 times with the tail uppermost. That is not the case. But the Probability Theory is still a convenient one for testing whether a prediction is accurate, for the coin is apparently independent: it doesn't remember how it last fell – if it has come down tails 65 times, the chances of it coming down tails on the 66th occasion is no different that when it was thrown first: still one in two.

Happily, the more chances that are available, the more dependable the Theory becomes. Take a pair of dice, for instance, and consider the chances of throwing two sixes. The chance of throwing one six is obviously six to one; so that of throwing two sixes is 36 to one. Throw two double sixes with the dice, and the chances become 36 × 36, which is 1,296. Both scientists and seers were quick to see that the Theory of Probability could be used to test various means of prediction: if someone correctly predicted an abnormally large number of throws of a coin or turns of a card, then something very odd indeed (scientifically speaking) was happening.

This "something odd" began, early this century, to intrigue those more open-minded scientists. Despite increasing familiarity with what seemed to be the

J. B. Rhine (*above*) in the 1930s was one of the first investigators to study people's predictive powers on a scientific basis. Using cards marked with crosses, circles or squares, he found some people could tell which had been chosen far more often than would be expected – in fact, they were clairvoyant. This machine (*below*) was designed to test further the subject's ESP potential, by eliminating all chances of telepathy.

42

invariable laws of the universe, they were not convinced that there was an obvious scientific solution to every known phenomenon. J. B. Rhine, an American working in North Carolina, began in the 1930s to examine the undoubted fact that some people are remarkably good at making simple predictions: they "feel" that an event will occur, and it does. Most of us use the faculty simply enough: following a hunch, we might turn up early at the bus stop, to find that the bus is five minutes early. But it is used more importantly in other ways: every medical man, for instance, will tell you of the importance of intuition in medical diagnosis.

Science and ESP

Rhine, deciding to look at this strange but familiar talent, used a set of 25 cards marked with simple symbols – a square, a circle, a diamond – and invited people to guess, without seeing the card, which one had been selected from the pack. To get 5 of the 25 right would be about average. But some people, Rhine found, were considerably more accurate than that, even when the cards were mechanically or electronically chosen, and they were asked to identify not a single card but a whole run. The success rate was often more than a million times higher than chance – one nine-year-old girl, for instance, named all 25 cards correctly on one occasion, and 23 on another.

It was interesting that while people chosen at random scored more highly than chance would allow, but not spectacularly so, those who felt a special sympathy with the experiment or the scientists conducting it made spectacularly successful "guesses". This is in line with those clairvoyants or ESP practitioners who claim that an unsympathetic atmosphere can throw up an insurmountable barrier between them and success; that they simply cannot exercise their talents surrounded by people who, even secretly, do not believe they can do what they claim.

Experiments like Rhine's have been repeated again and again, and often with equally remarkable results: a man called Basil Shackleton, working in London in the early 1940s with cards bearing images of animals, "guessed" correctly 1,101 out of 3,789 times – which, as Lyall Watson points out, is a result so successful that it could not have been achieved by chance "even if the entire population of the world had tried the experiment every day since the beginning of the Tertiary period, 60 million years ago."

It is fair to point out that what Shackleton and his many fellow subjects were doing was not foretelling what cards *would be* chosen from a pile, but telling which cards *had been* chosen, even if their vision of the card chosen was often almost simultaneous. Their talent was inexplicable enough, but it was not the same as a talent for prediction. Yet it surely is of the same nature, and it would not be unreasonable to claim that there was some connection between the two.

A similar gloss on the talent of the seer comes when we examine PK, (psychokinesis), or the ability of some people to have a physical effect on things without being in contact with them. The Israeli Uri Geller is the best-known modern example of someone who can bend metals without touching; he has been accused of being a trickster, but has never been caught cheating. Neither has the equally extraordinary Russian Kulagina.

It seems a strong possibility that we "choose" a particular Tarot card or rune in the same way; that we "force" three coins to fall in a particular pattern when we throw them to determine the lines of the hexagrams of the *I Ching*. Everyone who has chosen a set of runes or cards will be familiar with the strong force which appears to draw them to particular stones or cards. The question presents itself whether we choose the cards or they choose us. So, does the future impose itself upon us, or do we – *can* we – choose it?

Scrying or "peeping" into the future with crystals became popular in the 19th century. This group (*above*) is relying on their mental powers which become concentrated and focused by the crystal.

A fortune teller from Trivandrum, India displays a wide range of prediction techniques, including some not common in the west, such as astro-palmistry. In fact, palmistry and astrology *are* connected – the mount of Venus in the hand links to the planet Venus. Most predictive disciplines are ultimately interrelated.

Xylomancy, or divination by throwing sticks, (*above*) has long been common as a form of prediction throughout East Asia. This fortune-teller from Vietnam is relying on the same basic powers in his ancient approach as any of Rhine's subjects.

Scientists who have observed ESP and PK have done little to suggest how they might operate, let alone explain them. Both phenomena run counter to scientific theories of space and time – space seems to have little to do with the success or failure of either, for experiments conducted over great distances by radio or TV have been as successful as those in a small room. It has been thought that some new form of energy or field of force is involved; Jung's theory of the collective unconscious has been invoked – a great pool of indefinable and unexplained energy, manifesting in primorlial images or "archetypes" with which some people find it easier than most to remain or to get in touch. The "projection hypothesis" suggests an undefined power of the mind which can act outside the known laws of nature. But as to why or how some people can apparently make use of this energy, while others cannot, has not so far been explained.

Yet gradually the outlines of the mysterious talent of the medium, seer or fortune-teller are being filled in. We know that (perhaps surprisingly) extroverts are better at PK and ESP than introverts; that reward and punishment inhibit results – supporting the insistence of seers that their powers are too sensitive to be insulted by such worldly considerations as profit or loss. And we need not despair when some scientists tell us that the long catalogue of successful experiments is not enough to convince them that PK and ESP exist. Many scientific theories remained unproved for years, but were eventually successfully demonstrated. (It took over a century for the heliocentric theory first propounded by Copernicus to be generally accepted, for example.) However, that catalogue of experiments does offer the soundest modern approach to prediction for those who are uneasy either about the possibility or wisdom of predicting events: it leads us to the conclusion that whether or not we can foretell what is going to happen, some people can to some extent make and shape the future, if only in predicting the turn of a card. Can they do more? The prediction of events in human life is vastly more difficult because of the myriad intangibles involved. If we are asked what we want of the future, it is often difficult to reply; we rarely see our human situation clearly, and find the

43

Michel Nostradamus
(*above*) was probably the
most famous of all seers –
the only one whose books
still sell four centuries after
his death in 1566. Some of
his visions of the future have
been proved right.

44

**An astrological swimming
pool** in Hollywood illustrates
the modern revival of
astrology. Now it is part of
everyday language, and
enormously popular in all
Western cultures as well as
in the East.

complexities of life perplexing and difficult to rationalize. Ask us what we
expect to happen, and similarly we find it difficult to say. We either hedge
our predictions with numerous qualifications, or decline to make a forecast (often because we superstitiously fear that to state a wish openly is to
ensure that it will not come true). If we examine the history of prediction,
we find that while those who consult seers appear to be asking what is
going to happen, what they are really asking is, "What am I to do?", or
"What should I expect?" And if we look at the answers given by the seers –
whether at Delphi or in a clairvoyant's consulting room – we find that far
from making a firm prediction they are directed at persuading the querant to discover his real intentions, and act to accomplish them.

Professional predictors

Astrologers, Tarot readers or rune masters are always being asked to
foretell events. On the evidence we so far possess, it seems impossible to
predict the future in any detail. The few highly successful astrologers or
clairvoyants who claim that they can make firm correct predictions must
answer one simple question: why, then, are they not powerful and rich?
Can it be doubted for an instant that someone capable of invariably successful prediction would be world famous, employed by presidents or
prime ministers, retained at enormous salaries by business concerns? A
few do indeed advise businessmen, geologists and even (in California)
police forces. But not, it seems, with sufficient success to make their masters or themselves multimillionaires or world rulers.

This contrasts sharply with past ages, when astrologers found ready and
lucrative employment at the courts of the mighty. Nostradamus, the great
16th century French seer, was appointed to the court of the French king
Henry II and managed to predict the exact time of the king's death four
years later. What evidence we have suggests that information so strangely
received comes to us along lines about which we know nothing. It also
suggests that we all have "antennae" which we can use in this way,
provided that we accept the irrational intuition which enables us
somehow to see the future now.

This book has two purposes. In describing the major methods by which
men and women have, over the past 5,000 years, attempted to look into
the future, it enables us to sharpen those nebulous and irrational instincts
which the best clairvoyants have grasped and honed to make them seem-
ingly capable of the incredible. We believe that, with care, we can all learn
to use those instincts which, perhaps by grasping signals which cannot be
measured in conventional terms, enable us to intuit the future.

The second thing that this book does is to offer readers just those
techniques which have enabled us to shape the future so that it coincides
with what we hope or want of it.

It is not impossible that the future does exist, somewhere, in some
sense we cannot understand; and perhaps if that is so, then it exists absolutely – so that we cannot change it. If it does exist but we *can* change it, it
can only be by personal intervention; to intervene, we must in some way
project ourselves into the future; if we do that, then the future becomes,
for us, the present, and we will have abolished it!

But by using the *I Ching* or the Tarot, we can learn to see future possibilities more clearly, and can learn to live with them, whatever they are.
We can see what the future may be, and accept it. When it holds no terrors
for us, we can reject the need to know about it in detail. Then, indeed, we
will have abolished the future: what we will have is a progressive *now*, in
which everything is possible and therefore knowable. We will have
learned, as T. S. Eliot put it, "While time is withdrawn, [to] consider the
future / And the past with an equal mind . . ."

Perhaps, then, we will no longer need to know "what the future holds".

Predictive Techniques

Tarot

Traditionally linked with divination, the unique Tarot deck of 22 picture cards, the Major Arcana, *depicts haunting, mysterious subjects such as the Hanged Man, the Magician, the Fool, the High Priestess (or Popess), and the Wheel of Fortune. Such images represent potent symbols which may provide a key to the future and to our inner selves.*

In addition to the 22 picture cards of the Major Arcana, the Tarot comprises the *Minor Arcana* of 56 number cards and court cards, much like those of an ordinary pack. The combination of the two packs, making a total of 78 cards, occurred in Italy during the 14th century. This 78-card deck was used to play a game called Tarrocchi, but it also provided a means of divination in which the symbols of the Major Arcana play an essential role.

The 56 cards of the Minor Arcana are divided into 4 suits, each with 4 court cards (King, Queen, Knight and Page) and 40 cards numbered from 1 to 10. Instead of Hearts, Spades, Clubs and Diamonds, these suits are Swords, Batons (or Wands), Cups and Coins (or Pentacles). In fact, Cups relate to Hearts, Coins to Diamonds, Swords to Spades, and Batons to Clubs.

An attempt has been made to link the Tarot with the Jewish mystical system known as the *Kaballa*. JOD, the first letter of the divine name JEVE, represents eternal force, wisdom and divine royalty, and may be associated with the King court card and the suit of Wands or Sceptres. The second, HE, symbolizes creation and motherhood, and may link with the Queen court card and the suit of Cups or Hearts. The third letter, VAU, represents the bond of love, the mystery of union and the Tree of Life, and is associated with the Knight and the suit of Swords. The fourth letter, HE, represents the association between physical and spiritual, humanity and divinity, corresponding with the Page and the suit of Pentacles or Coins.

However, the Tarot contains many symbols from other sources, deriving partly from Greek and Roman myth, partly from much older symbols and half-forgotten legends, and partly from Christian teaching. It also has strong associations with astrology. For all its antiquity, the pack still presents to us today a recognizable symbolic picture of the world around us, so that when we consult it, we are able to identify the various elements and apply them to our questions.

There are various kinds of Tarot pack and various designs, both ancient and modern. It is desirable that you simply choose the one that appeals most strongly to you (we cannot illustrate them all here, but most specialist bookshops will have a number of packs on offer). In the following pages we use the standard Marseilles pack (c. 1557) – its traditional illustrations are perhaps easiest for a beginner. In contrast is the highly pictorial 19th century Rider Waite pack, which shows clearly the symbols and images associated with the 22 cards of the Major Arcana.

These strangely illustrated cards, also known as the Greater Trumps, are unrelated to conventional playing cards, and represent a unique feature of the Tarot. They follow a sequence from "The Magician" (I) to "The World" (XXI) and are numbered in Roman numerals. They are introduced by "The Fool", which is not numbered and may have affinities with the Joker of ordinary playing cards.

How should the cards be used?

As we explain in the following pages, the fall of the cards and their relationship to each other in a particular spread provide the answers to the questions asked. When drawn in a reading, the cards relate to your hopes and desires and will sharpen your attitude, whatever sphere of your life is under scrutiny.

However, like the *I Ching*, the Tarot does not offer a firm picture of what is going to happen, but a vista of possibilities, a commentary on your own state of mind as you ask your question about the future, the approach you should make, the climate that may await you, and how you should react to it.

Each card represents an individual and distinctive principle (see pp.48-55) and has a title which gives a clue about its appearance and interpretation. All are used in divination: they are chosen by the person asking the question (the querant), and laid out in one of the patterns described on pp.65-71. They may then be interpreted either by a Tarot interpreter or by the querant. However, it is usually better to read the cards for others, or have them read for you, than to attempt to read them for yourself. Distancing yourself from your own problems is notoriously difficult, whereas others are not affected by your inner prejudices and fixations, and may be able to see more clearly the symbolism's application to your problem.

Major Arcana

The evocative symbolism of the Major Arcana, reaching deep into the unconscious, distinguishes the Tarot from a mere fortune-telling implement. The cards certainly offer an interpretation of the future but their symbols also inspire the seeker to understand his or her motives and state of mind. Familiarity with these cards is an essential starting point for anyone wishing to use the Tarot effectively.

The gallery of cards given below presents the Major Arcana one by one in traditional numerical order.

Packs vary in their depiction of them and the descriptions given here are most appropriate to the Marseilles pack. Discrepancies in illustrations are not important; what matters is your reaction to your own choice of cards and the interpretation they suggest.

The interpretation of each card shown here carries a summary of the symbolic meaning of the card, followed by its practical application. It must be stressed that complete comprehension of the Major Arcana depends on a thorough knowledge of both aspects if a sound interpretation is to be achieved.

TAROT
Words in *itals* = keyword associated with each card.

LE MAT
THE FOOL

LE BATELEUR
THE MAGICIAN

LA PAPESSE
THE HIGH PRIESTESS

0 The Fool – *Everyman*
The Fool represents human nature with all its strengths and weaknesses. He is urged on by his dog (is the dog friend or foe?) and is well prepared for his journey. He carries a bundle which may represent inherited knowledge, instinct or intuition; but will he use these provisions wisely?
Message: Listen to your wiser self. This card alerts you to your weaknesses and stresses that self-awareness is the key to psychological and spiritual wholeness. It urges you to think twice: thoughtless action leads to regrets. Immature behaviour, folly and indiscretion will cause difficulty in any sphere of your life. If you are at the outset of a new project, you should examine the situation closely. Perhaps you have been viewing it through rose-coloured spectacles?

I The Magician – *Skill, adaptability*
The Magician presides over all the suits of the Minor Arcana and may call on them to further his own progress and development. His hat bears a horizontal representation of the figure 8 – the figure attributed to Hermes in occultism (see Mercury p.110). The Magician is original, creative and flexible but he is also very cunning and capable of manipulating others for good or ill.
Message: This card suggests you should not be apprehensive about taking positive and determined action. Weakness of will and an unoriginal approach will impede progress. You are in a strong position to influence others; be compassionate but forceful.

Variations in title – the Major Arcana

Titles of the Major Arcana vary from pack to pack and are sometimes given in French or Italian. Below we list some of the main differences as well as the French and Italian titles. This will help you identify the cards in your particular pack and link them to those set out in the following pages.

0 The Fool: The Foolish Man, *Le Mat, Le Fou, Le Fol, Il Matto*

I The Magician: The Juggler, The Thimble-Rigger, The Cup Player, The Mountebank, The Pagad, *Le Batteleur, Le Joueur de Gobelets, Il Bagatto, Il Bagattel*

II The High Priestess: The Female Pope, The Popess, Junon, *La Papesse, La Papessa*

III The Empress: *L'Impératrice, L'Imperatrice*

IV The Emperor: *L'Empereur, L'Impereur*

V The Pope: The Hierophant, Jupiter, *Le Pape, Il Papa*

VI The Lovers: The Lover, *L'Amoureux, L'Amant, Gli Amanti*

VII The Chariot: *Le Chariot, Il Carro*

VIII Justice: *La Justice, La Giustizia*

VIIII The Hermit: *L'Ermite, L'Ermita*

X The Wheel of Fortune: *La Roue de Fortune, La Rota di Fortuna*

XI Strength: Force or Fortitude, *La Force, La Forza*

XII The Hanged Man: *Le Pendu, Il Penduto*

XIII Death: *La Mort, Il Morte*

XIIII Temperance: *La Temperance, La Temperanza*

XV The Devil: *Le Diable, Il Diavolo*

XVI The Tower: The Tower of Destruction, The Lightning-struck Tower, The House of God, The Hospital, The Tower of Babel, Fire of Heaven, *La Maison de Dieu, La Torre*

XVII The Star: *L'Étoile, La Stella*

XVIII The Moon: *La Lune, La Luna*

XIX The Sun: *Le Soleil, Il Sole*

XX Judgement: The Last Judgement, *Le Jugement, L'Angelo, Il Giudizio*

XXI The World: The Universe, *Le Monde, Il Mondo*

II The High Priestess (Popess) – *Discrimination*
Quintessentially feminine, the High Priestess poses a challenge to masculine dominance. She is usually shown reading a book and her expression is calm – but does her composure merely serve to mask her emotions?
Message: The High Priestess symbolizes wisdom. She is willing to share her knowledge with others and advises introspection. Listen to what others have to say but analyse it carefully. Be organized and discreet; hidden influences may be at work. Let intuition and your positive emotional responses guide you. The High Priestess also has a bearing on health and diet and is perhaps urging you to review these two areas of your life.

III The Empress – *Security*
The Emperor's consort and the feminine principle, the Empress represents desire in all its forms. She symbolizes emotional and financial security, suggesting an enjoyment of earthly pleasures and material comfort. Often depicted as pregnant, she stresses fertility and fruitful union. She brings harmony and partnership to personal or business relationships. Her nature is creative and resolute, passionate and honest. She may represent any dominant female in your life: mother, daughter or wife.
Message: Be confident and decisive in financial matters but also diplomatic. If you are about to make an important decision, she warns you not to be tempted to take the line of least resistance. An assertive approach will bring success. You may have to help your partner; be encouraging and supportive and motivate him or her for your mutual progress, but beware of being too possessive. Resist the temptation to squander money or to take part in backbiting.

L'EMPEREUR
THE EMPEROR

LE PAPE
THE POPE

L'AMOUREUX
THE LOVER

IV The Emperor – *Action*
The Emperor signifies temporal power achieved through action. He has attained his position of authority by virtue of his brave and energetic approach. Formerly aggressive and violent, he is now mellowing, although he is still a fiery character prone to impulsive and extravert behaviour. He has nonetheless learnt from experience and gained wisdom. He is the archetypal male, assuming the roles of father, brother and husband, as the Empress (his companion) represents the female counterparts.
Message: The Emperor bestows strength and firmness in the attainment of goals. He suggests we channel our energy and use it positively. His advice offers the benefit of his experience: be wary of premature action and immature behaviour. He appreciates the strength of the desire to win, but the means of victory should not involve a ruthless attitude towards other people. With power comes responsibility. Don't let your passionate nature rule your head.

V The Pope –
Enlightenment
The Pope wears the triple crown – symbol of power in the three worlds of Man, the Soul and Eternity. His authority is absolute, but he is a sympathetic and compassionate ruler. He is merciful and just and sets a good example. He encourages you to stick by the rules – perhaps the rules

of your own conscience. You have the right to choose to obey or disobey, as symbolized by the two pillars behind him.
Message: The Pope stresses the value of integrity: look deep into your heart, then act with the courage of your convictions. Banish superficial considerations and focus your mind on more important matters.

VI The Lovers (The Lover)
– *Love, harmony, choice*
Cupid shoots his arrow, endowed with energy from the Sun, at a young couple below. In many older decks a young man is shown standing between two female figures, "Virtue" and "Vice", who represent alternatives and imply that a choice needs to be made. In other packs a couple are shown exchanging marriage vows. The card is rich in symbolism; on one level it represents human love in its finest form, but there is also an implicit warning: Cupid inflames the passions, and the Lover must preserve a sense of honour and trust if a long and lasting spiritual love, as well as sensual pleasure, is to bless their union.
Message: If embarking on a new love affair or trying to revitalize an existing relationship, remember the Lover's warning: Don't fall in love with love, this may be just an infatuation.

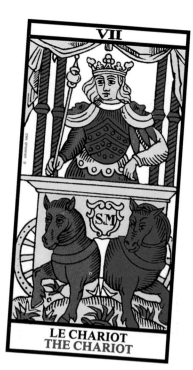

LE CHARIOT
THE CHARIOT

L'HERMITE
THE HERMIT

51

LA JUSTICE
JUSTICE

VII The Chariot – *Vitality*
A handsome young hero rides resplendent in his chariot. Crowned and carrying a sceptre, he represents youth, movement, achievement and popularity. He appears to have been in battle and is returning home triumphant. His two horses, sometimes depicted as sphinxes, represent his spiritual and sexual drives, but there is a hint of conflict here as the two appear to be travelling in opposite directions. The upturned and outward looking faces on his epaulettes reinforce this impression.
Message: The over-riding message of this card is to have faith in yourself. It stresses victory through self-awareness. Our capacity for achievement is a measure of our ability to balance mental and physical strength. Success will come through a combination of hard work and careful reflection. You should be feeling optimistic, but are you pushing yourself to your full intellectual capacity? Now is the time to fulfil your potential. This card is also auspicious for travellers.

VIII Justice – *Balance*
Justice maintains the balance between positive and negative. She is equable and fair. The pillars behind her throne represent moral strength and integrity. She has the gift of clear judgment; the ability to differentiate between right and wrong.
Message: Justice advises you to be reasonable, impartial and restrained. However, this does not mean you should sit on the fence and refuse to make a decision. She is essentially practical and encourages you to analyse your situation practically. Perhaps you should be more self-critical, but don't dwell on problems for too long; worry can be self-defeating if it is not applied practically.

IX The Hermit – *Truth, knowledge, prudence*
Although the Hermit has acquired sage-like wisdom and experience during a long life, he continues to seek truth. His lamp symbolizes his continual quest for knowledge. Occasionally he may withdraw from the world but he also realizes that too much knowledge can become a responsibility, and is therefore willing to put it to practical use by counselling others.
Message: The Hermit stresses the value of wisdom; he may use this either to his benefit or that of other people. He warns you never to assume you know everything there is to know. Keep an open mind in all situations and be receptive to new developments. Perhaps you should withdraw and assess your situation critically. Be cautious in your actions and discriminating in your choice of friends and colleagues. The Hermit's ability to stand back from a situation allows him to remain flexible and avoid stubborness.

LA ROUE DE FORTUNE
THE WHEEL OF FORTUNE

LE PENDU
THE HANGED MAN

LA FORCE
FORCE

X The Wheel of Fortune –
Equilibrium, change
Three creatures, two monkeys and a sphinx (or in some packs a monkey with lion's claws), are trying to balance on the ever-turning wheel of fortune. One monkey is definitely on the downward path while the other is making his way towards the peak of success. The third creature is poised comfortably on the top. He looks confident but the wheel of fortune is in perpetual motion, so his security is questionable. In some decks the angel, lion, ox and eagle – Evangelist symbols – decorate the corners of the card. They represent permanency and serve as a contrast to the ever-changing world.
Message: The menagerie reminds us of change: the flux of fortune and the fine balance between success and failure. You may be about to enter a new cycle, or perhaps you are coming to the end of a problematic period. In either case your circumstances are about to change.

XI Force or Strength –
Fortitude, conquest
A beautiful woman battles with a lion and appears to be winning without too much trouble. Gentle determination gets the better of brute strength – the iron hand in the velvet glove. Like the Magician, she wears a large hat decorated with the figure 8 (the occult number attributed to Hermes or Mercury, see p.110). This symbolizes the combination of conscious and unconscious power.
Message: This card advises you to develop your powers of understanding by listening to your intuition. The obstacles that appear to be impeding your progress may be imaginary. Self-awareness breeds confidence and is the best route to success. You have spiritual power on your side, so rid yourself of nebulous worries and take determined action.

XII The Hanged Man –
Transition
The Hanged Man here is very much alive. He is in a state of inactivity, perhaps experiencing a moment of calm before the truth is revealed. If you are not familiar with the Tarot's symbolism, you may find this violent image somewhat alarming, but the Hanged Man does not represent physical pain. It is a symbol which has been traced to the Florentine custom of painting criminals on walls: if they were still at large they were shown hanging by the ankle as in this card.
Message: The Hanged Man may herald a change of mind or opinion, or perhaps signify a period of respite between two events. Be patient, use this time wisely to collect your thoughts. You will instinctively know when the time is right to move on. Rest, but don't completely relax your guard – you may have a rival working against you, causing more havoc than you realize. Be alert.

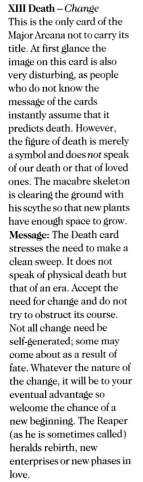

XIII Death – *Change*
This is the only card of the Major Arcana not to carry its title. At first glance the image on this card is also very disturbing, as people who do not know the message of the cards instantly assume that it predicts death. However, the figure of death is merely a symbol and does *not* speak of our death or that of loved ones. The macabre skeleton is clearing the ground with his scythe so that new plants have enough space to grow.
Message: The Death card stresses the need to make a clean sweep. It does not speak of physical death but that of an era. Accept the need for change and do not try to obstruct its course. Not all change need be self-generated; some may come about as a result of fate. Whatever the nature of the change, it will be to your eventual advantage so welcome the chance of a new beginning. The Reaper (as he is sometimes called) heralds rebirth, new enterprises or new phases in love.

XIV Temperance – *Moderation*
Temperance is orderly, disciplined and careful. She is in control of the situation, able to transfer water from one urn to the other without spilling a drop. The water is said to represent the essence of life, and her action may be seen to symbolize the merger of past with future. The difficulty of her task emphasizes the value she places on diligence. She is a kindly mother figure who urges hard work. The open landscape stretching behind her may symbolize opportunity. She is also said to be the Angel of the Moon, and is often shown standing by a flowing river.

Message: The symbols of water and the Moon are traditionally associated with the emotions. The figure of Temperance in this context therefore advises you to control your emotions. A sense of fulfilment, peace and harmony will result. The open landscape stretching behind her suggests you draw on your natural resources: use your talents to attain your goals. Work hard and your efforts will be rewarded, and strive for harmony in your relationships with others. You are probably better liked and more respected than you imagine. You may be about to deepen an emotional relationship. If so, this card is very positive.

XV The Devil – *Self-awareness*
The Devil is one of the most striking figures of the pack; a macabre (in some packs androgynous) figure, his image dominates the card. Man is represented by the two figures tethered to his pedestal. But look carefully, their bonds are not secure and they could easily slip through them.
Message: This card holds a warning: the individual is not trapped, but merely thinks he is. You can liberate yourself from the chains that bind you and beat the devil within. The devil never disappears entirely, but you can counteract his influence by being aware of your weaknesses. Don't rely on others or allow yourself to be tempted into lazy, self-destructive ways.

53

XVI The Tower of Destruction – *Risk, breakthrough*

A bolt of lightning strikes down a solid tower. This violent image symbolizes a great revelation: truth shattering an illusion. The Tower represents old beliefs and appears to be firm, but it cannot withstand the natural force of the lightning. In this pack the Tower only has three small windows, emphasizing a limited outlook.

Message: This violent image creates an instant impression of destruction, indicating shattered illusion, revelation or drastic change. It represents a complete break with the past. You are likely to take risks in the near future. Tread carefully, you are also very accident-prone at the moment. Expect the unexpected and be confident that, whatever the change, it will be to your eventual advantage.

XVII The Star – *Hope*

The maiden on the card is called Proserpine, traditionally destined to spend one-third of the year with Pluto, King of the Underworld, and the rest of the time with her mother Ceres. She is pouring the water of life and bringing moisture and thus fertility to earth. The large star is that seen by the Magi; the seven smaller ones represent hope. The promise of renewal is reinforced by the birds and the shrubs in the background.

Message: Proserpine tells us to be optimistic and positive. She represents pure spiritual love which lends insight. The presence of this card in a reading begs a question – have you been too restless or superficial in the past? The influence of the Star is positive. Your outlook is bright and you are continually becoming psychologically stronger. You may be feeling restless; be constructive, this is a good time to make firm decisions about your long term future. Don't allow negative thoughts, worries or inhibitions to obstruct your progress. Be determined but remain sympathetic to others. Consistent effort will be rewarded.

XVIII The Moon – *Susceptibility, deception*

The Moon herself is the dominant image of this card. She is beautiful but, like moonlight, can also be deceptive. Note too how the dogs, supposedly man's best friend, look like wolves. The presence of the crab or crayfish in the water below symbolizes fears or inhibitions, and reinforces this card's emphasis on the hidden.

Message: Above all, the Moon warns against self-deception. You should ask yourself whether the conditions of your life are what they appear to be. Could you be labouring under some illusion? The presence of the crab or crayfish points to our inner fears, the hidden anxieties which prevent positive psychological development. Perhaps your emotions are affecting your judgment. You may have been overemotional or perhaps you have overreacted to a situation. Be wary of false friends or rivals.

LE SOLEIL
THE SUN

LE JUGEMENT
JUDGEMENT

LE MONDE
THE WORLD

XIX The Sun – *Joy*

The Sun heaps energy, warmth and happiness on a young, contented couple who are about to embrace. They appear trusting and uninhibited; an example of pure love. They represent contentment, fulfilment and true friendship. Even so, the Sun also has a harsher side; its rays can be damaging.

Message: Fire is a good servant but a cruel master. Do not be lulled into a false sense of security by the apparently positive influence ruling your life at present. Avoid the trap of complacency. The Sun gives vitality, energy and creative power – exploit these talents to the full. Take pleasure from pure, simple things and the arts. The Sun is a particularly auspicious card if you are about to marry or have a child. The message is essentially positive, but it does carry a warning: beware of pride.

XX Judgement –

Transformation

An angel summons men from their graves. The figure appears to be offering atonement for past mistakes and the possibility of a new beginning. Misdemeanours are being exposed and absolved, allowing sinners to be transformed and to live their lives on a higher plane of existence.

Message: This card calls for self-analysis. It suggests that if you examine your faults and weaknesses, awareness of them will transform you and make you more sympathetic, less resentful and therefore more humanitarian. Perhaps you need to forgive and forget; bitterness can be a canker of the spirit. Be careful that no one is taking unfair advantage of you, but also be honest with yourself, consider your own actions. These may be adversely affecting other people. If this is the case, the consequences are not irremediable. The symbolism of ressurection in this card indicates a second chance.

XXI The World –

Achievement

In modern terms this woman has "made it" and is surrounded by a laurel wreath, symbol of success. A lion and bull support her and an angel and eagle, symbolically the guardians of truth, stand behind her.

Message: Success and fulfilment, both worldly and spiritual, are indicated by this card. Your efforts are about to be rewarded. You are entering a very positive phase during which you will enjoy the fruits of your labour. You are experienced in worldly matters and you will use your knowledge wisely for your own benefit and that of others. As the last card of the Major Arcana, the World represents the end of a journey, the ultimate: enjoy your work, leisure and love.

Minor Arcana

The Minor Arcana consist of four suits – Wands, Swords, Coins and Cups. Each suit has four court cards – a King, Queen, Knight and a Page. While the Major Arcana are said to relate directly to the querant, the court cards of the Minor Arcana represent other people: those close to the querant or about to enter his or her life. When they appear in positions relating to past events in a reading, they represent those who have influenced us in the past. As a general rule, Kings represent men and Queens women. Pages signify young people of either sex. The Knight is an exception, either representing our thoughts or signifying a messenger. When a King or Queen appears upside down in a reading, its sex is reversed. (For example an inverted King represents a woman). An inverted Knight signifies a delay in the message he bears, but a Page bears the same message whether upright or inverted.

An indication of the physical appearance of the person signified by a court card is revealed by the suit of that card, since each of the suits is associated with a specific physical type. Wands, for example, indicate fair-haired blue-eyed people (see individual suit entries). Each of the four suits is also linked to one of the four elements and the traditional qualities associated with it. For example, Wands are of the Fire element and denote spirited, volatile people.

The Court Cards

Cups

Cups are of the water element and the qualities attributed to this suit emphasize the emotions, intuition and the unconscious, stressing feelings more than intellect. They represent love, happiness, gaiety and joy, passion and deep feeling. (Cups after all often hold water which is a symbol of pure pleasure and of the unconscious). The positive qualities associated with this suit make it the most humane of the four. The physical type personified by the suit of Cups has light brown hair and hazel eyes.

ROY DE COUPE
THE KING OF CUPS

REYNE DE COUPE
THE QUEEN OF CUPS

CAVALIER DE COUPE
THE KNIGHT OF CUPS

Knight of Cups
The romantic portrait of a young man riding gracefully. He may be a messenger bearing an invitation or news of an opportunity. He is dreamy and has difficulty concentrating. He may be someone in love. His preoccupied state of mind may serve as a warning: be on your guard against trickery or deception.

VALET DE COUPE
THE KNAVE OF CUPS

King of Cups
An elderly king balances his cup confidently on his knee, his left arm relaxed on the arm of a solid throne. The type of person signified by a King is probably a bachelor. He is responsible and well-educated, and may be a lawyer or businessman but someone who is also creative and artistic. At worst he is someone crafty and dishonest who is capable of double-dealing.

Queen of Cups
Like her husband, the Queen holds her cup sedately balanced on her knee. Her throne has a protective canopy and she holds a spear in her left hand. She is a warm-hearted woman, poetic yet practical, intelligent, honest and imaginative.

Page (or Knave) of Cups
In some packs the Page contemplates a fish in his cup, in others he merely holds it obediently. The card represents someone with the ability to step back from a situation, someone withdrawn and calm who can make objective judgements. He is thoughtful, studious and imaginative.

56

Coins

Coins (also known as the suit of Money, Deniers or Pentacles) are of the air element and represent the material world. This suit gives indications about financial matters and progress in business or career, but also provides insight on a more personal level. The cards may comment on your career progress, but will also indicate the extent of your personal involvement with your work. The physical type associated with this suit has very dark hair and dark eyes.

ROY DE DENIERS
THE KING OF MONEY

CAVALIER DE DENIERS
THE KNIGHT OF MONEY

Knight of Coins

The Knight is a confident materialist who experiences little difficulty in attaining his goals. He represents someone mature, reliable and methodical. He may ask whether you are thinking enough about increasing your prospects. Should you keep an eye on your health and perhaps change your diet?

King of Coins

The King proudly displays his coin, and wears the figure 8 hat (see the Magician and Strength in the Major Arcana). The person represented by this card is a successful man with sharp business acumen who seldom misses an opportunity to increase his wealth. He prizes financial and material comfort very highly. He is a loyal friend whose faults are a tendency to gamble or over-invest.

REYNE DE DENIERS
THE QUEEN OF MONEY

Queen of Coins

The expression of satisfaction on the Queen's face as she looks down at her coin reveals a character who values financial security. She may indicate someone who is wealthy, generous and charitable, perhaps a mother figure. Her faults are a reluctance to trust others, and fear of failure.

57

Page (or Knave) of Coins

Unlike the other court cards of his suit, the Page appears completely uninterested in his coin. (In some packs he has lost it). He is an attractive dreamer but although he may seem superficially carefree he represents someone who can concentrate on study, and who has plenty of ideas and originality. The type of person signified by the Page is not necessarily a student, but can be anyone with a tendency to become absorbed in a subject.

THE KNAVE OF MONEY

VALET DE DENIERS

Swords

Swords (or Epées) are of the earth element and emphasize mental strength, implying courage, authority, ambition and aggression. They urge activity and accomplishment. However, the results may be good or bad. In some packs the swords are shown surrounded by clouds, a symbolic representation of truth penetrating illusion. The presence of a Sword card in a reading may therefore signal some kind of change or transformation. The physical traits associated with this suit are dark hair and hazel eyes.

CAVALIER D'ÉPÉE
THE KNIGHT OF SWORDS

Knight of Swords

Like the King, the Knight is a shrewd combatant, but his approach is more chivalrous. He is willing to confront problems directly, but sometimes his reactions are too hasty and his approach ill-advised. The presence of the Knight may therefore be suggestive of one who rushes too fearlessly into the unknown. It may also indicate someone who is preoccupied by a single thought.

VALET D'ÉPÉE
THE KNAVE OF SWORDS

ROY D'ÉPÉE
THE KING OF SWORDS

REYNE D'ÉPÉE
THE QUEEN OF SWORDS

King of Swords

The King's alert, inquisitive expression is reminiscent of that of the Charioteer (Major Arcana VII), and indicates a powerful and authoritative personality. With his unsheathed sword symbolizing his readiness for action, the King represents an energetic and determined person with an analytical mind, perhaps a doctor, an engineer, or someone in the armed forces. He may be someone who urges caution. His faults are a capacity for cruelty and selfishness.

Queen of Swords

The Queen's severe expression suggests someone who has suffered. She may literally represent a widow or merely someone who has suffered a loss. She is associated with sadness but she has known considerable happiness in the past. She is generous, kind, quick-witted and capable. Her faults are a tendency to be narrow-minded and to nag.

Page (or Knave) of Swords

The Page is vigilant and discerning, active and ambitious. Note however that he holds his sword in his left hand, so perhaps these qualities are not immediately apparent. His powers of insight are excellent. If such a person is influencing you, try and learn from him but be careful, don't rely on him completely. Alternatively, this card may be urging you to stop ignoring minor symptoms and have a medical check-up.

Wands

Wands (Clubs or Batons), are of the fire element. This is the suit of enterprise, energy and growth. In many decks the wands are shown shooting new leaves, symbolizing life's constant process of renewal. The presence of Wands cards indicates inventive ideas and progress. The character type associated with this suit is a hard-working, innovative person. The physical type has blond hair and blue eyes.

Knight of Wands

The Knight of Wands is completely fearless, ready to meet whatever the future holds. This card suggests you may be about to change your address or travel, and warns of possible quarrels or a change in relationships. On a positive note, it encourages you to think about ways in which to expand your business interests.

CAVALIER DE BATON
THE KNIGHT OF CLUBS

ROY DE BATON
THE KING OF CLUBS

King of Wands

His Majesty sits on the throne in a somewhat informal pose, giving the impression that he is restless and has little time to spare. He is noble, honest and conscientious but his emotions are easily inflamed, so while he may be a wise, mature father figure, he may also be short-tempered on occasion. He is usually married. His faults are a tendency to be austere, to exaggerate and be too dogmatic.

REYNE DE BATON
THE QUEEN OF CLUBS

Queen of Wands

The beautiful Queen, unlike her male counterpart, appears very regal and completely at ease on her throne. She represents someone who enjoys life but has a lot of common sense. She is open and honest, sympathetic and loving, and extremely feminine. Her sincere interest in other people makes her an excellent hostess. Her faults may be jealousy and deceit.

VALET DE BATON
THE KNAVE OF CLUBS

Page (or Knave) of Wands

The Page seems at peace with the world as he contemplates his baton, which is planted quite firmly on the ground. He represents a very loyal and faithful person, perhaps a lover or a messenger bearing important news. He warns you against indecision and the problems generated by idle gossip.

59

Pip Cards

Apart from the four court cards, there are ten other cards in each suit. These are known as the pip cards. They are numbered from one to ten and their individual meanings bear out the collective meaning associated with their suits. In addition, the meaning of the pip cards is qualified according to a set of subject categories or "principles". The same number of each suit shares the same principle. But since each suit relates to a different sphere of life, the numbered card of one suit sometimes signifies the opposite to the same numbered card of a different suit, even though they share the same principle. For example, success is the overriding principle of Sevens, but whereas the Seven of Wands signifies success in an enterprise, the Seven of Swords indicates success of an enemy. The following key outlines the ten basic principles:

Characteristics of the Suits

Cups — *Emotions, the unconscious, fantasy*

Coins — *Prosperity, hard work, practical concerns*

Swords — *Mental activity, truth, tact*

Wands — *Action, adventure, achievement*

Aces – *commencement*

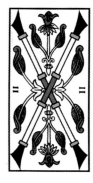

Ace of Cups
A love affair. News of a loved one. A new home. Travel for family reasons. Advice from a friend.

Ace of Coins
A turn in fortune. An unexpected gift or inheritance. A short journey. Money from professional work. Entertaining incurs expense. A union of ideas.

Ace of Swords
A turn in fortune. An unexpected gift or inheritance. A short journey. Money from professional work. Entertaining incurs expense. A union of ideas.

Ace of Wands
Enterprise and energy. New ventures. A business opportunity or trip. Challenge and scope for initiative.

Twos – *opposition*

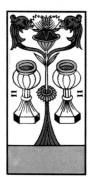

Two of Cups
Romantic impulses. Emotions need to be controlled by reason. A shared intellectual interest. Harmonious union. Love reciprocated. Renewed passion.

Two of Coins
The need for consolidation. Responsibility may cause nervous strain. A profitable partnership. Original money-making ideas.

Two of Swords
Problems. Responsibility for a friend's actions and the risk of making too many sacrifices. Disappointment in social life. Duplicity.

Two of Wands
Analysis prevents misunderstanding. Leisure hours and working schedule may need attention. A surprise, possibly promotion. Enjoyment at work. Caution.

Threes – *realization*

Three of Cups
Resolution of a problem.
Fulfilment, solace and
satisfaction. Romance.
Uncontrolled bursts of
emotion and undue
sensitivity. Creative work
makes good progress.

Three of Coins
Profitable partnership.
Involvement in a variety of
projects – perhaps too
many. Possible exhaustion
of energy. The need for
discretion.

Three of Swords
Collaboration resolves
problems. Responsibility
could inhibit progress.
Misunderstanding or
deception. Absence or
sorrow. A law suit or divorce,
separation or
postponement.

Three of Wands
Successful business
partnership. Enterprise,
negotiation and commerce.
Self-confident and
aggressive action gets
results. Consistent effort is
rewarded.

Fours – *obstacles*

Four of Cups
Obstructions to love.
Harmony leading to satiety
in love. Over-tiredness may
reduce vitality and promote
discontent.

Four of Coins
Financial difficulties.
Careful organization to
improve finances. Patience
brings success. Temptation
to hoard.

Four of Swords
Delays and difficulties.
Persistence wins through;
regrets impede progress.
Time off revitalizes. The
need for solitude.

Four of Wands
Counteracting difficulties.
Elimination of obstacles.
Achievement. Prosperity
brings peace.

61

Fives – *victory*

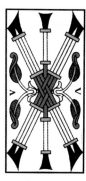

Five of Cups
Love conquers eventually.
Beware hypersensitive
reaction. Struggle, then
success. Indecision may
cause problems.

Five of Coins
Eventual success and
recovery of losses. A careful
discussion with a partner
eases a financial burden.

Five of Swords
Caution – rivals may
succeed. Obstacles need to
be eliminated before the
way ahead eases.
Impulsiveness leads to error.

Five of Wands
Determination brings
victory. Fierce competition.
Challenge. Valuable advice
from elders and advisers.

Sixes – *opposition may succeed*

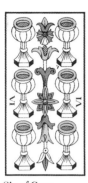   

Six of Cups
Dynamic attraction. The possibility of a new love affair. Infatuation. Idealized love. News of a happy event.

Six of Coins
Share profits. A small donation to charity may be appropriate. Good financial opportunities should not be passed up. Beware dishonest dealings.

Six of Swords
Rivals are powerless. The battle is almost won. Discipline necessary to organize work and delegate tasks. Cooperation with others vital.

Six of Wands
Possibility of failure when success seems sure. Success depends on a philosophical approach to delays, an alert frame of mind and patience. Extremes and aggression in business should be avoided at all costs.

Sevens – *success*

Seven of Cups
Success for you and your loved ones. Daydreaming may be harmful. Accurate decisions require coolness. A domestic crisis will end.

Seven of Coins
Assured success. A large fortune. The fruits of hard labour are reaped. A profitable business trip. General progress.

Seven of Swords
Success of rivals. Dishonesty. Insubordination. Need for positive thinking and careful strategy.

Seven of Wands
Success of your enterprise. Calculated risks pay off. Initiative and an individual approach secure success. A strong position is maintained in spite of rivals.

Eights – *partial success*

   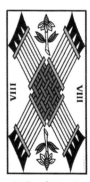

Eight of Cups
Difficulties in relationships. Selfishness and ambition cause harm. Possessiveness. Divided loyalties.

Eight of Coins
Success and money from hard work. Dissatisfaction. The need for reassurance. Perseverance will pay off. Financial dealings.

Eight of Swords
Frustration through problems. Confusion. Hesitation and self-doubt impede progress.

Eight of Wands
Think before taking initiatives. Additional responsibility and prestige likely. Promotion through planning.

Inverted cards

Note that when a card is inverted (that is if its image appears upside down to the reader when set out in a spread), its message will be modified. For many centuries, an inverted card was considered an unpropitious signal, often indicating the opposite of the orthodox meaning. You will still find this effect noted in traditional books on the subject, and even in some of the booklets supplied with packs.

Here, we follow modern interpretive theory which proposes that an inverted card indicates a delay in the outcome of the prediction or that the positive qualities usually associated with the card are somewhat dimmed. If, for instance, a Minor Arcana card is inverted and placed next to a strong, positive Major Arcana card, the Major Arcana card – the stronger influence – will be affected by the weaker, but only to a moderate extent.

Nines – *equilibrium*

Nine of Cups
Emotional stability. Parenthood. Sexual passion combines with true love. Jealousy may prove destructive. Good health.

Ten – *conclusion*

Nine of Coins
Financial security. Further study may stimulate the mind and improve finances. An unexpected gift or bill. Enjoyment of nature and peace of mind.

Nine of Swords
Loss of friendship. An acute problem. Love overcomes difficulties. Admission of faults resolves problems. Worries can be rationalized and hence dissolved.

Nine of Wands
Keep calm, be prepared. A strong position at work may be temporarily shaken by change or deception. A prudent, intuitive approach helps weather the storm.

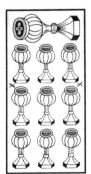   

Ten of Cups
Happy family life and friendship. Success. Fulfilment. Possibly a new love affair or revival of an old. Changes at home.

Ten of Coins
Prosperity. Deals go through smoothly. Inventive and original investment is fruitful, but danger of over-speculation.

Ten of Swords
Sudden loss. Insecurity. Disruption. Possible loss of employment. A minor setback if dealt with calmly; don't over-react.

Ten of Wands
Achievement. Solution of problems. Temptation to place too much emphasis on power. A possible career change or transfer at work.

How to Read Tarot Cards

You and your cards

Having chosen a set of Tarot cards, it is important that you treat them with respect. Remember that they are yours and should only be used by you and your querant.

First get to know your cards. Take them out and look through them, shuffle them, then put them in sequence – the Major Arcana from the Fool to the World and then the Minor Arcana. Then go through the pack again, studying the picture cards in detail and soaking yourself in their symbolism.

Learn to look after your cards; try not to expose them to an unsympathetic atmosphere such as a busy office. If this is unavoidable, keep your pack stored in a wooden box (pine is traditional), wrapped in a piece of pure silk. Tradition decrees that you choose the colour of the silk with equal care: it is supposed to reflect your personality – your vibration or aura in esoteric terms. The cards will be equally happy nestling under a coverlet of your favourite, or perhaps your zodiac, colour. (see p.96ff.)

How to develop your Tarot skills

When you start working with the cards you will probably need to experiment. It is generally better to read other people's cards because it is difficult to remain objective about your own. But for the purpose of practice and until you feel confident of your skills you can begin by reading your own cards. It is advisable, however, not to do more than one reading a day since the prevailing atmosphere really does seem to influence the cards, as does your current mood. By the following day or when you are ready to have your next session, the world will have turned on its axis, your mood will have changed, and you and the cards will be ready to work afresh.

If you really want to progress with your Tarot studies you must be systematic in your approach. When you have chosen a spread (see p.66ff.) lay the cards carefully in position, turn to the description of the cards (see p.48ff.) and write down their meaning in note form. We also suggest that you draw out, on paper, a series of rectangles in the appropriate pattern, each representing a card in the spread. Write the layout number beneath each card and, inside the rectangle, write the name of the card that has been drawn. You will then have a plan of the spread. From your full interpretation notes, you can then align what the cards say with your own situation or that of the querant.

It is a good idea to keep a full file or notebook containing the readings you have done, both for yourself and for others, adding your own final conclusions (and any eventual outcome) to the notes. You will then be able to look back and see just how accurate you have been. For future readings you can take out the file and compare the selection of the cards on the first and subsequent occasions. Use it as a source of reference, a means of monitoring not only the querant's progress but the development of your own skill.

Shuffling and handling the cards

Traditionally the Tarot pack is shuffled and cut three times. Your querant should always be the one to shuffle the cards. It can be quite difficult to handle all 78 cards and you may prefer to divide the pack into three, shuffle and cut each of the three sections in turn, and then group them together again. An alternative is simply to swirl them clockwise, then gather them together. If the querant has a specific question to ask of the cards, he or she should speak the question aloud while shuffling the pack. The querant will know instinctively when the cards have been sufficiently shuffled.

Tradition also suggests that the left hand is negative and the right hand positive; the left has the negative flow of the Moon, the right the positive flow of the Sun. So to tune in to this magnetic flow it is as well to lay the cards from right to left unless the spread that you are using suggests otherwise. When you have laid the cards out (and of course at this point they are always face down), the way in which you turn them over is important. We think that the best method is to turn them from top to bottom so that a card which is inverted within the pack remains so when seen by the reader (sitting opposite) rather than the querant.

Attitude and atmosphere

The question of intuition is a vital one. In the beginning you should keep it well under control. Don't allow yourself to get carried away once the cards are in front of you. Keep to the basic interpretations given on pp.66-71. As time goes on your skill and in-depth knowledge of the cards will combine with intuition to help you draw your conclusions. You will also learn to recognize how the cards work individually and how they relate to one another within the context of a spread. Remember that the traditional interpretations have been gathered and elaborated over many centuries. In summarizing them for this book we have tried to glean the best from both ancient sages and modern specialists, to give you a sound background from which to work.

The cards only suggest atmosphere, situations, possible actions; they don't and can't compel our attitudes or behaviour – we as human beings are in control. Heed the Tarot's warnings but also take up its suggestions. You will find the cards often give encouragement and reassurance.

The atmosphere in which you work is important; the lighting should not be glaring, and it is best if there is no noise to distract you. If you live with a constant background of music, keep the volume very low and choose music that is really soothing, not too emotionally charged and cer-

Inverted cards

As we have seen (p.56 and 63), cards appearing upside down in the reading have their message modified as a result. Remember too that the cards are interpreted according to the way they face *you*, and that the court cards represent people as well as principles. Always bear in mind that when a male court card is inverted it represents a woman, and when a female court card is inverted it represents a man. In some packs it is very difficult to tell when the pip cards are inverted. In this case, put a tiny arrow on the face of each card to show which is the top. (Note that this should not show on the back of the card.)

Perhaps the most important thing to remember when starting a reading is that you must concentrate and really focus your mind on the problem under scrutiny. You and the querant will find that some cards simply cry out to be selected. When this happens you will know that you and the cards are really working in harmony, and their wisdom will be a positive help and source of enlightenment to you.

tainly not of the sort where sudden chords will distract your attention from the cards. As it is desirable to keep your cards in a wooden box, so it is preferable that you lay them out on a wooden surface. Ideally you should have a pine board made for the purpose. If this is not possible, put down a dark-coloured cloth, choosing a shade that appeals to you. From the start, encourage your friends not to be too light-hearted. You need not be grim but you should be calm and collected.

The simple yes/no spread

This spread is recommended if you simply want to ask a direct question requiring a "yes" or "no" answer. Unlike most spreads it does not depend on interpretation of the Arcana.

1) Shuffle the cards.

2) Deal the top five cards (face down) from right to left and put the rest of the pack aside.

3) Turn the cards.

4) Interpretation of the cards according to this method depends not only on their positions in the spread but also on a points system. The centre card (number 3) is a key card which counts as two points. The other cards have a value of one point each. A card that is the right way up indicates "yes" and an inverted one, "no". Using the points system count up the number of points for yes and no. If your score is even (3 votes for yes and 3 for no), the cards have decided that they cannot offer a definite answer at this time. Maybe you are not ready to make your decision yet and should defer it. You may not be taking your problem seriously enough, perhaps your attitude is too flippant or you lack concentration. Perhaps you don't really want to know the answer!

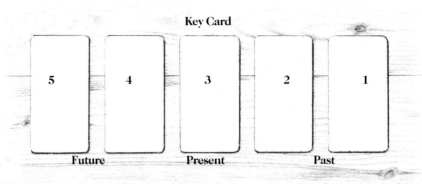

Key Card

| 5 | 4 | 3 | 2 | 1 |

Future   Present   Past

Card 5: 3 of Swords
Also relates to the future. Its message warns the querant that he should beware of under-handedness in the future. He is in charge of the project and therefore responsible for it. If he is not careful his future prospects might be inhibited. However, the fact that the card is inverted means that its negative influence is somewhat mitigated.

Card 4: The Queen of Cups
This relates to the future and, since it is inverted, represents a man rather than a woman, with brown hair and hazel eyes. (At the time of reading the querant did not recognize such a person but later contacted us to say that a new member of staff joining the project fitted that description and was proving helpful).

An alternative:

The five card spread can be developed to give a fuller answer than a simple "yes" or "no". Take the centre key card to represent the present, the cards to the right to represent the past (and events leading up to the present), and those to the left of the key card to represent future trends.

Example

A businessman working on a project needed the support and approval of his colleagues to carry through a good but complicated idea. He asked whether his next meeting with his colleagues would be amicable.

The querant shuffled the cards and the reader dealt them. The points indicated four votes for "yes" and two for "no", so the answer was affirmative. A closer look at the cards told him more.

It is worth noting that three of the cards in this spread are Swords, a suit which places emphasis on caution and tact. The overall message of the spread suggests that the querant is living through a difficult period during which he needs to tread very carefully; an over-assertive or overly aggressive attitude could seriously affect his progress.

Card 3: 9 of Swords

This is taken to represent the present, and underlines the querant's problem by its key words, "loss of friendship". However, the overall message of the card is positive and reassuring, suggesting that the querant will not lose friends provided he is decisive without being stubborn.

Card 2: 8 of Swords

This shows quite clearly the querant's hesitation and his realization that he must be alert.

Card 1: Major Arcana XIV Temperance

This card suggests that, in the past, hard work had enabled him to gain control of the situation, and hence his colleagues probably rate him more highly than he realizes. The landscape depicted in the card suggests the opportunities his project might bring.

67

Ten-card spread

This is a useful and versatile spread which encapsulates the querant's problem and also extends his or her perspective of it. The answer given to any question will be enhanced by the guidance, reassurance, and words of warning and wisdom which always accompany the cards.

1) Separate the Major Arcana from the rest of the pack.
2) Give the cards to your querant to shuffle and cut.
3) When the cards are ready they should be handed

back to you and set out face down in the pattern and order shown below.

4) Turn the cards over, turning them from top to bottom if you are reading for another person, and like the pages of a book if you are reading them for yourself. (Note the position of card 1 half hidden by card 2. Naturally you will have to move them out of position when you come to look at the cards closely, but while you are setting them out it is important to observe the correct layout).

Card 1: *Present Position* – XIV Temperance

The querant has more control over her situation than she realizes but Temperance warns her to control her emotions and encourages hard work. Opportunities are likely to come to her and she will achieve her goals provided she makes the most of her natural talents. She is better liked and respected than she realizes.

Card 2: *Immediate Influences* – XVII The Star

Her outlook is bright. She must not give up hope or allow negative thoughts or worries to impede her progress. She may well be feeling restless. She must try to ignore this; consistency of effort will pay off.

Card 3: *Goal or Destiny* – V The Pope

This card is very reassuring. The querant is in a good position to take advantage of fortunate influences and should develop inner strength and will power. She must have the courage of her convictions. (Note how well this card blends with cards 1 and 2. An excellent pattern is emerging).

Card 4: *The Distant Past* – XX Judgement

She had a difficult childhood, perhaps a domineering father. She has undergone a transformation but the card warns her that if she harbours any resentment this will dampen her spirit. She must forgive and forget if she is to fulfil

the potential indicated by the previous cards.

Card 5: *The Recent Past* – III The Empress

The querant had indeed sacrificed financial security in the recent past. She had become disillusioned with her previous job and given it up without having any real prospects. The card warns that she should not now be tempted to take the line of least resistance. She is prone to do this and needs to be careful.

Card 6: *Future Influences* – XIII Death

One of the most interesting and revealing cards of the spread in terms both of position and message. Important changes are about to take place: all the cards up to this point appear to have been leading to a climax. The querant appears to be on the point of a considerable breakthrough and must take courage and remain hopeful (keeping the message of card 2 in mind).

Card 7: *The Querant* – XV The Devil (inverted)

Another extremely revealing card, symbolizing self-awareness. The querant should realize that in many ways she is her own worst enemy, but she is in a position to break her bonds and move forward. She must counter her negative traits with positive ones. However, the fact that the card is inverted means that its message is softened and less dynamic.

Card 8: *Environmental Factors* – VI The Lovers (inverted)

Although the predominant theme of this card is love, it also signifies choice. The latter is more appropriate to the querant's situation. She is sensitive to environment and had rejected jobs in the fashion industry if they involved working in dreary, dimly-lit basements. The love indicated in the card refers to her goals. In the course of discussion we discovered that she would love to design stage costumes. We had uncovered her heart's desire. But the card was inverted, so she would have to be patient.

Card 9: *Inner Emotions* – XVI The Tower (inverted)

The querant must expect

the unexpected, be willing to break with the past and prepare herself emotionally for a new phase in her life. She should not take foolish risks. She would soon be ready to move forward to the next phase of her life. The Tower warns her not to fritter away her energy, which is something she tends to do.

Card 10: *The Final Result* – XI Force

A very good card to have in the final position. The querant will win. She will eventually realize exactly what she wants and at this point will be near to getting it. She will encounter little difficulty, especially if she listens to her intuition. This card suggests that the obstacles in her path are largely imaginary; firm action will bring success.

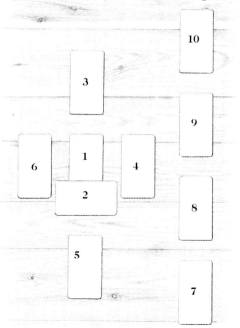

5) Study each card closely with reference to the stage in time it represents according to the layout. (See diagram).

Example

The querant, an imaginative and inventive dress designer in her late twenties, had sound qualifications and good experience but was out of work. She felt confused and uncertain about her future and sought reassurance from the cards. She asked the cards whether she would get a new job (see below for reading).

This was a powerfully positive reading. While it did not say "Yes, you will get a job soon", the cards strongly hinted that she would. The reassurance and good advice offered were remarkable and helped her, as a good tool of prediction should, to look at her problem objectively. Having taken heed of the warnings given she was far more confident that she would win through.

The Ten-Card Spread

Goal/
Destiny

The
Final
Result

Present
Position

Inner
Emotions

69

Future
Influences

Immediate Influences

The
Distant
Past

Environmental
Factors

The
Recent
Past

The
Querant

The pyramid spread

This is one of the most common spreads used in Tarot and one of the most interesting to learn. Others may be more comprehensive and provide more detail, but there are enough cards in this spread to enable you to assess any situation: its past, present and future. The pyramid spread can be used to shed light on problems of all kinds, to answer questions and relate your current situation to future trends in your life.

Use the full pack. Shuffle, cut and turn over the cards following the instructions on p.65, and set them out in the pattern shown below. Note that the first card is placed in the bottom right hand corner and the rest should be set out in the sequence indicated by the

Card 1: Major Arcana XIII Death
This card, interestingly placed as the first of the spread, represents change, in this case the change in the husband's behaviour.

Card 2: Major Arcana XIV Temperance (inverted)
This card shows that the querant is in control of the situation. Although upset, she did not react over-emotionally, showing the characteristic moderation associated with this card. The card is inverted, which implies that she may find it difficult to maintain a calm attitude and will need to make a conscious effort to control her emotions.

Card 3: 9 of Swords
An acute problem. This relates directly to the wife's distress. But the card also bears the message: love will overcome difficulties. She was anxious about her loved one but not timid in her approach.

Card 4: 10 of Cups (inverted)
A happy card but, because inverted, it could mean that full happiness will be delayed. However, it shows the revival of old love and indicates that the querant is responsive to the mood.

Card 5: Key Card – 6 of Cups
This card combines well with the fourth card and confirms its message of devotion and harmony.

Card 6: Major Arcana IV The Emperor
Action. The couple must take action to resolve the problem.

Card 7: Page of Cups (inverted)
A younger person may be somehow involved.

Card 8: 8 of Coins
The querant may not feel sufficiently rewarded for her efforts but the card encourages her to persevere.

Card 9: Key Card – Major Arcana III The Empress
This is an excellent card and well placed. The immediate future shows that the querant will feel more emotionally secure. She should be decisive, assertive and self-confident and is warned against taking the line of least resistance.

Card 10: Ace of Coins
In this case the Ace would seem to represent a union of ideas and nicely complements the message of the Empress.

Card 11: 2 of Swords (inverted)
This is a warning that the querant must beware of duplicity and must not make too many sacrifices.

Card 12: Page of Coins
In this case the Page may represent the husband who may well be able to learn from past mistakes.

Card 13: Key Card – Major Arcana XX Judgement (inverted)
Here is another Major Arcana card in a key position, and therefore giving crucial information. The fact that it is inverted may indicate difficulty or delay, but the key word, transformation, is very hopeful. The card suggests the querant must be aware of bad decisions. It warns her not to be resentful; to forgive and forget. The card also warns that someone may be taking unfair advantage of her.

Card 14: Major Arcana XVIII The Moon
A further warning. This time it speaks of deception. She must be cautious.

Card 15: King of Wands
This excellent card represents wisdom. As it is a court card and these refer to other people, the card can be taken to mean that the querant's husband will eventually become wise.

Card 16: Major Arcana XIX The Sun
This is a symbol of satisfaction, pure love and true happiness, and therefore a very encouraging card, but the querant must not allow pride to spoil this.

Card 17: Key Card – Knight of Coins (inverted)
Here we have another interesting key card showing that the querant should be confident and that the husband will be mature and responsible, with the ability to complete the task of reconciliation. The card in this key position implies strongly that the problem will be resolved.

Card 18: Major Arcana XV The Devil
This card's keyword, self-awareness, says it all. The people concerned are in a position to free themselves from their problem. All the answers they need lie within themselves. Once they have pinpointed the problem, the card indicates that they may need to reassess their situation and make changes for the future.

Card 19: 5 of Cups
True love conquers all! But there is also a warning here: the querant must not be too emotional or sensitive if she is involved in a struggle.

Card 20: Major Arcana XII The Hanged Man (inverted)
Transition. A period of respite perhaps before the message of the final card is borne out.

Card 21: 6 of Swords
This card in the final, most important position confirms the generally hopeful tone of the reading. The problem will be resolved provided she is firm and does all she can to help her husband in the future.

numbers 1-21. Note also how the cards are grouped according to meaning, and that each group has one particularly significant card which dominates the others – the key card. The most important of these is the final key card, 21, which indicates the eventual outcome of the problem or situation.

Example

A happily married woman was upset by changes in her husband's behaviour. At the time of the consultation she wanted reassurance that together they could analyse the problem and with her help he could resolve it. The querant shuffled the cards and the reader dealt them in the order shown below.

The Pyramid Spread

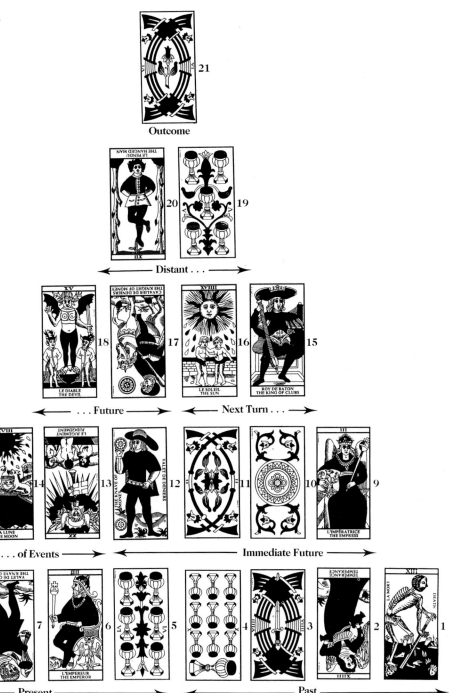

Outcome

Distant . . .

. . . Future

Next Turn . . .

. . . of Events

Immediate Future

Present

Past

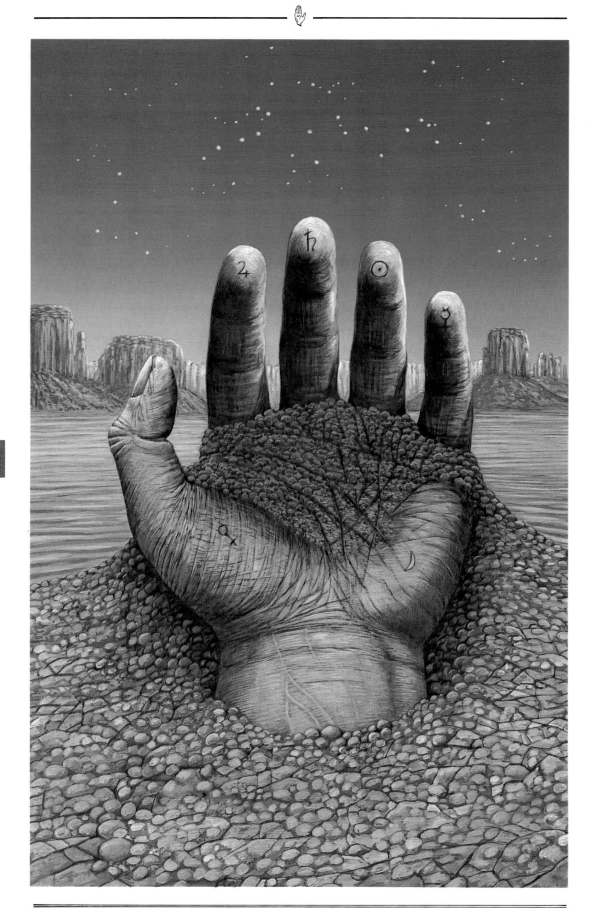

Palmistry

The belief that the hand – and more particularly the lines and other markings on the palms – reveal both character and the future seems to stretch back into the Stone Age. Palm prints have been discovered in caves around the world where paleolithic men lived, which may have been used for palmistry.

Palmists maintain that the art of palmistry originated in ancient Sumeria and Egypt. More definitely there are references to palmistry in Indian literature of the Vedic period (c. 1500BC) and Aristotle in the fourth century BC wrote on it at length. Palmistry may have been practised throughout the Middle Ages, as a covert discipline; certainly it was condemned as a type of witchcraft in 17th-century England but at the same time it was being taught as a reputable discipline in Germany at the universities of Leipzig and Halle. Eclipsed in the 18th century, it re-emerged in the 19th, Cheiro being one of its more famous practitioners.

In the present century, palmistry has even won some degree of recognition from the scientific establishment, for evidence from numerous experiments appears to support the palmist's theories. Hand analysis is already being used by some doctors to assist in the diagnosis of illness. The famous Swiss psychologist C. G. Jung was convinced that palmistry techniques were "of essential importance for psychologists, doctors and educationists" and he emphasized its "valuable contribution" to character research.

Many people believe that the lines of the right hand illustrate the characteristics you are born with while those on the left hand reflect what you make of yourself; likewise, the former indicates your "fate", while the latter shows how this may be avoided or mitigated. But modern palmistry no longer accepts this view. Not only do lines on both palms continually change and develop, but it is now generally accepted that the right and left hand relate to the two hemispheres of the brain – the left hemisphere controlling logic, speech and other "intellectual" areas, while the right refers to emotions, artistic creativity and intuition. Neurologists have shown that the left hemisphere controls the right side of the body and the right hemisphere the left.

When, for example, there is a blockage or mark (called an "island") on one of the major lines of the right hand, a difficult period in wordly affairs is suggested. The other hand would indicate something more personal and emotional. Sceptics sometimes object that people who do much physical hard work are likely to have more lines on their hands than office workers; but this is not strictly true. The lines of the palms are still there, although a different skin texture could veil some of the manual worker's lines.

The older school of palmistry traditionally recognized seven basic hand shapes, but in many ways it is more convenient to look at four basic shapes, subdividing these according to the shape of the palm and the length of the fingers. This provides a flexible but simple system. You may see at once that the hand in question is one of four basic shapes; if not, relate the description of the fingers to the hand shape to help reach a conclusion. Remember that "combination" hands are very common. When the types of hands and fingers fall into the same category, this enhances the strength of the characteristics represented. Different combinations combine different influences. If dealing with a "combined" hand, think of the interpretation of the palm first, and then of the fingers to provide a gloss on it (see pp. 74-75).

Before taking a hand-print (see p. 86 for how to do this) examine the hand itself. Is it firm or flabby to the touch? Flabbiness may indicate lack of energy or low metabolic rate – or it might suggest laziness or lack of self-confidence. A rough hand will naturally suggest hard labour, and also a practical person, especially if the hand is square. A very smooth contact may reflect a possibly guillible or easily influenced personality.

Colour is also an important indicator. For white people, the darker the skin colour the more extraverted, even aggressive, the subject is. Pale hands, by contrast, point to introspection. A pink hand reflects an outgoing and sympathetic personality, while vividly red hands can indicate aggressive tendencies. Very bright pink colouring might suggest high blood pressure, while a yellowish, dry palm could show kidney trouble. (Any such diagnosis from palmistry or any other form of divination should be checked by medical examination).

Examine the handshake too. A warm, friendly handshake shows someone forthcoming, interested in others and probably sympathetic; while a weak, half-hearted one may reflect a similar temperament. Beware the firm handshake that turns your hand so that the subject's is on top – this could reveal someone with a power complex. Check if the palm shapes confirm these findings.

The hand explained

Here we go through the different types of fingers, thumbs and palms and their interrelationship.

The fingers

Speaking generally, when fingers are short compared to the palm length, the individual is interested in the overall pattern of life and projects. Those with longer fingers enjoy disciplined thinking and reaching conclusions. Ideally, fingers should be straight and stand upright on their base. Usually, the broader the fingers the greater the self-confidence and open-mindedness. Very thin fingers can point to narrow-mindedness and an austerity in life – such people not giving either money or love readily.

Knotted finger-joints, if not the result of arthritis or an accident, can point to a tendency to worry over detail and possibly get bogged down in it. But palmistry combines the theoretical and the practical, so remember that knotted fingers, if the result of arthritis, could have been caused by a continual tense gripping of the hands, which itself says something about the subject's character.

The following descriptions of the four finger types are only a rough indication; you will find some longer spatulate fingers, some shorter psychic ones.

The square finger
Short and rather stubby, these are usually thick and firm, the nails square, complementing the solidity of the fingers and often the hand itself. These indicate an analytical approach, a love of detail in work.

The conic or round finger
These are somewhat longer than the palm, but usually in proportion to it. They are neither fat nor thin and mostly firm; the nails are well-formed and overall both elegant and energetic. They suggest a love of beauty and harmony.

The spatulate finger
The diagram exaggerates a little but this finger type is easily recognizable. The fingers are usually of medium length and very muscular. Their possessors are often unconventional and energetic, taking novel approaches to problems and ideas.

The psychic or pointed finger
Long and sensitive, often very smooth, these will be used expressively, seeming to act as antennae for their extremely intuitive and sensitive owners, who have quick minds and a strong desire to communicate.

The phalanges

Fingers are divided into three bands called phalanges, traditionally assigned the following proportions: 2 to the first (nearest the fingertip) 2½ to the second, 3 to the third. It is the relative proportions of each that count. The first phalanges, if noticeably longer in all the fingers, may indicate the person has cultivated that area – the spiritual – more fully than the others. If the second phalanges dominate, they emphasize the subject's primarily mental and analytical approach to life. Puffy phalanges here may show smugness, narrow ones rigidity of belief. The bottom phalanges, usually the longest, illustrate how physical needs usually dominate much of our lives. If even longer, they reveal a very physical approach to life.

The thumb

A baby unfolds its thumbs before any other finger and the thumb can tell much about a person as it traditionally signifies the mind. The phalanges have the same three levels as those of the fingers, except that the lowest forms part of the girdle of Venus (see p. 79) showing vitality and sex drive.

The angle between the fully opened thumb and the index finger denotes thrift and independence. If the angle is 90° or more, the subject may be generous and even extravagant. Below 60° may indicate miserliness. Between 60 and 90° is average.

The length and thickness of the thumb should also be checked. The normal thumb is slightly shorter than the little finger and, in width, it is about 1¼ times that of the widest finger. A narrow short thumb may indicate someone with problems in attaining goals, whereas a long, wide thumb denotes someone with a strong drive for success.

To gauge the placement of the thumb, the subject should hold the first finger out straight and close the thumb against it. The fold that goes downward between thumb and finger will normally appear about halfway down the mount of Venus. A higher than average fold can indicate a closed mind or selfishness, whereas a low-placed one may suggest the other extreme – someone overly generous and easily swayed by others.

The hands
Here we relate each finger type to one of the four kinds of hand.

The square hand
The square hand indicates a practical, down-to-earth character. Square-handed people are not afraid of hard, physical work such as gardening or building. They find it easy to make practical decisions in the various spheres of their lives. However, they may tend to be stubborn, fixed in their opinions, sometimes missing opportunities through fears of a threat to their

security. Self-disciplined and liking routine, they cope well with financial matters. Many square-handed people like working in offices, but need fresh air and the countryside: basically they are productive but "earthy" people.

Sometimes this type of hand has a distinctive curve at the outer edge, opposite the thumb. This is known as the *percussion* edge. If the curve is pronounced, it shows creative ability, and the querant may show considerable aptitude at working with wood and natural materials. He or she may be gifted with a good singing voice.

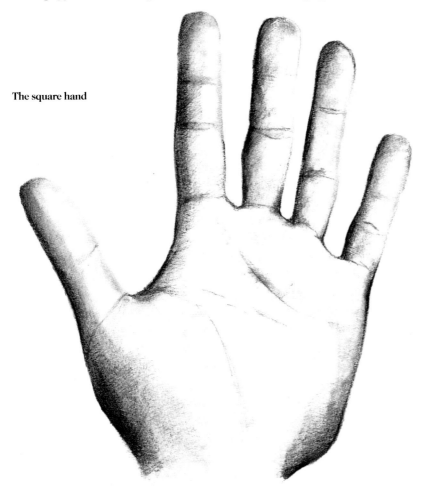

The square hand

75

Square fingers strongly emphasize the characteristics of a square hand, underlining stubbornness and the inability to escape from routine. Determination is probably increased, and discipline comes naturally. It is not surprising that (contrary to myth) many concert pianists have this type of hand (think of the hours of practice involved).

Conic or round fingers on a square hand add adaptability and mitigate stubbornness. There will be an element of versatility, and the mind will be far more open. Possibly the outlook will be less conventional, and any stick-in-the-mud tendency will give way to a freer spirit.

Spatulate fingers lighten the stolid qualities of the square hand, adding an inventive, original flair and a livelier thought-pattern. Intellectual prowess will be increased, and the high energy level will be invigorated and directed towards sport as well as practical hard work.

Psychic or pointed fingers on a square hand offer a marvellously interesting combination of the totally down-to-earth and practical and the dreamy and out-of-the-world. It may well be that here is a true psychic, for reality and the spiritual are combined, essential for those who want to be involved in the occult, who must resist the temptation to "dabble", and must study thoroughly and sensibly. But this is one way in which this type of combination is helpful: the characteristics will be an asset too in other areas of life – perhaps especially in the expression of love. Inspiration works on a practical level.

The conic or round hand

Those with a conic hand are intelligent and "bright", usually quick to learn. They hate routine, and, needing plenty of vitality and change, see that they get it. They have excellent powers of communication, and enjoy working with others; they hate being alone. They do well in the media or in public relations; they are good at selling and any agency work. They are often impatient, but are excellent organizers, with quick reactions. They are also usually very intuitive.

Some people consider this sort of hand typically "feminine". If the creative curve on the *percussion* edge is well-developed, they will be artistic – the women are excellent at sewing and dressmaking, though making a good effect rather than being notable for superb technique. They should guard against inconsistency, laziness, sensuality and superficiality. Many of these characteristics are similar to those of the Zodiacal sign of Gemini.

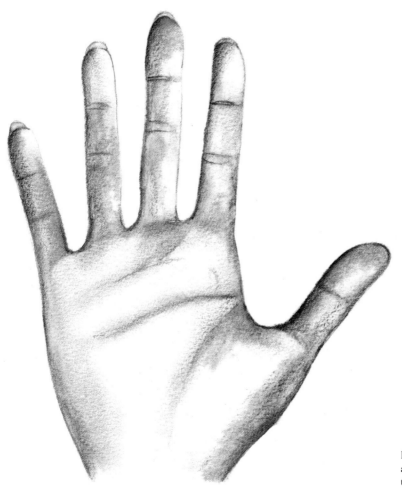

Square fingers add stability and common sense – qualities which are expressed through a good business sense. The communicative powers of the conic hand blend nicely with the practical. These fingers will also help the conic type to be patient, thorough and consistent.

Conic or round fingers emphasize the qualities of the conic hand, and the individual must be careful not to allow superficiality, inconsistency of effort and restlessness to mar progress. Changes must be made for the sake of progress rather than for their own sake. Liveliness, versatility and communicative ability are second to none.

Spatulate fingers indicate that general impatience could be offset by an extremely inquiring mind. If this is applied to study, they have the potential to go far, but they may tend to become somewhat prone to gossip and backbiting, so it is necessary for them consciously to maintain breadth of vision, and not get bogged down in detail.

Psychic or pointed fingers add idealism and the ability to combine inspiration with logic. An element of scepticism will colour the attitude, so that whatever is under examination will be studied carefully and logically, and some interesting conclusions will emerge. These people are capable of originality, but sound reasoning will support their theories even if an element of unworldliness is present. Intuition and a logical mind will be joined by insight and incisiveness in argument.

The spatulate hand

Here is someone who is extremely energetic, with enormous reserves of physical and intellectual ability. They are achievers, always doing something, with tremendous enthusiasm, optimism and breadth of vision. Inventive and original, they sometimes lean toward eccentricity or eccentric friends, and this trait should be recognized and if possible controlled. Many do extremely well in sport, and will often succeed as professionals; but it is important that they develop their intellectual resources as well as physical ones. Here are the travellers and explorers of the world. Their capacity and need for study is probably more important than they may realize (especially when young); if the creative curve is prominent, they may have a flair for literature. If broader at the base, spatulate hands reveal a need for physical activity; if broader at the top, for mental stimulation.

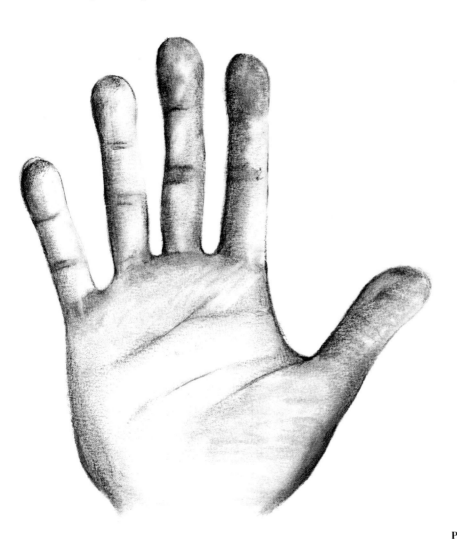

Square fingers on a spatulate hand reveal steady enthusiasm and control youthful wildness so that the individual learns from mistakes. Additional practicality could inhibit imaginative potential but will certainly add staying-power and determination.

Conic or round fingers in many ways complement the spatulate characteristics but will unfortunately increase any tendency to restlessness. The individual must bring versatility under control, expressing it perhaps in a great many areas of *one* interest. Consistency of effort must be achieved if dissatisfaction is not to follow on lack of direction.

Spatulate fingers emphasize the characteristics of the spatulate hand, with positive and negative features enhanced. Restlessness and the need for change, perhaps an unusual insistence on independence, may be problems. Awareness of negative possibilities will help the individual to come to terms with them.

Psychic or pointed fingers lend inspiration, which may be expressed in a particular faith or the study of comparative religion. An interest in yoga or some such contemplative discipline will be enormously beneficial. All kinds of philosophical study and a wise but intuitive attitude towards others will be an asset. Here is an indication of considerable intellectual ability.

The psychic hand

People with this hand are not necessarily psychic in the strict sense of the word, and it goes without saying that if they wish to develop such an instinct this should be done under the strictest supervision. But they are highly sensitive – dreamers, sometimes highly-strung and acutely aware of atmosphere, and as a result suffering from migraine and other nervous disorders. They are extremely imaginative, and often out of touch with reality, wearing rose-coloured spectacles for too much of the time. They may suffer from hypersensitivity and lack of practicality. They can be unpredictable, and need strong, understanding partners if their potential is to be realized. They often make marvellous designers and photographers – though coping with the practical side of running a studio can be difficult for them; personal finances are often difficult enough! They should use their highly-developed intuition to learn who are their true helpmates, and who are simply out to dominate and "use" them. This type seems most closely aligned to the Zodiacal Pisces type.

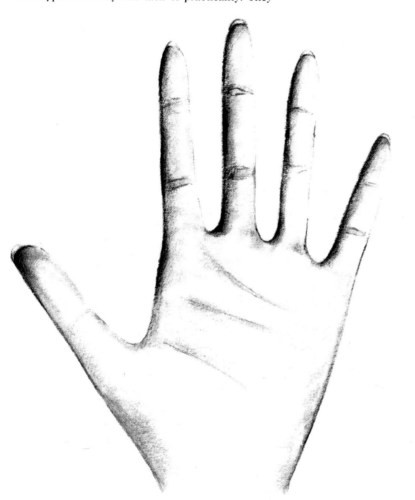

Spatulate fingers contribute abundant physical and intellectual energy which, provided the constitution and the psychological motivation are in balance, can be marvellously expressed. However, the tendency for this type to have difficulty in coping with life could also be emphasized. If these people realize their potential and allow themselves to develop it gradually, they could achieve much; but they will certainly need their strong, supportive partners or friends if that potential is not simply to become a burden – another form of conflict.

Psychic or pointed fingers further enhance the characteristics of the psychic hand. Querants with this emphasis should either work on other disciplines set out in this book, or perhaps take up palmistry seriously in order to learn to counter the powerful but confusing characteristics with which they are endowed. There may well be other areas of the hand which will show the ability to counter unworldliness – and this type of person needs protection; sometimes a reclusive or contemplative life is suitable, and a sense of vocation is likely. Benefit may come through meditation or psychoanalysis.

Square fingers are only rarely combined with the psychic hand; when this is the case it presents problems, for the individual may well be constantly pulled in two directions, simply never knowing what the best course is. If he or she recognizes that the down-to-earth side of their nature gives them stability rather than inhibiting their flights of fancy, they can forge psychological wholeness.

Conic or round fingers are excellent on the psychic hand, giving the individual a more logical approach to problems and life in general, and the ability to be more objective and less purely emotional and intuitive.

They will also have a useful intellectual capacity which enables them to express dreams and flights of fancy creatively, especially if there is a creative curve (see diagram 0). Inner restlessness and perhaps dissatisfaction could be a problem. Consistency of effort must be aimed for.

The palm
The palm of the hand is divided into distinct areas, which are comprehensively called *mounts,* and are named after the Sun and planets. Each has its own place in the interpretation of character. The diagram below shows the geography of the palm.

The mount of Venus
Anatomically, this mount covers one of the largest blood vessels of the hand. Generally speaking, it should be springy and firm. Well-developed, it is an indication of robust health, a strong constitution, a high energy level, and the ability to give and receive affection freely. It also denotes someone with a strong sex drive and a keen interest in sexual relationships. If the Mount of Venus is not clearly seen, the querant

often lacks vitality and the personality may be somewhat dreary; there will be little sympathy for others, and perhaps the lack of any capacity for the enjoyment of life and a low sex drive. Too highly developed, it indicates over abundant exuberance and sexuality, and a tendency to exaggerate.

The mount of Luna
Traditionally the Moon governs the unconscious side of life. A well-developed Mount of Luna shows that the querant has refined taste, is imaginative and somewhat a romantic – sensitive and aware of the prevailing atmosphere and the moods of others, and with a true apprehension of their problems. He or she will feel at one with nature, and probably have a liking for poetry and imaginative literature.

The Mounts:

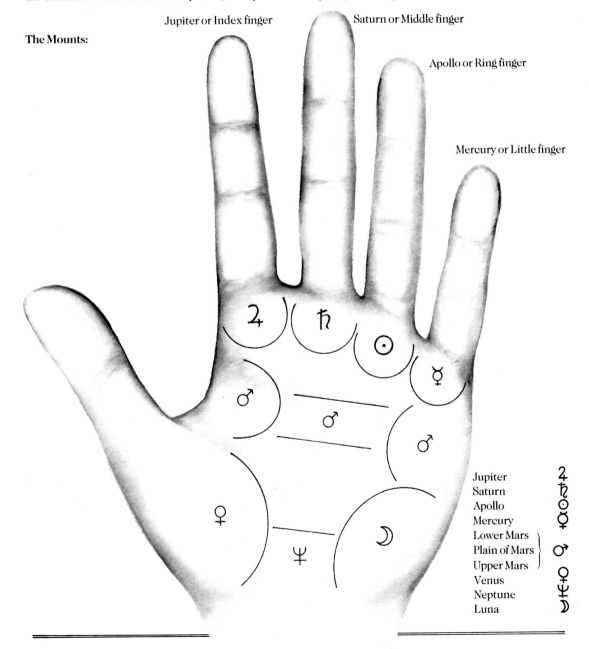

Jupiter or Index finger

Saturn or Middle finger

Apollo or Ring finger

Mercury or Little finger

Jupiter
Saturn
Apollo
Mercury
Lower Mars
Plain of Mars
Upper Mars
Venus
Neptune
Luna

The mount of Neptune

This mount is not easy to see, for it is not usually very prominent. Research on its significance is continuing, but it seems agreed that those with this area pronounced are usually good speakers with strong voices. They are also generally kind and sympathetic.

The mounts of Mars

There are three areas of the palm named after this planet.

Upper Mars

Well-developed, this indicates passive courage and the ability to endure – someone who will cope well under difficult circumstances, not giving in to pressure. Strong moral principles are suggested and these people will do much to defend the weak. If this area is under-developed, it usually indicates a lack of moral courage.

Lower Mars

This area shows the individual's level of active, physical courage; if it is overdeveloped, there is a tendency to aggressiveness. Normal sturdy development indicates someone who delights in challenge and takes bold risks. A well-developed lower Mars mount is excellent for sportsmen and complements a spatulate palm and fingers. If the lower Mars seems much higher than the upper, the person will bravely begin projects but find it difficult to carry them through.

The plain of Mars

In most people this will appear concave, so it is relatively high if raised at all or even flat; a very high plain of Mars signifies someone overbearing and proud. If this area feels soft, a certain selfishness is indicated; if thin, there may be a lack of common sense; but if it is thick, the individual will be no fool, resisting any temptation to be easily led by others who may try to gain advantage. Flabbiness here denotes laziness and self-indulgence; firmness, someone with good reserves of energy; if too firm, this could show a lack of adaptability.

The mount of Jupiter

When well-developed, this suggests a person with an excellent sense of justice, who will treat others fairly and be a good leader. The individual will know his or her weakness and strengths, and balance them. An unusually high Jupiter mount shows possible arrogance and pomposity. A low mount shows diffidence and a tendency to worry.

The mount of Saturn

Concerns life's problems, and how to deal with them. A good mount here indicates someone who deals with setbacks positively, and also perhaps a marked religious sense. Overdevelopment may point to pessimism and depression. A low mount indicates someone who tends to withdraw from others – in religion perhaps a hermit – and also musical appreciation and ability.

The mount of Apollo

Apollo is strongly linked to the Sun, so this is the mount which, well-developed, denotes a sunny and open disposition and indicates creativity, especially if the curve of creativity is marked. The subject should be encouraged to develop creative potential in suitable ways. Extraversion is probable; an over-developed mount will stress these – the person may wear too much jewellery, for instance, or have a startling personal appearance. A low mount of Apollo suggests that the individual will consider it wasteful and extravagant to spend time, money and energy on the acquisition of the beautiful or luxurious. He will lack the capacity to enjoy such things.

The mount of Mercury

If this is well-developed, it indicates a good business sense. High development suggests ambition and also skills in communication and sometimes a potential for medicine or even the occult. Low development can denote limited self-confidence or ambition or simply a lack of interest in the business world, depending on the rest of the hand.

The major lines

Ideally, the lines of the hand should be clear and easy to see, as free of breaks and islands as possible (an *island* is similar to that found in a river: the line diverges, then joins again). But that is like saying that we should all sail through life with no problems or challenges to test us. In other words, life is not like that. But theoretically, it is true that the clearer and more free of markings the lines are, the smoother and more rewarding life will be.

White people usually have pinkish lines, while black people with pink palms have easily discernible brown lines. If the lines are deep and fine, it is fair to say that the personality is outgoing and positive. Wide lines tend to show that the possessor is easily distracted, with powers of concentration less well-developed than they might be. The shape of the hand will comment on this: the psychic hand, for instance, will show that developing the powers of concentration will be difficult.

Those with many chains or islands will tend to be worriers; broken lines show many changes in the life, because the subject is restless by nature (look again at other features to confirm this). Sometimes, however, broken lines can be indicative of a mineral deficiency. Decided breaks in a line show distinct changes in the life style, or that the individual has suffered physical injury at that time (to time events, see p. 85).

The head line

Most modern analysts consider this line the most important. A *clear and strong head line* indicates power to cope well with the various aspects of life; career, outward expression of the self and personal objectives are shown by the right hand of a right-handed subject, and emotions by the left hand of a right-handed person. The indications are reversed if the subject is left-handed.

A *faint head line* shows indecisiveness; if the line is interrupted by islands or chains (see below), there is a tendency to timidity or weakness of character; but here again, remember to assess the shape of the hand and finger and the strength of the mount before reaching a final conclusion. Dots can mean headaches, crosses head injuries.

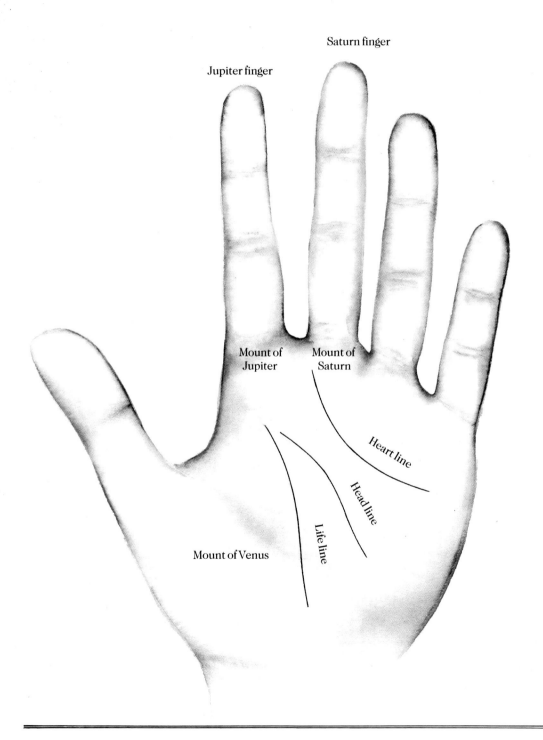

A straight head line

This denotes a morally "straight" person. If it is wavering, the person can be easily influenced by others. A *short but clear headline* denotes someone much involved in business and moneymaking.

Curved head line

This usually shows a rich imagination, which can lead to depression since it can work negatively. Changes of mood readily occur when this type of line is present.

The Writer's fork

Sometimes this line ends in a fork, with a branch line across Upper Mars. This is known as the writers' fork, and besides showing writing potential, it seems to strengthen intellectual capacity.

Branches reaching down from the head line indicate worries. Branches pointing up show interest in whatever finger the line reaches. A branch towards Jupiter indicates social interests. If the subject's head line is *very fine*, you should suggest an approach to work in short spurts with frequent brief rests, for there may be a tendency to overdraw on mental and physical energy.

It is often the case that the head and heart lines are joined at their beginnings (diagram 3 a). This indicates caution, and often suggests a childhood and youth spent in a close family atmosphere. Should the lines coincide for some time, they can show a slow developer.

The life line

The first thing to emphasize is that a short life line does *not* indicate a short life although this is what people often ask palmists. Many people with long life lines have been killed in accidents, while others with a very short life line have lived into their nineties. The life line shows the individual's vitality and awareness of the life force, and as it skirts the mount of Venus we should think of the strength of the relationship between them.

Traditionally, the life line should be narrow and deep, and the freer it is of breaks, irregularities or crossing lines, the better. Where breaks occur illness can be indicated; a return to clarity indicates a return to health.

82

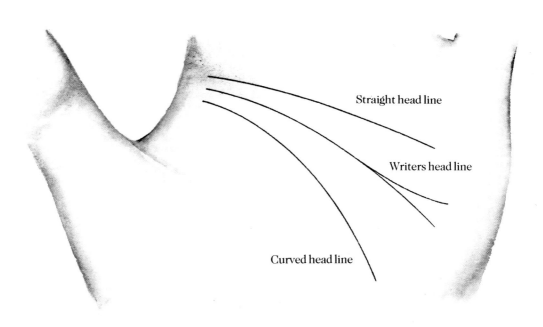

Straight head line

Writers head line

Curved head line

If the life line consists of many short, sketchy lines and looks as though it has been sketched by a rather amateur artist, there is a possibility that the subject does not enjoy robust health.

Islands or chains at the beginning of the line shows physical weakness as a child; from the point when the islands or chains vanish, the complaints of childhood and adolescence are left behind. Overlapping of breaks clearly indicate a change of life style, usually to the individual's advantage, with life opening out if the new section of the line begins outside the old one, but less advantageous or perhaps limiting if the new area of the line begins inside the old one.

If the subject's life line is very short, look to see if there is a very fine line branching from it near its end, and joining it to the fate line. This is an indication of an extremely exciting, important and perhaps drastic change. A life line which gets fainter at the end can signify ill health in old age.

All lines branching from the life line – known as *effort lines* – show increased power, finance and material success. Do not miss the significance of the word "effort", however.

The heart line

As its name suggests, this line relates to our emotions and attitudes to personal relationships; it also has a bearing on health. It usually begins between the Jupiter and Saturn fingers. It is the first line to traverse the palm below the fingers, and as a rule the higher and closer to the fingers it is the more logical and intellectual the approach to the emotional life will be. A line which lies lower on the palm shows someone freer in the expression of feeling. The former person will make sure the head rules the heart; the latter that the heart rules the head.

Should the subject's heart line spring from the middle of the mount of Jupiter, the attitude to love and marriage will be over-romantic. These individuals may well be more susceptible to emotional damage than others, just because they expect too much. If the line rises almost at the base of the index finger, there is a tendency for the individual to be jealous. Dots or cuts on the line show a tendency to worry too much about those close to them.

A very sketchy line with many little lines rising from it is a sure indication of a flirt, someone who may well

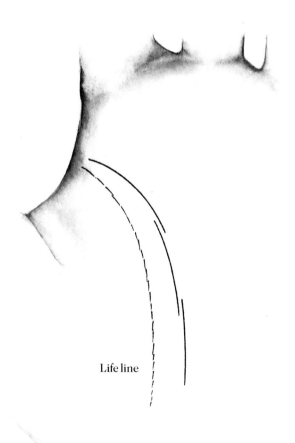

Life line

have many flighty love affairs, and who may be less capable of a long-term partnership, or may even be incapable of a deep-rooted and really meaningful relationship. Look carefully to see if this line rises from the mount of Saturn. If it does, the querant may feel contempt for the opposite sex. If this is the case, deep-rooted psychological problems obviously exist; and many years of study will be necessary before a hand-reader can assess these in detail.

It almost seems too simple to say that if the heart line is deep red, the individual is likely to be passionate; but this is nevertheless the case. If it is pale and broad, the attitude to love is much cooler.

As with breaks in other lines, breaks in the heart indicate breakdowns in relationships. It is very positive indication if the line begins with a fork on the mount of Jupiter, for this is an excellent indication that the subject is capable of deep love, and has an honest nature and great enthusiasm. It is sadly true that someone with a very insignificant heart line probably lacks the ability to love deeply – though this can be a sign of someone who possesses very deep feelings but is unable to express them. Look for the line that begins on the mount of Saturn. This shows an individual who seems only to require sex from a relationship, and may not find it at all easy to develop friendship or good day-to-day rapport with a partner.

Those with very straight heart lines will tend to put their careers first – a tendency which will be strengthened if the mount of Saturn is at all pronounced, or if ambition or ruthlessness shows in others areas of the hand. These people will often neglect their partners or children in order to make more money to better the family's life style, and this will distance them from those they love. In such cases, encourage the subject to invest time on simple pleasures with the family.

Where health problems are concerned, islands, especially under the Jupiter and Saturn fingers, can mean hearing problems, and there is evidence that such a marking under the Apollo finger can mean the same thing. Calcium deficiency can be shown on this line when chaining is present; but look to see if this indication is supported elsewhere.

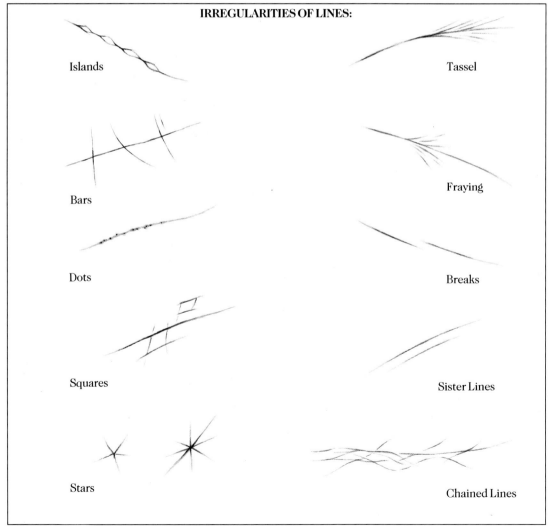

IRREGULARITIES OF LINES:

Islands

Tassel

Bars

Fraying

Dots

Breaks

Squares

Sister Lines

Stars

Chained Lines

The timing of events

Over the years, several methods of timing future trends and events have been developed. One of the major difficulties is that timing depends on accurate measurement of the lines on the palm, and it is often difficult to find an obvious and precise starting-point. So timing is often innaccurate. We describe below a method accepted by modern hand analysis, which has been thoroughly researched, and has proved reliable. Try it for yourself.

When timing future events, measurements of three major lines on the palm are made away from the thumb in the case of the life and head lines (*a* and *c* in diagram 1) and from the wrist up towards the fingers in the case of the fate line (*b*). These are the only three lines used in palmistry prediction.

For accurate measurement, it is better to work from a hand-print (see p. 86) rather than directly from the palm itself. The basic rule is that one millimetre represents one year of life, though if the subject has particularly large hands allowance may have to be made for this. If you are in doubt, try to discover a major event such as a bad illness, or a remarkable change in life style; these will be expected to show up on the hand, and can be used to adjust the time scale.

The life line is the most accurate on which to assess future trends. As a starting point, draw a line from the join between the Jupiter and Saturn fingers to the life line (diagram 2). The point at which it meets the life line represents the querant's twentieth year. From this, mark off the coming years in 5-millimetre intervals. (If you run out of line at what appears to the 40th year, adjust your measuring technique to allow for about 70 years (remembering that a short life line does not necessarily mean a short life).

In order to establish the time scale of the fate line, discover the point on it which marks the 35th year. This is done by using one of the three lines, or *rascettes*, at the base of the palm. Draw a line from the topmost rascette to the base of the Saturn finger, measure it precisely and determine the halfway point: this marks the 35th year (diagram 3). Again, clearly not everyone is going to live precisely 70 years – so analysts usually allow rather more than a millimetre for each year of life until about 50, and a little less from then onward.

To time events from the head line, draw your guide line from it to the join between the Jupiter and Saturn fingers and another to a point just beyond the base of the Saturn finger (diagram 4). The first point of intersection marks the 20th year, and the second the 35th: the millimetre-to-a-year rule obtains, and there should be about 15mm between the two points. Additional years are measured from these points.

Another significant marking on the palm is not a line but the space between the head line and the heart line, called the quadrangle. An unusually narrow quadrangle shows someone rather closed to others who does not allow much space between thought and emotion which people can enter. If the quadrangle does not narrow at all, it suggests rigidity. If it narrows excessively, it may reveal weakness or susceptibility to others.

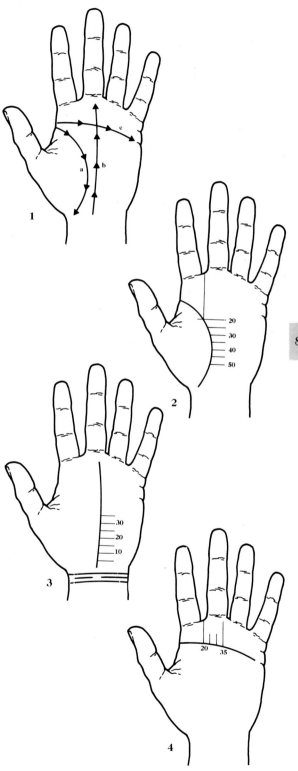

Sample interpretation

These readings were taken when Martin was 15 years old. For most of his childhood, though otherwise strong and healthy, he suffered from asthma and from an allergy to certain foods. This shows remarkably clearly on both palms. Note the group of islands on the life line of both hands and on the left hand the heavy *via lascivia* – a textbook indication of allergy. The left hand is the intuitive hand, and it is reasonable to conclude that the allergies are due to tension or worry of some kind, aggravated by emotional sensitivity rather than being purely physical. There is a strong possibility that Martin will grow out of his complaints, for the islands cease at about the 16th or 17th year.

Heart line

Martin is a warm and affectionate young man with a great deal of charm: the shape and placing of the heart line shows this (note the fork at the beginning, clear on both hands). An island on the Apollo mount indicates that he may have some tendency to eye strain, while the chaining on the heart line indicates possible mineral deficiencies.

Fate line

The fate line is stonger on the right hand than the left, so Martin's approach to his career will be materialistic rather than emotional. His square hands and square fingers show that he is practical, and will want to make

SAMPLE READING:

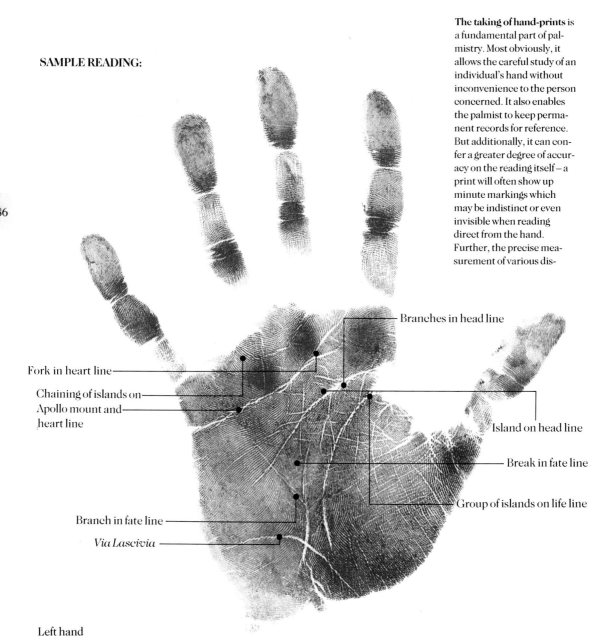

The taking of hand-prints is a fundamental part of palmistry. Most obviously, it allows the careful study of an individual's hand without inconvenience to the person concerned. It also enables the palmist to keep permanent records for reference. But additionally, it can confer a greater degree of accuracy on the reading itself – a print will often show up minute markings which may be indistinct or even invisible when reading direct from the hand. Further, the precise measurement of various dis-

Branches in head line

Fork in heart line

Chaining of islands on Apollo mount and heart line

Island on head line

Break in fate line

Group of islands on life line

Branch in fate line

Via Lascivia

Left hand

money. Looking at the progress of the fate line, there is a decided branch on the left palm, which veers directly towards the index finger, accentuating business and success in commerce, or perhaps one of the sciences. He will surely achieve a considerable break through when he is about 25 – this is clearly shown on the left hand-print by the branch and change of direction; on the right hand it is indicated by a narrowing and firming of the line, so greater stability and security will develop from that age. There is another indication of change at about 35, shown by a break in the fate line on the left hand and a turn of direction on the right. Martin will then, perhaps, change job or location; this will affect his personal life.

Head line
Martin's head line is well shaped, and on both hands several branches spring upward from it. This shows a number of successes over the years, though one bar on the right hand indicates a setback when he is about 21. However, a little further on there is a nice, upward-sweeping branch at the age of 22, so a good recovery will be made, and the setback will be temporary.

An island on the left-hand head line supported by the indications on the fate line of both hands, shows the possibility of an emotional upheaval of some kind at about 35. Here again there is an excellent strong branch shortly afterwards, showing that he will bounce back.

tances along or between lines (as when working out the timing of events for example, see p. 85) are much easier to take from paper.

The simplest method of taking a hand-print nowadays is by using a photocopier. Ensure that the hands are clean and dry and lay them, palm down, on the glass. Cover them with a white cloth to block out any extraneous light and take the copy. Label the result with the date and the subject's name.

Alternatively, you can

obtain a good hand-print by using printer's ink. Place your piece of paper on a slightly cushioned surface, ink the palm using a rubber roller, and press the hand down firmly on the paper.

Then peel the paper off the hand, beginning at the wrist, and allow to dry.

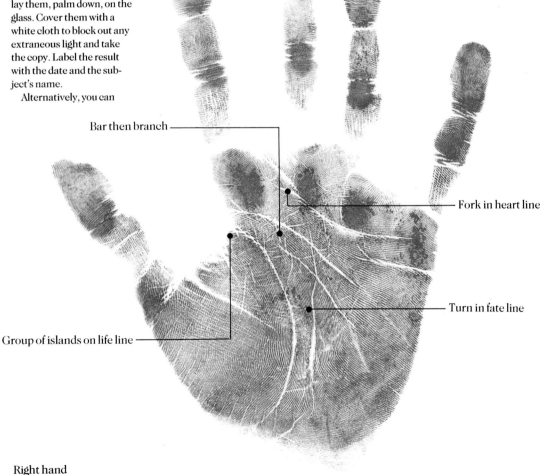

Bar then branch

Fork in heart line

Turn in fate line

Group of islands on life line

Right hand

87

Dice

The use of dice for divination and prediction dates back to at least 2000BC. The Egyptians knew and used a form of dice, as did the Greeks and Romans. Derived from bones used in sacred rites, early dice were also used in a great variety of games. In Asia, they were made of precious materials to increase their powers.

The use of dice for prediction probably derived from sortilege – divination by the casting of lots. One type of sortilege, astragalomancy, used forerunners of today's dice. Called astragals, these were the vertebrae or anklebones of sheep. With four clearly identifiable faces, they were easy to read, for each face had a set value. Astragals continued to be used alongside more modern sorts of dice until the tenth century by the Romans and the Byzantines.

The Arabs, instead of throwing dice, devised a method of spilling out pebbles into a compact heap and then drawing them out one by one at random, reading the omens as they came. This is "psephomancy", from the Greek for pebble; it was also the Greek word for a vote, hence today's art of *psephology*

– the analysis and prediction of elections, though not by casting stone or dice.

With stones, special markings were not usually needed if one stone differed sufficiently from another to be clearly distinguishable. Normally, the diviner who knew the meanings implicit in the stones kept his knowledge secret. To this day, witch doctors among African people such as the Nandi of East Africa, still prophesy with a bagful of "wise stones".

Celtic peoples had an ancient method of divination that used stones in a "singling-out" form of sortilege strongly tinged with magic. In Scotland, it was customary to place a circle of stones, each marked by one of those taking part, around a bonfire on Halloween. The next morning, if any stone had moved from its place, its owner would be doomed to die the following year. The casting of dice is also connected with the casting or choosing of runes (see p.189).

The Romans also used to write their own letters on bits of wood, then cast them and read the words – or gibberish – so formed. Many Amerindians divined by casting a handful of carefully marked holy arrows and reading from their patterns – a type of prediction called "bellomancy" which can be traced back to ancient Babylon and was also used by the Arabs.

In modern Brazil, shells called *buzios* are thrown in a form of religious ritual that is probably of African origin, brought over in the course of the slave trade. Deities controlling the forces of nature, called *orixas*, communicate through this ritual of shell-throwing with diviners who have undergone arduous and lengthy training. Originally *buzios* were thrown to determine who would be a tribe's special or tutelary *orixa*, but today it is used only to ask questions of the god(s). Sixteen different *buzios* are thrown each time in a complex ritual that allows 256 different answers (similar to the *I Ching*). At the end of the ceremony, the sacrifice or obligation necessary from the querant is interpreted from the shells' patterns.

In practically all these castings, it seems possible that the mind of the person throwing the dice or other objects somehow affects the way they fall; there is some experimental evidence to back this up. With so many methods, often secret, there is doubt about how even the most obvious form of divinatory dice-throwing was done. Most modern systems are based on books published in the 19th century, in which a series of questions and answers offered arbitrary solutions to questions such as, "Shall I be happy in life?". The method we are following here is partly influenced by numerology and is probably the most interesting path, but it is by no means the only one used today.

Some people maintain that the dice should only be cast on someone else's behalf, others that the dice should be thrown in complete silence; yet others believe that cool weather and a calm atmosphere are essential preconditions. We suggest merely that, as with other systems, it is probably best to acquire and retain your own dice and to keep them in some special place; they should not be used casually and you should be in fairly serious mood when you question them. Whilst shaking the dice – and it is best to do this in a container of some kind, though they can be shaken in the palm of the hand – keep the question in mind before rolling them onto a flat surface. Then apply the following suggestions to your questions. Of course, as with all simple means of fortune-telling or prediction, the answers may often not seem to fit the questions; but a moment's thought will usually help interpret the clues in useful ways, offering you a new perspective on any problem.

The Oracle

If you have no dice, the combinations of numbers produced by throwing two dice can be represented by drawing a grid containing all the combinations, placed within 21 squares. Then shut your eyes and place a pin, a pencil or some other sharp instrument on the grid, and interpret the contents of the square as shown.

Six and Six: Concentrate on not becoming too upset; emotional turmoil will make the right decision more difficult. Try to forget everyone else and concentrate on what will be good for you; provided the conclusion you reach isn't entirely selfish, you should put it into practice.

Five and Five: The least likely solution is probably the one to go for: originality is what is needed rather than looking for a conventional way out. In a romantic entanglement several people may be involved, and you may be very confused. Someone else may make the necessary decision.

Five and Six: You are the kingpin of the situation and, provided you take an overall view of the problem and don't get tied down to small details, the solution you see will be the right one; you should suggest it strongly to your associates.

Two and Two: Caution is wise, but too much criticism can create waves. Cultivate a sense of sympathy with the weaknesses of others. It is sometimes worth spending money and affection freely, so do not allow caution to become meanness.

Two and Three: Natural tact and thoughtfulness can help problems as long as you don't allow yourself to be emotionally upset by others. Money spent on impulse may not necessarily be wasted, but rely on your own resources to refill the coffers.

Two and Four: Sound background work rather than any outward display will be best. In a strong need for partnership don't be misled into over-trusting. A battle between thrift and

generosity must be fought realistically.

Two and Five: Don't force your general views on other people, whose narrower look at the subject may be worth studying. Your forceful arguments may tip the balance the wrong way, so hold back a little. If someone seems to be behaving strangely, again consider whether they may not be in the right.

Two and Six: If somebody can use the present situation to take advantage of you, they may well do so. So if your problem involves another person, think carefully about their motives before relying on them. Think too whether, if you give them an inch, they may not take a mile or otherwise exploit you.

One and One: The question needs serious thought; all the evidence must be carefully studied. Emotion should play no part in your decision. More than one solution may offer itself, and this is no bad thing, you can take the one which seems most likely to lead to a satisfactory conclusion.

One and Two: Careful thought is needed, but you should take note of what your intuition tells you. You may need security in emotional concerns, but lack the capacity to offer emotional security in return. In financial matters check and double-check, but beware of causing offence because your natural shrewdness makes you suspicious.

One and Three: "Peace at any price" is one thing; but don't give way if all your reason tells you not to do so. Consult your partner and anyone else in a position to give relevant advice on the problem. But don't feel obliged to accept advice – weigh it carefully. If money is involved, don't be swayed by the apparent chance of an easy buck or quick gains.

One and Four: Your resourcefulness and intelli-

gence should see you through provided you don't weaken and don't overspend (money or energy). Any jealousy expressed towards you will be counterproductive; but try to understand the motives and make allowances.

One and Five: Tolerance is invariably useful in helping to resolve personal problems; don't let your rational mind limit it. But be sincere rather than affecting an attitude you don't mean. If the problem tempts you to gamble in some way, think through the situation which will arise if you lose.

One and Six: If the whole setup has gone too far and you feel that strong action is called for, you may be right and your energy should shake the situation up until it falls into place. Life is a switchback: don't feel that either the ups or downs are going to be permanent, and take both in your stride.

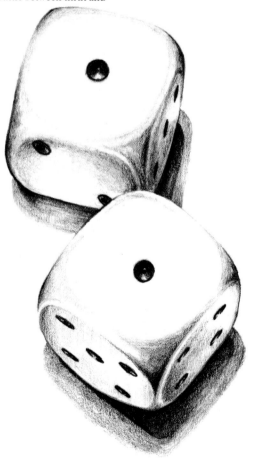

Three and Three: "Peace at any price" is rarely a rewarding solution to any problem. Nor will it help simply to shut your eyes to it. If you got yourself in this fix, only you can release yourself; there is no use in relying on outside help. Reject any offer of easy money; but hard work put into a scheme should ensure success in the long term.

Three and Four: The fact that risk-taking sometimes seems to pay off should not blind you to its dangers, especially in emotional matters. Following your personal inclinations can have its rewards, but this time watch out, especially if a partner (business or emotional) is concerned.

Three and Five: If the problem involves a partner, give them the benefit of the doubt; they may be in the right. But don't go so far as to trust them unconditionally. Following their advice may be wise but only if you do so on your own terms.

Three and Six: If someone else is involved, take a strong line and lead rather than follow. Your convictions are the result of deep natural instincts; don't fight them. Whether it is in light-hearted or serious matters, let them be your guide.

Astragalomancy

As an alternative to the above method, you might like to try the modern version of astragalomancy. Originally, a pair of astragals (normally the left and right anklebones of a sheep) would have been employed, but today it is perfectly acceptable to use an ordinary pair of dice. This method enables you to use the dice to answer particular, direct questions.

First, draw a circle on the ground or table about 12 inches (30 cm) in diameter. Then concentrate on your question and throw the dice onto the circle. (If one of them falls outside the circle, count it out.) Add together the numbers on the dice and then consult the list of answers given here:

One: Yes	**Seven:** Have faith
Two: No	**Eight:** Be patient
Three: Take care	**Nine:** Certainly
Four: Be wise	**Ten:** Doubtful
Five: Good luck	**Eleven:** Nonsense
Six: Of course	**Twelve:** A chance

Four and Four: Ambition can be crippled by excessive caution, so any opportunity which offers advancement should be grasped without too much concern for what might happen if you fail. In the leisure sphere, ambition is excellent; seize on anything new and enjoy it.

Four and Five: You should take advice, for at the moment you need it. Consider what others say, of course, but if they contradict your own instincts, question the latter very strongly. Others are not always wrong, although your strong self-assurance may suggest it.

Four and Six: If an emotional problem presents itself, it will not easily be solved; whether you or someone else is at the heart of the predicament, you should not ride roughshod over everyone else. There is likely to be a sudden resolution, either because you quickly see the solution, or because someone else forces it on you.

Sun-sign Astrology

Astrology is an immeasurably old discipline, and has exerted a powerful influence on whole civilizations. It developed in the Middle Eastern "cradle of civilization", some 5,000 years ago, but there is evidence to suggest that its origins may go back to paleolithic times. Certainly, it has played no small part in directing the course of events, if only because powerful leaders from the dawn of history to modern times have been strongly influenced by it.

The earliest surviving specific astrological records date back only to the 7th century BC, but fragments of documents from the reign of Sargon of Agade in Mesopotamia indicate that the positions of the sun, moon, the five known planets and other phenomena such as the comets were used for making predictions as early as 2870BC. There are even older star charts from Egypt, but it was the Chaldeans of Babylonia who, with their detailed observations, laid the basis of the astrological system still in use today.

From the time of Assurbanipal of Assyria in the 7th century BC to the early 17th century AD, there was almost no change in astrological theory. The Assyrians normally used astrology for predicting public events like floods or wars rather than for private affairs and it was not until the Greeks had adopted astrology for their own purposes, from 250BC onwards, that personal horoscopes became common. In the Roman empire, astrologers were immensely popular. Future emperors frequently consulted them, existing rulers sometimes forbade anyone else to do so to discourage plots against them; it was under the Romans that the greatest of astronomers, Claudius Ptolemy of Alexandria in Egypt, compiled his *Tetrabiblos* in the 2nd century.

This, the first modern astrological textbook, survived both attacks from early Christians – hostile to the pagan elements in astrology and to its possible restrictions on human free will – and the fall of the Roman empire, to re-emerge in the Middle Ages as the standard text. During the Renaissance, astrology flourished once more – even popes like Sixtus IV enthusiastically adopted it.

In past centuries, large claims have been made for astrological prediction. Guido Bonnati, one of the most famous astrologers of the 13th century, wrote:

"all things are known to the astrologer. All that has taken place in the past, all that will happen in the future – everything is revealed to him, since he knows the effects of the heavenly motions which have been,

those which are and those which will be, and since he knows at what times they will act, and what effect they ought to produce."

It was only with the advent of the scientific revolution in the 17th century – when Galileo and Newton seemed to prove that the universe was no more than a giant clock and astrology therefore a discardable superstition – did astrology fall from favour with educated and intelligent people. Not until this century, as 17th-century certainties have themselves collapsed, has it re-emerged.

Most modern astrologers do not claim to be able to predict exact events – rather they restrict themselves to issuing general warnings, as meteorologists do, about the coming "climate". They may suggest periods more suitable for relaxation or vigorous work: times when one might be accident-prone or careless; times propitious for certain activities. Apart from this they concentrate on counselling and on helping people with personal problems such as career guidance or their personal relationships.

Sun-sign astrology – the newspaper columns (usually headed "Your Stars", although stars have little or nothing to do with astrology) which claim to tell you what the day, week or month ahead has to offer – is a very recent phenomenon. Astrology has a written history of 4,000 years; Sun-sign astrology was born when the British astrologer R. H. Naylor, having apparently foretold the crash of the R-101 airship in 1930, was asked to write a regular column for the London-based *Sunday Express*. He devised the idea of publishing 12 paragraphs, each making predictions for one of the 12 Sun-signs (i.e. the signs of the zodiac such as Aries, Virgo, etc).

Sun-sign astrology has since then taken a tremendous beating from those who claim that it is too generalized to be of much use as a means of prediction. Yet it has proved almost impossible for any popular newspaper or magazine to do without a Sun-sign column. The British Opinion Research Centre

93

found recently that over two-thirds of the adult British public read the astrology columns; in France, the figure was 58 percent, in Germany 65 percent and in the US a dazzling 73 percent. And of course television too has its popular astrological pundits.

It is easy to mock Sun-sign astrology: the idea that one-twelfth of the nation should drive particularly carefully on a specific Wednesday morning, or bring their partner a small present on the following Friday, is undisputably comic. So can this kind of astrology be of any use to us?

It is clearly less useful than predictions made on the basis of the fully calculated birth chart, for which larger claims can certainly be made. But, sensibly used, Sun-sign predictions do have a place.

In this book we reveal, for the first time, how the professional astrologers write their monthly, weekly and daily columns. As with astrology in general, there is nothing weird or psychic about this; anyone reading these words could, with much hard work, become a successful professional astrologer. Certainly anyone reading this can, with experience, learn to write a Sun-sign column for themselves.

Because astrologers produce their columns in the same way, using the data based on the same textbooks (the oldest of which is Ptolemy's *Tetrabiblos,* published 1,800 years ago and still in print) it follows

that the paragraphs for Aries in all the world's newspapers for a particular day should be much the same. But it is not quite as simple as that. Different astrologers, with different degrees of experience and marginally different training, will emphasize different aspects of the "solar chart" (the Sun-sign chart) which they use for their predictions. But nothing they say, if they are reputable and properly trained, will come off the top of their heads; it will be based on information collected over the centuries and summarized on the following pages.

And should you take notice of it? That of course depends on your temperament and ultimately your experience. If you find after a time that you can predict trends for particular periods, it is foolish to ignore them. There is surely a point in being cautious on a day when 2,000 years' experience of the activities and influence of Mars tells you that you are likely to be careless with sharp tools; there may be a point in making a special effort to find work when Mercury (which traditionally has a beneficient effect on communications) is positioned favourably.

The following pages explain in detail how the Sun-sign columns are written for each of the 12 signs of the zodiac. Initially, you will probably be most interested in working out the monthly trends for your own sign.

Your Sun-sign

Although it sounds absurd to suggest that the whole human race can be divided into 12 sections, we should remember that far broader divisions are accepted – male and female, or extravert and introvert (for psychologists). And modern statistical analysis has shown that Sun-signs can be remarkably useful in delineating character and in suggesting, for instance, the occupations in which we may be happiest.

The following lists can be used in various ways for forward planning: if you are uncertain about a holiday destination, for example, consult the list of places traditionally associated with you or your partner's Sun-sign. Similarly, you can use the Sun-sign associations when planning Christmas presents or dinner parties, for example.

It is important, however, not to put too much emphasis on the Sun-signs, for we are influenced not only by the Sun but by all the other planets, each of which appears in our full birth chart in one sign and house or another. Then there is the effect of the ascending sign – the one rising over the eastern horizon at the moment of our birth – which ancient astrologers believed to be stronger than that of the Sun-sign.

With this book, when using astrology to evaluate possible future trends, try to relate them to your astrological character: a Sun-sign Geminian, for

Star chart on the domed ceiling of the Frederiksborg Palace, Hillerød, Denmark. The chart, painted by Chris Overgaard, dates back to the reconstruction of the palace which took place at the end of the last century.

instance, will be specially affected by the planet Mercury, which "rules" that sign – that is, has over many centuries had a strong symbolic connection with it. Take into consideration your ruling planet, listed below, and also your Sun-sign's *element* or *triplicity,* and *quality* or *quadruplicity* which are also traditional.

The Elements

Each sign is traditionally governed by one of the four elements: fire, earth, air or water. Remember that a fire sign contributes enthusiasm, an earth sign practicality, an air sign gives an intellectual, communicative approach to people or problems and a water sign a highly emotional, intuitive character. The fire element tends to give people a fiery enthusiasm for sex and a determination to enjoy this aspect of their lives; those with earth signs are sensual but need security in their love lives; air signs are romantic but enjoy sexual experimentation, and water signs have a high emotional content and can be very considerate lovers.

The Qualities (or Quadruplicities)

Cardinal signs are outgoing and enterprising, fixed signs resist change, mutable signs are adaptable and even fickle. Signs are also masculine or feminine, positive or negative; the former tend to be more introverted and thoughtful, although the division is a very rough and ready one. Astrologers give each sign a keyword, summarizing crudely the way it shapes its denizens' approach to life in general. These are given below.

Your Sun-sign date

Some people born on particular days are uncertain under which Sun-sign they fall. Born on November 22, for instance, you may be uncertain whether you are a Scorpio or a Sagittarian (though you will almost certainly feel more in tune with the characteristics of one sign than the other). There is unfortunately no short cuts to discovering your true Sun-sign; you must either obtain an ephemeris (a table showing the position of the planets) for your year of birth, which will tell you at exactly what time the Sun changed signs on your birthday, or ask an astrologer to find this out for you.

Some people born on these days will assert that because they are born on the "cusp" – that is, near the starting point of a new sign – they therefore possess some of the characteristics of both signs. This is not possible; you have either one Sun-sign or the other. But you will certainly be affected by both Venus and Mercury, which, because they are always placed very near the Sun, emphasize the effect of the signs next to your sign on your approach to thought or love. This is not a Sun-sign influence, although it may well be mistaken as such.

95

Aries

Dates: March 21 – April 20
Key words: assertively, urgently
Positive, masculine
Ruling planet: Mars
Triplicity or element: fire
Quadruplicity or quality: cardinal
Colour: red
Gemstone: diamond
Metal: iron
Flowers: honeysuckle, thistle
Trees: all thorn-bearing trees
Herbs and spices: capers, mustard, cayenne pepper
Foodstuffs: onions, leeks, hops
Animals: sheep, rams
Countries: England, France, Germany
Cities: Naples, Florence, Krakow, Birmingham (UK)

96

Taurus

Dates: April 21 – May 21
Key words: possessively, permanently
Negative, feminine
Ruling planet: Venus
Triplicity or element: earth
Quadruplicity or quality: fixed
Colour: pink
Gemstone: sapphire or emerald
Metal: copper
Flowers: rose, poppy
Trees: ash, cypress, apple
Herbs and spices: cloves, sorrel, spearmint
Foodstuffs: wheat, berry fruits, apples, pears, grapes
Animals: cattle
Countries: Ireland, Switzerland, Iran
Cities: Dublin, Mantua, Leipzig

Gemini

Dates: May 22 – June 21
Key words: communicatively,
adaptably, versatilely
Positive, masculine
Ruling planet: Mercury
Triplicity or element: air
Quadruplicity or quality: mutable
Colour: most colours, especially
yellow
Gemstone: agate
Metal: mercury (for jewellery,
platinum)
Flowers: lily-of-the-valley
Trees: nut-bearing trees
Herbs and spices: aniseed,
marjoram, caraway
Foodstuffs: nuts, vegetables grown
above ground, carrots
Animals: small birds, parrots,
butterflies, monkeys
Countries: Wales, Belgium, USA
Cities: London, Plymouth (UK),
Cardiff, San Francisco, Melbourne

Cancer

Dates: June 22 – July 22
Key words: protectively,
sensitively
Negative, feminine
Ruling planet: the Moon
Triplicity or element: water
Quadruplicity or quality: cardinal
Colour: silvery grey
Gemstone: pearl
Metal: silver
Flowers: acanthus, convolvulus,
white flowers
Trees: trees rich in sap
Herbs and spices: saxifrage,
verbena, tarragon
Foodstuffs: milk, fish, fruits and
vegetables with high water content
Animals: creatures with a shell
covering
Countries: Scotland, Holland
Cities: Manchester (UK),
Amsterdam, Tokyo

Sagittarius

Dates: November 23 –
December 21
Key words: widely, freely,
exploratively
Positive, masculine
Ruling planet: Jupiter
Triplicity or element: fire
Quadruplicity or quality: mutable
Colour: dark blue, purple
Gemstone: topaz
Metal: tin
Flowers: pinks, carnations
Trees: lime, birch, mulberry, oak
Herbs and spices: sage, aniseed,
balsam
Foodstuffs: bulb vegetables,
grapefruit, currants, sultanas
Animals: horses, hunted animals
Countries: Spain, Austria,
Hungary, South Africa
Cities: Toledo, Stuttgart,
Budapest, Cologne, Sheffield,
Washington DC

98

Capricorn

Dates: December 22 – January 20
Key words: prudently, aspiringly,
calculatedly
Negative, feminine
Ruling planet: Saturn
Triplicity or element: earth
Quadruplicity or quality: cardinal
Colour: dark grey, black, dark
brown
Gemstone: turquoise, amethyst
Metal: lead
Flowers: ivy, hemlock, heartsease
Trees: pine, elm, yew, medlar
Herbs and spices: hemp, comfrey,
knapweed
Foodstuffs: potato, barley, beet,
spinach, malt
Animals: goat, all cloven-hoofed
animals
Countries: India, Mexico,
Afghanistan
Cities: Oxford (UK), Delhi, Mexico
City, the administrative areas of all
capital cities

Aquarius

Dates: January 21 – February 18
Key words: independently, humanely
Positive, masculine
Ruling planet: Uranus (ancient ruler, Saturn)
Triplicity or element: air
Quadruplicity or quality: fixed
Colour: turquoise
Gemstone: aquamarine
Metal: aluminium
Flowers: orchid, golden rain
Trees: fruit trees in general
Herbs and spices: those with a sharp or unusual flavour
Foodstuffs: food which can be conveniently deep-frozen, preserved foods; dried fruits
Animals: large birds capable of sustained flight
Countries: USSR, Sweden
Cities: Moscow, Salzburg, Hamburg, Leningrad

Pisces

Dates: February 19 – March 20
Key words: nebulously, impressionably
Negative, feminine
Ruling planet: Neptune (ancient ruler Jupiter)
Triplicity or element: water
Quadruplicity or quality: mutable
Colour: soft sea green
Gemstone: moonstone or bloodstone
Metal: titanium or tin
Flowers: water-lily
Trees: willow, fig, trees that grow near water
Herbs and spices: succory (chicory), lime, flowers, mosses
Foodstuffs: cucumber, pumpkin, turnip, lettuce, melon
Animals: mammals that like water, fish of all kinds
Countries: Portugal, the Gobi and Sahara Deserts
Cities: Jerusalem, Warsaw, Seville, Alexandria, Santiago de Compostela, Bournemouth

Leo

Dates: July 23 – August 23
Key words: creatively, impressively, powerfully Positive, masculine
Ruling planet: the Sun
Triplicity or element: fire
Quadruplicity or quality: fixed
Colour: the colours of the Sun from dawn to dusk
Gemstone: ruby
Metal: gold
Flowers: sunflowers, marigolds
Trees: palm, bay, orange and lemon, laurel
Herbs and spices: saffron, peppermint, rosemary
Foodstuffs: rice, honey, vines and crops in general
Animals: big game, especially the cats
Countries: the South of France, Italy, Romania, Sicily
Cities: Rome, Prague, Bombay, Madrid, Philadelphia, Chicago, Los Angeles, Bath, Bristol

Virgo

Dates: August 24 – September 22
Key words: critically, analytically Negative, feminine
Ruling planet: Mercury
Triplicity or element: earth
Quadruplicity or quality: mutable
Colour: navy blue, dark brown, green
Gemstone: sardonyx
Metal: mercury or nickel
Flowers: all bright-coloured, small flowers
Trees: nut-bearing trees
Herbs and spices: those with bright yellow or blue flowers
Foodstuffs: vegetables grown beneath the earth
Animals: all domestic pets
Countries: Greece, the West Indies, Turkey, the state of Virginia, USA, Brazil, New Zealand
Cities: Boston, Heidelberg, Paris, Athens

Libra

Dates: September 23 – October 23
Key word: harmoniously
Positive, masculine
Ruling planet: Venus
Triplicity or element: air
Quadruplicity or quality: cardinal
Colour: shades of blue from pale to ultramarine; pink and pale green
Gemstone: sapphire, jade
Metal: copper, perhaps bronze
Flowers: blue flowers; hydrangea, large roses
Trees: ash, poplar
Herbs and spices: mint, cayenne
Foodstuffs: tomato, pear, asparagus, beans
Animals: lizards and small reptiles
Countries: Austria, Burma, Japan, Argentina, Upper Egypt, Canada
Cities: Copenhagen, Johannesburg, Vienna, Lisbon, Frankfurt, Nottingham

Scorpio

Dates: October 24 – November 22
Key words: intensively, passionately
Negative, feminine
Ruling planet: Pluto (ancient ruler, Mars)
Triplicity or element: water
Quadruplicity or quality: fixed
Colour: dark red, maroon
Gemstone: opal
Metal: steel or iron
Flowers: geranium, rhododendron
Trees: blackthorn, thick bushy trees
Herbs and spices: aloes, witch hazel, catmint
Foodstuffs: most strong-tasting foods
Animals: crustaceans, most insects
Countries: Morocco, Norway, the Transvaal, Algeria
Cities: New Orleans, Fez, Milwaukee, Liverpool, Halifax, Hull

How to do Sun-sign astrology

1. You will need: paper; a sharp pencil; felt-tip pens; a pair of compasses; a protractor; a ruler; adhesive tape; a length of fine string (preferably coloured); scissors; and an ephemeris for the current year (obtainable from large or occult bookshops).

2. You must be able to recognize the symbols or *glyphs* of the planets and Zodiac signs:

♈ = Aries
♉ = Taurus
♊ = Gemini
♋ = Cancer
♌ = Leo
♍ = Virgo
♎ = Libra
♏ = Scorpio
♐ = Sagittarius
♑ = Capricorn
♒ = Aquarius
♓ = Pisces

☉ = Sun
☽ = Moon
☿ = Mercury
♀ = Venus
♂ = Mars
♃ = Jupiter
♄ = Saturn
♅ = Uranus
♆ = Neptune
♇ = Pluto

3. Using your compasses and protractor, copy diagram 1. Your circle should be at least 4″ in diameter. Remember the *glyphs* must face inward, and that each of the twelve segments must be of equal size i.e. 30°.

4. Turn to the page of the ephemeris giving details of the month you wish to study. Look at the top grid headed *Longitude*.

LONGITUDE **NOVEMBER 1987**

DAY	☉ ° ' "	☿ ° '	♀ ° '	♂ ° '	♃ ° '	♄ ° '	♅ ° '	♆ ° '	♇ ° '
1	8♏ 1 32	0♏ 5R	26♏ 19	14♎ 57	22♈ 54R	18♐ 33	24♐ 12	5♑ 46	9♏ 50
2	9 1 33	29♎ 11	27 33	15 36	22 47	18 39	24 15	5 48	9 52
3	10 1 35	28 28	28 48	16 15	22 39	18 45	24 18	5 49	9 55
4	11 1 39	27 55	0♐ 3	16 54	22 32	18 51	24 21	5 51	9 57
5	12 1 45	27 34	1 18	17 33	22 25	18 57	24 24	5 52	10 0
6	13 1 53	27 25D	2 32	18 11	22 18	19 3	24 26	5 54	10 2
7	14 2 2	27 27	3 47	18 50	22 11	19 10	24 29	5 55	10 5
8	15 2 13	27 40	5 2	19 29	22 4	19 16	24 32	5 57	10 7
9	16 2 26	28 3	6 16	20 8	21 57	19 22	24 35	5 58	10 9
10	17 2 42	28 35	7 31	20 47	21 51	19 28	24 38	6 0	10 12
11	18 2 59	29 16	8 46	21 26	21 44	19 35	24 42	6 2	10 14
12	19 3 18	0♏ 4	10 0	22 5	21 38	19 41	24 45	6 3	10 17
13	20 3 39	1 0	11 15	22 44	21 31	19 48	24 48	6 5	10 19
14	21 4 2	2 1	12 29	23 23	21 25	19 54	24 51	6 7	10 22
15	22 4 27	3 7	13 44	24 2	21 19	20 1	24 54	6 8	10 24
16	23 4 53	4 18	14 59	24 41	21 14	20 7	24 57	6 10	10 26
17	24 5 22	5 32	16 13	25 20	21 8	20 14	25 1	6 12	10 29
18	25 5 52	6 50	17 28	26 0	21 3	20 20	25 4	6 14	10 31
19	26 6 24	8 10	18 43	26 39	20 57	20 27	25 7	6 16	10 33
20	27 6 58	9 33	19 57	27 18	20 52	20 34	25 10	6 17	10 36
21	28 7 34	10 58	21 12	27 57	20 47	20 41	25 14	6 19	10 38
22	29 8 11	12 24	22 27	28 36	20 42	20 47	25 17	6 21	10 41
23	0♐ 8 49	13 52	23 41	29 15	20 38	20 54	25 20	6 23	10 43
24	1 9 29	15 21	24 56	29 55	20 33	21 1	25 24	6 25	10 45
25	2 10 10	16 51	26 10	0♏ 34	20 29	21 8	25 27	6 27	10 47
26	3 10 52	18 21	27 25	1 13	20 25	21 15	25 31	6 29	10 50
27	4 11 35	19 53	28 40	1 52	20 21	21 21	25 34	6 31	10 52
28	5 12 19	21 24	29 54	2 31	20 18	21 28	25 38	6 33	10 54
29	6 13 4	22 56	1♑ 9	3 11	20 14	21 35	25 41	6 35	10 57
30	7♐ 13 50	24♏ 29	2♑ 23	3♏ 50	20♈ 11	21♐ 42	25♐ 44	6♑ 37	10♏ 59

The planet's positions will be listed for midnight *or* noon GMT, depending on the edition you have, but for this purpose there is no difference. The figures given refer to the fact that each sign is divided into 30° of arc; each degree into 60 minutes, and each minute into 60 seconds.

In our example (November, 1987) the Sun on day one (November 1) occupies degree 8 of Scorpio (Scorpio 8°); by the last day of the month, it has moved on to Sagittarius 7° (in Sun-sign astrology we ignore the minutes and seconds, using only the degrees).

5. Using your sharp pencil, mark the Sun on your chart, as shown in diagram 2. It is placed roughly where the eighth degree of the sign i.e. Scorpio is (counting anti-clockwise – all planets move through the signs in that direction). Add an arrow to show the distance the Sun travels during the month.

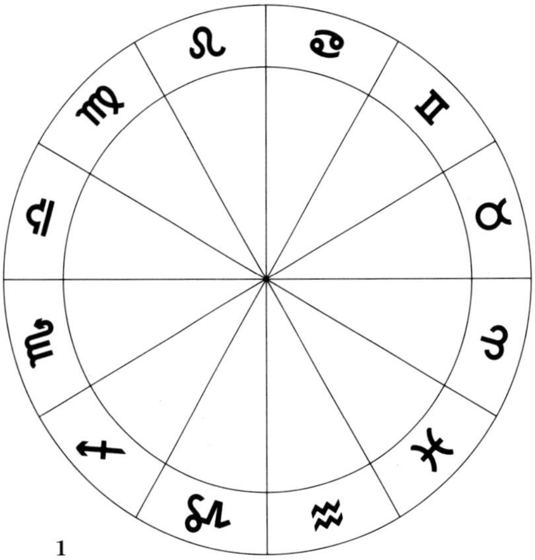

1

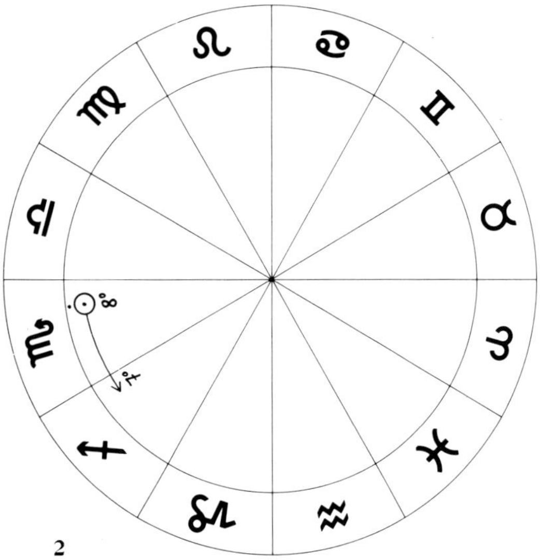

2

6. Now look in the *Longitude* grid for Mercury's movements. On November 1 it stands at 0° Scorpio *R,* on November 30, at 24° Scorpio. The *R* is important: it means that, as seen from earth, Mercury is *Retrograde* (appearing to be moving backwards) – indeed on the 2nd it has moved back into the previous sign, Libra. Look down the Mercury column, and you will see that on November 6 the planet's position is 27° Libra *D.* On that day, Mercury appears once more to move forward, so its motion is *Direct.* (All planets except the Sun and Moon sometimes change from direct to retrograde motion). Now draw Mercury on your chart (see diagram 3).

8. Repeat the process for all the other planets. Note that Jupiter is *Retrograde* all month, moving backwards from 22° Aries to 20° Aries. This completes the drawing of the chart (diagram 5).

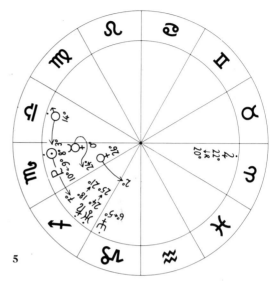

5

9. Take the ephemeris again. Ignore the panel headed *Declination and Latitude,* which does not apply to this area of astrology, and look at the small box which will show you the dates of the New and Full Moon. In the sub-division headed *Phenomena* you will see a column headed *d h m* – representing *day, hour, minute.*

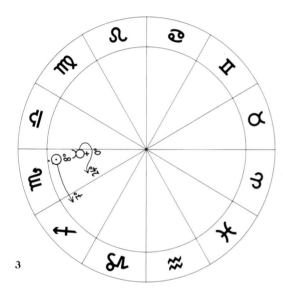

3

7. Next note Venus, travelling from 26° Scorpio right through Sagittarius to 2° Capricorn (diagram 4).

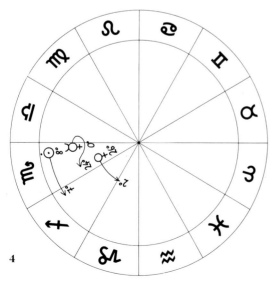

4

D PHENOMENA			VOID OF COURSE D		
			LAST ASPT	D INGRESS	
d	h	m	2	10am24	2 ♈ 1pm41
5	16	47 ○	4	1pm58	4 ♉ 6pm 3
13	14	39 ☾	6	4pm47	7 ♊ 0am17
21	6	34 ●	9	5am36	9 ♋ 9am11
28	0	38 ☽	11	8pm40	11 ♌ 8pm46
			13	11pm 6	14 ♍ 9am30
			16	11am 6	16 ♎ 8pm49
d	h	°	18	10pm39	19 ♏ 4am48
2	14	0	21	6am34	21 ♐ 9am17
9	10	28N35	23	10am48	23 ♑ 11am33
16	21	0	24	9pm27	25 ♒ 1pm14
23	12	28S30	27	2pm42	27 ♓ 3pm41
29	20	0	29	12pm 6	29 ♈ 7pm37
2	17	0			
9	12	5N 8		d	h
16	23	0		12	18 APOGEE
23	12	5S 4		24	15 PERIGEE
29	20	0			

In November the Full Moon falls on the 5th at 16.47 GMT and the New Moon on the 21st at 6.34 GMT. When the Moon is full it always occupies the sign *opposite* the Sun (in this case Taurus, with the Sun in Scorpio). When the Moon is new, it occupies the *same* sign as the Sun (in this case, Scorpio). Ignore the other two positions shown for the Moon.

10. Now look at the panel headed *Daily Aspectarian*.

DAILY ASPECTARIAN

(A dense ephemeris aspectarian table of daily planetary aspects with times is printed here.)

Some of the glyphs in this panel will be new to you: they show the *aspects* the planets make to each other through the month. Aspects (see below) are angular relationships between the planets as we see them from earth, and in astrology some have strong, some weaker effects. Aspect lines are plotted on the chart by placing a dot just inside and close to the planet's position. Oppositions and squares are conventionally indicated by solid black lines, trines and sextiles by solid red lines (shown below as dotted lines) and the minor aspects by broken black lines. Conjunctions are obvious anyway, so they are not marked.

Glyph		Examples (most are from the ephemeris for November 1987)	Strength of aspect
☌ **conjunction (a)** *(when two planets fall on the same degree of a sign)*		☉ ☌ ♇ Sun conjunction Pluto (November 2)	Very strong
☍ **opposition (c)** *(when two planets fall 180° apart)*		☉ ☍ ☽ Sun opposition Moon (Sun and Moon are always in opposition at the time of the Full Moon)	Very strong
□ **square (b)** *(when two planets fall 90° apart)*		☉ □ ♅ Sun square Uranus	Strong
△ **trine (d)** *(when two planets fall 120° apart)*		♃ △ ♄ Jupiter trine Saturn (November 21)	Strong
✳ **sextile (e)** *(when two planets fall 60° apart)*		♂ ✳ ♅ Mars sextile Uranus (November 16)	Moderate
⚻ **quincunx (f)** *(when two planets fall 150° apart)*		☉ ⚻ ♃ Sun quincunx Jupiter (November 14)	Moderate
∟ **semisquare (g)** *(when two planets fall 45° apart)*		☉ ∟ ♄ Sun semisquare Saturn	Moderate
□ **sesquare (h)** *(when two planets fall 135° apart)*		♀ ⚼ ♃ Venus sesquare Jupiter (November 9)	Weak
⚺ **semisextile (i)** *(when two planets fall 30° apart)*		♀ ⚺ ♇ Venus semisextile Pluto (November 12)	Weak

104

11. The *Daily Aspectarian* shows other details, too: the dates when planets change signs and when their movements change from *direct* to *retrograde* and back again. In addition (though as it happens, not listed for this particular month), you will sometimes see *SR*, when a planet is *Stationary Retrograde* before it returns to direct motion.

12. Now make a list of the elements in the Aspectarian which you will use in order to interpret the astrological moods of the month: the aspects, the times of the Full and New Moons, the times when the planets change signs. Especially when you are starting out, make sure you know which signs the planets are in when they make aspects.

13. *The Houses.* Apart from the Zodiacal signs, the *houses* are the next most important part of the structure, whether you are working on a full birth chart or a Sun-sign chart. There are twelve houses, and their effects are interpreted in full on pp. 108-109. For the moment remember that whatever *sign* you are interpreting, the *houses* remain in the same position, running from 1-12 anti-clockwise, the first house always being in the 8/9 o'clock position.

15. Cut out your completed chart drawing for November so that you have a simple circle containing all the details you need. Place this under the string with Aries in the 8/9 o'clock position. The string represents the horizon. Now, Jupiter will be in the first house, the Sun and Pluto in the eighth house, with the Sun moving into the ninth house during the course of the month when it enters Sagittarius. Mars is in Libra in the seventh house, moving on to the eighth house. The planetary positions and the houses they occupy show the basic trends for Arians during November 1987.

Move your circular disc so that Taurus is at 8/9 o'clock: and you have Jupiter in the twelfth house, Mars in the sixth moving into the seventh and the Sun spending most of November in the seventh before moving into the eighth – and so on. These are the trends for the month for Taureans.

So, revolving your chart so that each Zodiac sign in turn stands at 8/9 o'clock, and using the positions and movements of the planets through the Signs and Houses, the dates when they change signs, the dates of the Full and New Moons and of the aspects, you can interpret what the month holds.

105

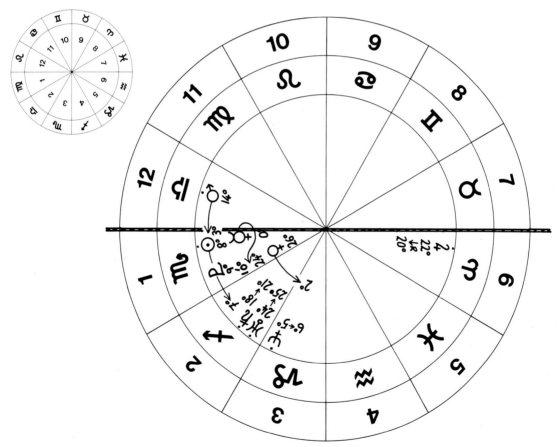

14. Now take your length of string and lay it flat across a sheet of plain paper, sticking it in position with adhesive tape.

Scorpio's Sun-sign chart for November 1987. Note that Scorpio is orientated so that it occupies the 8/9 o'clock position on the chart. Hence the planets are in their correct house positions for interpreting the monthly trends for Sun-sign Scorpios.

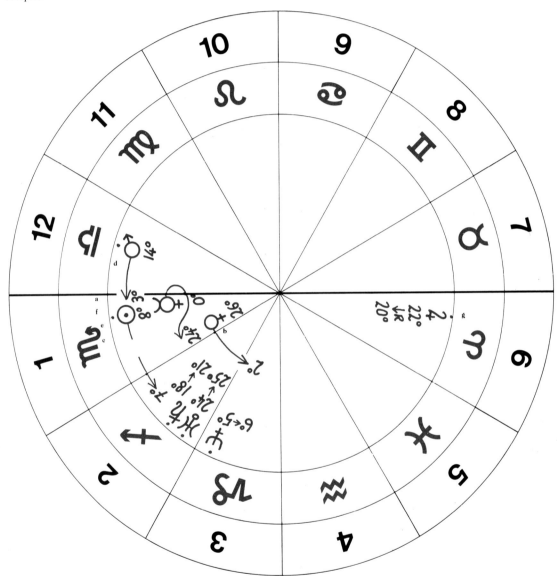

Reading the chart for Sun-sign Scorpio

a *Sun in Scorpio in the first house*
At the time of your birthday you experience your solar return – the Sun has returned to the first house, the position it was in at the time of your birth. You are at your best at this time of year, your personality is particularly strong and you are able to exploit your natural talents to the full.

b *Venus in Sagittarius in the second house*
For most of November Venus travels through the second house of Scorpio's chart. This is the house of money and possessions. The planet Venus's influence is very positive so financial gain is highly likely.

c *Sun conjunct Pluto*
Because each sign occupies 30° of the chart, and the Sun moves one degree each day, it is sometimes possible to interpret a very precise personal trend from it. Here the aspect, a strong conjunction, is exact on November 2 and as this is Scorpio's birthday month, the trend has a very potent effect for those born on that date whatever their age.

d *Mars in Libra in the twelfth house, Mars in Scorpio in the first house*
Although the twelfth house is the most private, introvert and secretive of all the houses, Libra relates to others so we can say that this trend involves another person. Once Mars moves into Scorpio and the first house, Scorpios will be better placed to act positively on behalf of loved ones. Mars makes us hasty so Scorpios under this influence may act rashly.

e *Sun in Scorpio in the first house*
This house rules our health, general well being and vitality. The Sun's passage through it will exercise a positive influence.

f *Mars in Scorpio in the first house*
From November 24 Mars, entering Scorpio and the first house, will give support to the good work the Sun has done in previous weeks. Mars will remain in this sign until January 8 1988 so long term projects should be successful.

g *Mars opposition Jupiter*
Mars in Libra in the twelfth house, Jupiter in Aries in the sixth house. Scorpios love to enjoy life and don't believe in half measures. Given this characteristic, such a strong planetary aspect could have adverse effects. The presence of Jupiter in Aries (another area of the chart concerned with health particularly the digestive system and bowels) highlights the potential problem.

Interpretation – Scorpio's Sun-sign column

Now is the time for you to steal the limelight, show off a little and make sure those who are important to you know what you can do. Ask favours and make the most of the powerful and positive energy of the Sun (in your sign until the 22nd) to get new projects of all kinds off the ground.

Your financial position this month is very good but being a Scorpio you enjoy life and like to do things in style so be careful not to jeopardize this by excessive spending. A big birthday celebration (a night out on the town with loved ones?) for example, may turn out to be more expensive than you can realistically afford.

Someone may have taken you into their confidence. Guard their secret zealously. In your eagerness to help, you run the risk of betraying their trust. It is advisable to suspend action until after the 24th when you will be in a better position to devote time and energy to friends and their problems.

Health-wise you should feel particularly fit and energetic. Indeed increased vitality is highlighted for Scorpios over the next few months. However, bearing in mind those birthday celebrations, watch out for the expansive influences of Mars and Jupiter in your sign this month around the 11th. If you're not careful you could have a shock when you get on the bathroom scales at the end of the month.

All in all Scorpios can expect to enjoy a very good month. In keeping with astrological tradition, we are always at our peak at the time of our birthday so make the most of it and enjoy life to the full. Birthdays also signal a new beginning so make some positive changes for the future. The strong planetary aspects in your sign during the months ahead will steer you in the right direction. But don't get too carried away by the thrill of success, remember there are a few pitfalls highlighted for you too this month; keep a tight rein on your purse and appetite!

The houses

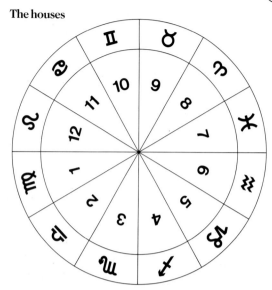

The astrological houses are the basis of all astrology of the sort we are dealing with here. Each house represents a different sphere of our lives. They are related to the Zodiac signs, and they also have a distinct relationship to each other. For instance, Aries, as a sign, tends to make its subjects somewhat self-centred: the first astrological house (known as the Aries house) is the most personal of the twelve; Taurean subjects show possessiveness, in one way or another: the second house (the Taurus house) represents possessions.

A comparison of the houses with the short descriptions of the Sun-signs on pp. 96-101 will give you a good general picture of the sphere of life revealed by each house. The houses are used in the same way in natal astrology.

The first house/the Aries house
Represents health and personal well-being, related to our attitudes to life, optimistic or pessimistic according to the influence of the planets passing through it at the same time. This house tells us when to be assertive or to hold back, when to show off a little or to keep a low profile. When the first house is emphasized, make important long-term decisions, taking a partner's decisions into consideration. The health aspect is extremely important, and which aspect is concerned can be learnt by interpreting planetary influences as they travel through the first house. It may be a good time to reassess the amount of exercise taken. The first house also tells us when to ask with good grace favours of others. Uncharacteristic, selfish behaviour could, at such times, mar progress.

The second house/the Taurus house
The house relating to money, possessions and earned income. It can warn against extravagance or praise financial sagacity. It also suggests times to make important purchases or sell unwanted things. Some-

times it is possible to assess when to be enterprising and perhaps start a business venture. If hoping for a pay rise, it can be obtained easily under favourable trends. If you have a favourable planetary transit through this house at times of department stores' sales you will probably get good bargains but may be tempted to overspend. Beware of stubbornness when this house is in focus.

The third house/the Gemini house
The house related to communications, young relatives, neighbours, cars or transport. When this is emphasized by planets passing though it, we often feel like speaking out, writing letters to the papers or getting our opinions across via 'phone-in radio programmes. Often relationships with neighbours are intensified – for good or ill. These are times to enjoy the company of young people – nephews, nieces, cousins. Sometimes conditions are favourable for buying or changing cars – it can be easier to pass a driving test when this house is in focus. Many more short journeys might be undertaken than is usual. Perhaps one of the best ways to use the third house is to discuss problems; we are usually able to analyse situations more clearly and speak more coherently. Be careful not to become superficial or restless when planets are transiting the third house.

The fourth house/the Cancer house
The house of home and family. With it in focus, parents or elderly relatives will often take up an above-average amount of time. They, or children, will give special pleasure or will present time-and-energy-consuming problems. We often feel the need to move house or to embark on ambitious home improvement schemes. More simply, we can enjoy making new cushion-covers or curtains, or even do extra cooking to stock the deep-freeze. Something that happened a long time ago may be remembered, or perhaps someone (a childhood friend of the family, for instance) will come back into our lives. We often feel nostalgic and sort out family photographs or souvenirs. Be careful not to be overemotional or uncharacteristically moody under a fourth house influence.

The fifth house/the Leo house
The house of creativity, sport, love affairs, children and risk-taking action. Great enjoyment is possible when favourable planets are travelling through the fifth house. Here are times to experience the Big Night Out, very often being particularly attractive to the opposite sex. If creative at all, we get the urge to start new artistic, often glamorous projects. Remember the planets will not encourage you to risk your shirt, whether in speculation on the stock exchange or at the race course. The house will indicate times to renew an active interest in sport, dance or other exercise – but don't take physical risks. Be careful not to be too bossy or dogmatic under its influence.

The sixth house/the Virgo house

The house relating to routine work, hobbies, diet, stresses and strains that affect our physical and mental well-being. When it is emphasized, we have to get "stuck in" to some routine work that we may have been shelving. It may be rather boring and perhaps physically demanding yet, when physically completed, will be very satisfying. If unduly worried, examine problems and always allow common sense and a practical outlook to help make decisions. It is usually good to reconsider eating habits and perhaps change them, adjusting diet. Healthier food while under this influence can lead to lasting improvement in health and perhaps much needed weight loss – or indeed gain, if underweight. There could be no better time to start a new hobby; it will give much pleasure. Beware of nagging and getting minor problems out of perspective when the sixth house is occupied.

The seventh house/the Libra house

The house representing emotional partnerships with spouses or lovers. But the theme of partnerships is not confined to them since the house also assesses attitudes to business partnerships and sometimes to important relationships between students and teachers. Indeed, all relationships other than that of parent and child are influenced by the planets as they travel through the seventh house. They present good opportunities for deepening a new relationship or reassessing one going through a difficult period. It can be the time for developing a love affair, perhaps started when planets were travelling through the fifth house. Now the relationship may become stabilized and permanent.

The eighth house/the Scorpio house

The house relating to money, insurance and inheritances. It also has a bearing on sexlives and sweeping changes in life. When emphasized, this house offers good opportunities for starting saving schemes and generally reorganizing financial commitments. These can be times when inheritances occur, or perhaps to make wills. On a psychological level, we sometimes make great changes – or, if suffering from some nagging problem, get to work on it. "Making a clean sweep" is an excellent phrase when thinking about the eighth house, but be careful not to throw out the baby with the bathwater. Quite often the sexdrive is increased; while satisfying it (and improving our sexlife is always desirable) be careful not to cause anxiety or emotional damage. With planets in this house, take care not to betray a confidence and do not allow abnormal jealousy or suspicion to cloud your thoughts or actions.

The ninth house/the Sagittarius house

The house relating to study, travel, the law and publishing. It also bears on the need for freedom and all kinds of intellectual challenge. When planets are travelling through the ninth house, the time is good for either planning or taking a holiday. Business travel will also be fruitful. Sometimes we lay down the law to our families – again a good thing to do, if their behaviour is not what you think it should be! If wanting to start a study course, this is the time to do so. If feeling the need for travel but unable to get away, it is rewarding to read travel books and allow yourself armchair journeys. Lives can suddenly feel restricted and claustrophobic, but don't exaggerate problems. Now is also the time to write a book or article or learn a foreign language.

The tenth house/the Capricorn house

Here the emphasis is on aspirations, ambitions, and careers. Planets travelling through this house make it easier to impress our employers, improving chances of promotion. When out of work, make a special effort to find a job, to persist and not to underestimate yourself or your achievements. Those not involved in a career can plan for the future, give additional support to their partners' careers or perhaps to their children. Sometimes we have to carry extra responsibility and may find it weighing heavily. If so, persist. Life can be very enjoyable, for you may find yourself attending formal functions or entertaining important people.

The eleventh house/the Aquarius house

Here emphasis is on friendship, social life, clubs and societies. With this house accentuated, it is a good thing to attempt to make new ties of friendship or perhaps deepen an existing acquaintanceship. You may feel the need to get out and about, so join a club or society to further an existing or new interest. If you are already a member of a club, you could be asked to serve on the committee or even become its chairman or president. Sometimes it is good to develop talents others do not think you possess. Informal entertaining is also enjoyable at these times, but when planets are travelling through the Aquarius House you can become somewhat intransigent and distance yourself from loved ones in an unusual, enigmatic way with eccentric or unpredictable behaviour.

The twelfth house/the Pisces house

The house related to the unconscious. When planets move through it, we can become secretive, sometimes with good reason, sometimes for less desirable ones. Rest is often needed and some form of restoration, away from a demanding career or young children. The help and support of therapists, priests or understanding older people may also be needed. This is a time for contemplation and for the rebuilding of physical and emotional resources. Often we get special pleasure from poetry, the arts or the cinema and religion can be unusually significant. But, when the twelfth house is emphasized, be very careful to avoid deceit and do not let others deceive you.

109

Planisphere from an astronomical manuscript. France, 15th century.

As the planets process around the Sun, they travel through each sign of the Zodiac in turn, and also through the houses of the solar chart. Because these pages concentrate on Sun-sign predictions, we concentrate on the influence of the planets in the houses – since their sign-influence relates character as deduced from the fully calculated, individual birth chart which is part of natal astrology, not covered in this book. Here, then, is a full interpretation of each planet's effects as it travels through the houses.

The Sun

The reason why Sun-sign astrology was invented was

that we know where the Sun is at the time of our birthday – it is in the sign which covers the period (roughly a month) coinciding with one of the 12 Zodiac signs. So we grow up knowing that we are "an Arian", "a Leo", or whatever. When the Sun enters our particular Sun-sign it also enters the first house of our "solar chart", and then proceeds through all the other houses and signs during the following 12 months.

Astrologers call the Sun a planet (although we know that it is really the only star used in astrology). As it passes through the houses, the Sun has a powerfully positive and energizing influence, which is interpreted in the same way as that of the planets we deal with below. Read the interpretations of the areas of life covered by the houses (pp. 108-109); the Sun will emphasize these in the most positive way. In the case of the Sun, you can ignore all of the more negative indications which are hinted at.

The Moon
The influence of the Moon is covered on pp. 120-122.

Mercury
Key-word: communication. The planet influences our thinking processes and also has a bearing on our nervous system.

Mercury in the first house
Think about yourself and plan what you want to do during the coming 12 months. With a positive outlook, you will be quick-thinking and will feel very decisive. Be careful not to allow impulsiveness to get the better of you. Your level of nervous energy will be specially abundant, and you will be able to grasp any situation speedily, but don't skip detail.

Mercury in the second house
You will certainly have a practical approach to problems, but you may take some time to think things through (unless you are a Sun-sign Geminian). Sell unwanted things or change your car. If looking for bargains, you'll do well. Think about a second source of income and pay attention to the small print on loans or hire purchase.

Mercury in the third house
Air your views; make contact with neighbours and, if necessary, sort out tricky problems – but avoid sarcasm. Concentrate on getting out and about as much as possible and enjoy young people's company. Arrange an interesting outing with them but watch out for nervous strain.

Mercury in the fourth house
A good time for planning changes to the home; you have an active imagination at the moment so new ideas should come easily. You will be liable to fall into a nostalgic mood. Don't get worries out of proportion or become irrational. If you fall out with anyone, do not be resentful.

Mercury in the fifth house
Concentrate on enjoying yourself. You will experience a keen appreciation of the company of children. A good time for creativity and stepping up social activity. You will find it easy to organize events at present, though you will be better at seeing broader pictures than attending to detail. Try not to take too many risks and don't be too dogmatic.

Mercury in the sixth house
Worries may get out of proportion. Take a practical outlook on life. When dealing with problems, try not to get bogged down by small, unimportant details.

Mercury in the seventh house
Your powers of communication are enhanced and this is an excellent time at which to discuss any problems with your partner. You will be tactful and diplomatic – but indecision may be a problem, so try to go straight to the point. Discuss the possibility of new joint interests, if necessary making minor changes to improve your life style.

Mercury in the eighth house
A good time to think about any psychological problem; discuss it freely with a friend or specialist. Your intuition will be well-tuned at present, and will often suggest the answer to a niggling problem. If someone else is involved, try not to be over suspicious or resentful. Study occult interests now, if you wish. Mystery, in fact or fiction, will appeal.

Mercury in the ninth house
Your outlook will be positive and optimistic and you should take up new challenges. Stretch your mind to benefit from new intellectual pursuits. A course of study started now may particularly appeal, especially in philosophy. Travel, physical and intellectual, is indicated but beware of risk-taking.

Mercury in the tenth house
Think about changing your job; ambition and patience combined coud lead to advancement. If out of work, write more letters, revamp your CV and make an extra effort to find new employment. Plan for the future, be ambitious, practical and shrewd, especially if dealing with superiors or prospective employers. If necessary, fight bureaucracy.

Mercury in the eleventh house
An excellent time to make a big effort to meet new people who share your interests. Concentrate on your social life: do new and different things, but avoid showing off. Stubbornness could also be a problem. Humanitarian work will benefit yourself as well as others. Your intuition is reliable; but try to be more flexible in your ideas.

Mercury in the twelfth house
This is a time for quietly thinking about important things. You may well feel more introverted than usual, needing to get away from the demands of daily life. You might, perhaps, want to extend any work you do for charities. There is some indication of secretiveness, even mysticism.

Venus

Key-words: love and relationships. The planet affects both areas of life, and has a very strong effect on the way we express affection. It also has powerful *financial* overtones, and affects our attitude to money. This sphere of our lives is often closely linked to our expression of love.

Venus in the first house

Your mood will be loving and romantic, and you will want to express warm, emotional feelings towards your partner. If unattached, you will probably be quick to fall in love. Watch out for selfishness, however. You will be looking and feeling good, but may procrastinate over work. Your social life should be particularly enjoyable, if rather expensive.

Venus in the second house

A good time for reassessing your earning power, and maybe asking for a pay rise. Important purchases, should be made at this time. You will get great pleasure from the arts, buying clothes and eating out in expensive restaurants, which may lead to a certain flabbiness. In your love life, avoid possessiveness.

Venus in the third house

A particularly good time at which to make contact with friends you've not seen for ages; you will enjoy visiting places of interest near home. Your capacity for friendship is underlined right now – write letters, make 'phone calls. Your attitude to love will be lively and light-hearted; remember you need friendship and intellectual *rapport* with a partner.

Venus in the fourth house

An excellent time to make your home more attractive. Experiment with all creative home-making crafts, especially cooking or sewing. Do not overcommit yourself financially, especially on home improvements. You may be overprotective, with a tendency to hug people to yourself – whether lover or family. Try to control overbrimming emotions.

Venus in the fifth house

This should be an enjoyable time, with the distinct possibility of a new love affair or the revitalization of an existing one. Passion and sheer affection are much emphasized but try not to put your lover on too high a pedestal. You will feel like living it up but don't allow your gambling spirit to get the better of you.

Venus in the sixth house

A time for reassessing your image, perhaps by changing your wardrobe or losing some weight. Spend time working out ways of improving your work schedule and increasing leisure time. At present you may be overcritical of those dear to you. Natural modesty may be inhibiting full expression of love.

Venus in the seventh house

If a sudden romance springs up, be careful; there is a tendency at present for you to fall in love with love. However, this is a splendid time to concentrate on an existing partner and perhaps sort out any problems in your relationship, for romance is indicated and there is no reason why you should not express it. This is also a good time to work on joint interests, including business projects.

Venus in the eighth house

Even if you haven't much money, now is the time at which to start a small savings scheme or to get involved in a business project. Review insurance policies and concentrate on financial matters in general. Think about improving your sexlife at a time when you feel passionate and emotional.

Venus in the ninth house

A wonderful time at which to enjoy a holiday abroad or contacts with loved ones from overseas. Watch out for laziness if studying. It is a good period for those involved in export or travel business. There is also a possibility of a sudden attraction to a foreigner. But any romance may run into difficulty if your partner wants to make it more permanent, for your love of freedom is paramount at present.

Venus in the tenth house

Good promotion prospects. Watch out for emotional involvement at work: this could be fun, but complications might arise. Relationships with parents or members of the older generation can be especially worthwhile.

Venus in the eleventh house

A time for socializing and extending your circle of friends. Give a party and invite your friends to bring along their friends. Generally extend your social life, perhaps by becoming a member of a club or society that particularly interests you. You may well be extremely attractive at present but, despite a feeling of high romance, this is not a time in which you are likely to become deeply involved emotionally.

Venus in the twelfth house

You are likely to fall into a quiet and perhaps somewhat reclusive, even mystical mood. This may be the result of your partner's actions; your loyalty is such that you have had to make sacrifices recently. Perhaps you are in love and do not feel strong enough to declare yourself at present. Don't worry – the time will soon come when you feel more assertive.

Mars

Key-words: physical energy, action, assertiveness, anger. The planet has a strong influence on our energy and the speed at which anger may flare up. Its influence is short and sharp; very often Mars is active when we are overhasty, so we become accident prone; it is also connected with rushes of adrenalin at moments of danger. The orbit of Mars falls outside that of the earth. It takes about two-and-a-half years to travel around the Sun, and thus stays in each sign and house for just over two months.

Mars in the first house
At present your energy will be stimulated and enhanced. Partly because of this you may be overhasty; be careful to avoid minor accidents when handling sharp knives or tools or hot dishes. You can do much, so do not hesitate to seize the initiative – but do give yourself time to think about your actions. Headaches could be bothersome.

Mars in the second house
Money will burn a hole in your pocket and you will be in the mood to make extra money and spend it. Try to keep a balance; overenthusiasm can lead to overspending and complications over payments. Keep calm dealing with such problems. You will work hard at present; try not to become too intractable.

Mars in the third house
Your intellectual energy may run ahead of your physical energy at present; it is important to concentrate if restlessness is not to hinder you. Take care not to exaggerate problems with neighbours or relatives. Try to do some community work under this influence.

Mars in the fourth house
You are likely to have a blitz clearing-out and cleaning your home or doing some practical work there. Your emotional level is high and you may, for some reason, feel fed up with members of your close circle. Try to be patient and not to show ill-temper. Work out your tensions through physical exercise.

Mars in the fifth house
Your enthusiasm for love and all the good things is abundant and your social life should go with a swing. Arrange some pleasurable experiences at this time but beware of overspending and exaggeration. Try to keep your temper under control.

Mars in the sixth house
You will be in a working mood and this is a good time to get on with any task you have been shelving. Spend more time than usual on sport and exercise and avoid overrich foods. If you expend energy on conventional career matters, you may have to fight a dislike of carrying responsibility and may suffer from stomach upsets as a result of worry.

Mars in the seventh house
It is possible to have a lot of fun and sexual pleasure with your partner when Mars is in the seventh house, for it makes you both romantic and passionate. But be careful; the energies can work negatively, causing minor quarrels to get out of proportion. At work, you could be energetic one day, lazy the next. Try to balance things more.

Mars in the eighth house
You may be concerned by a problem. Aim to talk it over with a sympathetic friend. Your emotions and sex life are highly charged at present. Express them openly for, if blocked, jealousy or obsession can take over. A good time to do some research.

Mars in the ninth house
You will be in an energetic, adventurous, enthusiastic and daring mood. Try to express these feelings as fully as possible, remembering you can cope with any kind of challenge that comes along. One of the best ways to expend overabundant energy is through sport, exercise or travel. Watch for a tendency to exaggerate or become boisterous: get rid of mental cobwebs.

Mars in the tenth house
You have extra energy on your side to put into your day's work and to achieve goals presently important to you. Try to control your energy; if in a career, your efforts will not be unnoticed. Keep your eyes open and use your initiative. If working at home, plan home improvements and give extra encouragement to the family. Do not get attached to power for its own sake.

Mars in the eleventh house
Be careful not to upset friends and acquaintances by overreacting negatively to what they say, nor by their slowness in responding to your suggestions. You are now in a good position to spur them on into greater enjoyment of joint interests. If you're a committee member, you can do much to further its objectives; enthusiasm can be channelled into charitable work.

Mars in the twelfth house
You may become atypically secretive. Perhaps you have something to tell others and instinctively know that the time is not yet right to do so. Should someone entrust you with a confidence, don't break it. Try to control your emotional energy, which could well be very charged at present; you may need calming so relax with music or books.

113

Jupiter

Key-word: expansion. Jupiter takes about 12 years to complete a journey around the Sun, so it stays in a sign, and therefore the same house of the Solar Chart, for about 12 months, giving a background theme of colouring to our lives. The effects of its particular house will be focused more strongly when other planets join it or make short term aspects to it. Traditionally, Jupiter has always been known as the most beneficial of all planets. With it working for us, we usually experience a time of opportunities. The planet also relates to the law, the church, publishing and industry. All types of study come under its wing, especially foreign languages.

Jupiter in the first house

A time when you will feel positive, assertive and optimistic. Put plans into action and set yourself goals to improve your life style. Generally a fortunate period. Remember too that "expansion" *can* mean weight gain and too much living it up can make you vulnerable to liverishness. Beware of overdramatizing problems and losing your sense of perspective.

Jupiter in the second house

The accent is on making extra money; by this time next year you should be feeling very satisfied with your bank balance, provided you have not been over extravagant. Think about starting a business project to give you a second source of income. Care is necessary not to allow emotions to get the better of you – you might be behaving too possessively.

Jupiter in the third house

You may need to get out and about more than for some time. Perhaps you need stimulating intellectually – especially if you are a mother with young children. Think about starting a group of some kind with others who share your interests. What about learning to drive, or taking an advanced driving course? If you have ever wanted to write pieces for your local paper or give talks on your local radio, now is the time.

Jupiter in the fourth house

As Jupiter settles down to transiting your fourth house, you will feel the need for a larger home. Try not to allow restlessness with your present home to cause you to rush into making changes but take your time. If a move is not feasible, home improvements should work out well. Sometimes we decide to "expand" our families under this influence – i.e. have another baby.

Jupiter in the fifth house

You will feel very optimistic and hence will be more than ready to take risks – both financial and emotional. But be very careful; your gambling spirit might get the better of you. If you control your feelings you'll make great progress. Time spent instructing children in what fascinates you will also be rewarding

Jupiter in the sixth house

Reorganize your work schedule and you will have more time for fun. Liverishness may occur, pulled thigh muscles and torn tendons if you are into sport. We sometimes become hypochondriacs under this influence. Keep up a sensible exercise programme and watch your diet carefully.

Jupiter in the seventh house

You should experience a happy and rewarding period with your partner. Work out ways to improve your joint lives and to develop new shared interests. But be careful, because often we expect too much from our partners, taking rather than giving. Our attitude and reactions to loved ones can become overdramatic.

Jupiter in the eighth house

Whether young or old, rich or penniless, now is the time to think about money in relation to the long term future. Start saving a few pennies weekly – or reassess your stocks and shares. If bequeathed a family heirloom, get it insured. Investments made during the coming months should prove worthwhile.

Jupiter in the ninth house

You should experience some exciting developments. If confronted with challenging situations, respond positively. All forms of study will progress excellently Try to arrange to travel – the further afield and the more exotic the better. Dealings with publishers, solicitors or the clergy should be advantageous.

Jupiter in the tenth house

This is a good period for business or career opportunities. Be confident, and look on obstacles as challenges rather than setbacks. Acting ability will stand you in good stead.

Jupiter in the eleventh house

You will derive special pleasure from the company of friends and acquaintances. If you want to ask a favour of a friend, do so – especially if Jupiter is influenced by Venus or Mars. You may have to take a more active role in running your club or society. Be generous with time and money for charity.

Jupiter in the twelfth house

During this period, you may benefit especially from philosophical or spiritual subjects. Religion, music, or the arts may mean more at such times. Give yourself time to think and contemplate. Yoga and meditation could be worthwhile. Avoid overreacting emotionally and excessive sacrifices for other people.

Saturn

Key-word: limitation. It takes about 29½ years for Saturn to complete a journey through all the signs and houses of the Solar Chart so it stays in the same house for about two and a half years. It too is a kind of background influence, dormant for long periods of time, then activated by aspects with other planets. Do not get its influence out of perspective, just bear in mind its position; at times it will work powerfully.

It is through the influence of Saturn that we learn from experience. While we may suffer setbacks, we often make important changes that affect our long-term future. We take on commitments of all kinds such as marriage or house purchase. Often promotion to a "top" job separates us from colleagues.

Saturn in the first house

At times you may feel a certain amount of frustration and find life difficult, but experiences now will help you greatly in the future. You may have to carry additional responsibility but this will add to your eventual progress. Keep a positive, constructive outlook. Watch your vitality – you might need additional vitamins, especially in cold weather. Be methodical and don't take unnecessary risks.

Saturn in the second house

Resign yourself to having to work extremely hard for every penny or cent you earn. Don't take financial risks – and if you can, put aside money for hard times. You may feel less inclined to be as generous as usual – perhaps from necessity.

Saturn in the third house

A period when you could experience a continuing problem with neighbours, or a young relative may take up more of your time than usual – if so, know you are being of enormous help. Sometimes we suffer from breakdowns in communications such as lost mail. Make sure your car is serviced regularly.

Saturn in the fourth house

Your parents or someone of an older generation may become more demanding. Perhaps you will have to carry additional responsibility. You might move to a bigger and more prestigious home (but be careful; the mortgage could become a heavy burden). Not a good time to embark on major alterations to your home.

Saturn in the fifth house

While you will enjoy life, you will take your pleasures rather seriously. If creative, allow your work to develop along the traditional lines of your craft. Your love life could become dreary – or you might be attracted to a much older person. Sometimes under this influence we are separated from our lovers. Your children may go through an uncooperative period.

Saturn in the sixth house

The accent is on your general health. Your vitality could become a little low and you may suffer from inexplicable aches and pains. Check your diet – it could be out of balance. If you become involved in a long, dull and demanding project, press on, since your efforts will not be wasted. Be disciplined.

Saturn in the seventh house

You may need to reassess your relationship with your partner. You could get married, for commitment is very much a Saturnine theme. Don't be rushed into any such decision, however. This placing can indicate the formation of a business partnership with an older or more experienced person.

Saturn in the eighth house

Long-term investments made now will be beneficial. A good time to make your will. You could find yourself attracted to horror or mystery fiction. Try not to let any psychological problems become obsessive. You will probably want to think deeply about many issues.

Saturn in the ninth house

Your outlook will be serious and philosophical. If studying, you will be able to apply your learning constructively to many areas but you may feel less optimistic than usual. You may enjoy travelling less than usual, experiencing frustrations and delays.

Saturn in the tenth house

Now is the time to go all out to achieve your ambitions. It may not be easy but the chances of promotion to a very important if lonely position are high. But do not let career or ambition cause neglect of your family. Be tactful and gentle; persuasion will pay off.

Saturn in the eleventh house

Responsibility will make its presence felt, involving something that means much to you. Under this kind of influence you can become chairperson of societies or clubs; committee work will be demanding. Sometimes older friends are important. You could gain from involvement in charitable work, perhaps fund-raising.

Saturn in the twelfth house

If you have problems, you could easily be very secretive about them, possibly leading to an obsessive attitude to what is bothering you. Do try hard to talk things over with a sympathetic friend or counsellor. Aim to use this positively, perhaps through devoting more time to helping others. Don't grumble about your problems: there are others worse off than you.

115

THE GENERATION INFLUENCES

Uranus, Nepture and Pluto

Uranus, Neptune and Pluto are known astrologically as the "generation influences". Their orbits are at such a great distance from the Sun that they stay in the same sign of the Zodiac and the same house of the solar chart for a great many years, therefore exerting an influence on a whole generation of people. Uranus takes 7 years to travel through each sign and house, Neptune takes 14 years to travel through each sign and house and Pluto takes between 13 and 32 years to travel through each sign and house.

These planets are not used in quite the same way in Sun-sign astrology. While, like Jupiter and Saturn, they will exert a long-term, background influence (depending on the house they inhabit) that influence will be ignited when the quicker-moving planets make aspects to them.

Do not overemphasize the long-term trends; if you concentrate on interpreting the house position of Neptune when you are working on a single month's trends, the effects will be to unbalance your conclusions. In the Sun-sign context, use these planetary influences only in relation to other planets. Here follows an interpretation of these planets' houses influences: use them carefully, remembering the warning above.

Uranus

Key-word: Change (disruptive or sudden). Uranus was the first of the three "modern planets" to be discovered (by William Herschel in 1781). It takes about 84 years to complete its journey through all 12 signs and houses of the Chart. This lively, enigmatic planet often sparks off our originality; we are susceptible to tension or excitement when it is operating and should be careful not to fall into eccentric behaviour. Uranus at its best makes us humanitarian, friendly and aware of the problems and sufferings of others. It is also energizing, so we can usually take positive action – but be careful to control the impulsive or unpredictable side of its influence.

Uranus in the first house

During this long period you will probably make an above average number of important changes. You could unconsciously be rather tense so don't allow yourself to rush into decisions, even if you feel like doing so. Once during your lifetime you will find that Uranus will occupy the same degree of the same sign as the Sun was in at your birth. This will make a key period for you. Life will be exciting and full of the unexpected; keep calm.

Uranus in the second house

You may well experience sudden financial fluctuations. Be prudent; put money aside regularly in case a job collapses unexpectedly or some money due to you does not materialize.

Uranus in the third house

This is a splendid placing intellectually; you could easily have bright or original ideas. Do not be apprehensive but try to act on them. Against this, you may experience transport problems – perhaps with your car. Watch out for nervous strain and tension and avoid sudden, unpredictable actions that might upset others.

Uranus in the fourth house

There could be tension in the home – perhaps your children are being fractious. Try to close any generation gap; don't, if you are upsetting your parents, persist. Especially if you want to move into your own apartment, demonstrate an adult approach.

Uranus in the fifth house

A marvellous, invigorating influence if you are creative; branching out into new areas of work will demonstrate your originality. You should get a lot out of this trend – especially when focused by other planets or when Uranus makes specific influences for you. Your love life could be changeable and perhaps erratic; affairs may be colourful but unstable.

Uranus in the sixth house

This trend may work adversely on your nervous system. If you are tense or a natural worrier, the planet may aggravate this condition. Try to burn energy evenly and take up an intellectual challenge or divert nervous energy into a new form of exercise such as badminton or fencing.

Uranus in the seventh house

This can be a dynamic, invigorating influence on relationships but it can also precipitate important decisions – whether to make amends or end your present partnership. This influence will be most strongly felt when Uranus makes a direct, specific influence to the Sun's position. In general, do as much as possible to enliven your partnership.

Uranus in the eighth house

Be extremely careful when dealing with investments – whether saving a few pounds a week or less, or running an international banking operation. Sudden changes can cause setbacks and problems. Look out for snags when committing yourself to house or property insurance, and be very careful if borrowing.

Uranus in the ninth house

Unexpected developments may occur when travelling abroad – perhaps dramatic holiday love affairs. Be prepared for less pleasant things, too – such as money being stolen, flights changed, hotels unready. This is an exciting influence for writers; students may be tempted to study spasmodically or try to impress tutors by being too clever by half. Concentrate instead on craftsmanship and technique.

Uranus in the tenth house

Sudden, unexpected developments will concern your job. You may be forced to take drastic action, but that in itself could goad you into aspiring to greater things. If you happen to be made redundant, remember that this could be a mixed loss.

Uranus in the eleventh house

This is a strong placing for Uranus. Your social life could take decided strides forward during the seven years that Uranus occupies this house. You may well become a dedicated member of some group or society. New interests could flourish and, as they do, your circle of friends and acquaintances will widen.

Uranus in the twelfth house

Be careful, you could be bothered by irrational worries – especially when Mars or perhaps Mercury make aspects to Uranus. The trend, however, is tiny and should not affect the whole seven years that Uranus takes to travel through your twelfth house. Use the indication well by exploring comparative religion, or spend more time being charitable. The twelfth house relates to sacrifices made for those suffering.

Neptune

Key-words: illusion, cloudiness and deception. Neptune was discovered in 1840 and takes about 146 years to complete a journey around the Sun, through all 12 signs and houses. So when interpreting its influence in a Sun-sign column, we must be even more cautious than with Uranus, for it remains in the same house for 14 years.

Read the following; then, with a view to extending your knowledge of how Neptune works from each house, use your interpretation of its house position only when other planets activate its influence – and then only with great discretion.

This planet is strongly connected with the idea of escapism and we often fall into escapist habits when it works negatively for us. But when it works positively, we become extremely perceptive and inspired. Sometimes we become overemotional and fail to see life as it really is.

Neptune in the first house

Neptune will only be in this house if you are a Sun-sign Capricorn, since it will travel through this sign until 1998. The chances are that it will tend to soften your strong Capricornian personality, you may become less practical, cautious and determined, and less sure of your real ambitions. It could add some interestingly gentle but also woolly-minded characteristics. Be on your guard against self-deception and make an effort to face up to reality.

Neptune in the second house

You may experience a tendency to squander money – perhaps to lend it to people who won't return it. Keep financial dealings on a businesslike footing; this is necessary if not easy, otherwise problems could drag on in a confusing way for ages. Watch out for self-indulgence.

Neptune in the third house

This placing could be to the force when Mercury makes aspects to Neptune. At such times you may suffer problems with your mail or telephone or become unusually suspicious. If so, do not let your feelings run away with you. You may feel inspired – perhaps to explore strange or exotic places. But remember this only applies when Mercury is busy with Neptune.

Neptune in the fourth house

There could be problems with the plumbing, especially when Mars contacts Neptune. If you live in a cold climate, make sure your pipes are lagged. Life can become colourful at these times, with interesting developments – you may go to a party where you meet unusual people. Don't be too hard on a troublesome member of your family; be understanding, remembering others may not be as uncomplicated as you.

Neptune in the fifth house

You could easily develop an unrealistic attitude towards your love life. Perhaps you are looking at your adored one through rose-coloured spectacles. Do not take any emotional or financial risks – especially when Venus makes contact with Neptune; things may not be as good as they seem. Allow your inspiration free rein in creative appreciation, expression or inventiveness.

Neptune in the sixth house

You could feel very lethargic over routine work. If you are allergic to drugs or have sensitive skin, Neptune may adversely affect you there – so avoid if possible even prescribed drugs and any foods which you know tend to aggravate your problem. Now would be a good time to take a course in counselling, or in the techniques of first aid.

117

Neptune in the seventh house

Until 1998 this placing will apply to Sun-sign Cancerians. You may take the easy way out of difficulties with your partner and perhaps not face up to reality. If at all worried, listen to your powerful intuitive sense, but don't allow it to be bolstered by your lively imagination, for together they could mislead you. Be cautious when there are aspects to Neptune from Venus.

Neptune in the eighth house

A liking for mystery and the occult could become a lifetime's study. If you want to get involved in clairvoyance, make sure you learn from a specialist with proper training. Be cautious financially.

Neptune in the ninth house

You could easily develop a philosophical outlook and become a useful adviser. Disciplined study, though not easy for you, is necessary. Channel your ideas constructively and you could influence others in the best possible way.

Neptune in the tenth house

This could be a decade for interesting career changes, perhaps after a deep involvement with a job moving to other areas. But you may lack positive direction and have to choose between a dull but secure job and one with overwhelming job-satisfaction and interest. Life can be tricky when a strong planet like Mars briefly appears or when Neptune makes a specific contact to your Sun.

Neptune in the eleventh house

You will develop ties of friendship with unusual, perhaps unworldly people. You could have fun. Don't feel inferior to them; you're not!

Neptune in the twelfth house

Here Neptune works at its strongest. You may need time apart for peace and quiet. Time to study what interests you – literature, photography, video-making. Be careful that under pressure you don't slip into negative escapism. Make sure your Neptunian influences work for, not against you. Strengthen your religious faith; help others but don't allow them to take advantage of you. All this is most likely when Mercury, Venus or Jupiter make positive influences to Neptune.

Pluto
Keyword: elimination. Pluto was discovered in 1930 – the most distant planet so far to have been found in the solar system. It takes 246 years to travel through all the Zodiac signs and the houses of the chart. Because its orbit is extremely eccentric, it takes between 13 and 32 years to move through a sign.

Because of the length of time it can stay in one particular house, you should not concentrate on its house position when dealing with Sun-sign astrology. Its specific influence in relation to the precise position of the Sun in your personal birth chart is very potent but in Sun-sign astrology it is only activated when the faster moving planets make aspects to it.

Pluto urges us to bring our problems out into the open. People often start psychotherapy when it is working for them, or make very drastic changes. We can find ourselves up against a brick wall; then, when the planet's influence has passed, the way ahead is clear. One colleague says that Pluto constipates – and indeed this is so, especially psychologically. The planet also has strong financial overtones; scrutinize investments and insurance.

Pluto in the first house

This placing only applies to Sun-sign Scorpios, Pluto not completing its journey through that sign until 1995. Its influence will be at its strongest when it makes a conjunction to the precise position of your sun. Generally during these years you will be able to

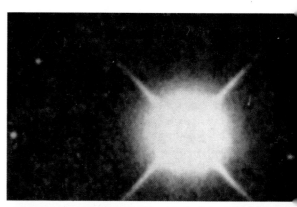

Pluto was discovered in 1930 when C Tombaugh's two photographs of the same region of the night sky, taken three days apart, revealed an unidentified,

express potently all your strong Scorpio qualities. Make sure that you are using them positively, and not allowing jealousy, vindictiveness or a deceitful tendency to get the better of you.

Pluto in the second house

If you are clever, you may increase your income under this influence – but be circumspect. These possibilities are most likely when Venus or Jupiter make aspects to Pluto.

Pluto in the third house

When Mercury or Mars are busy with Pluto, you may feel like having a short but violent row – perhaps with a noisy neighbour. But don't allow resentfulness to preoccupy you; keep it short. Otherwise from this house Pluto will not be a very strong influence for you.

Pluto in the fourth house

You could become very stubborn and dogmatic at times – especially when the Sun makes an aspect to Pluto, or Pluto makes a specific influence for you. At times you will feel frustrated but be careful and you will get what you want.

Pluto in the fifth house

Beware Venus contacting Pluto – you could easily

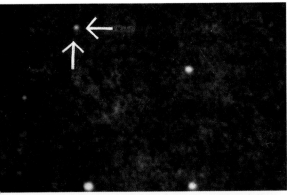

fast-moving heavenly body (marked by arrows). Pluto may once have been a satellite of Neptune – they certainly share common astrological ground.

fall passionately but hopelessly in love. The experience may be worthwhile but wearying. Do not take financial risks.

Pluto in the sixth house

When Mercury activates Pluto you may feel a build up of tension or frustration which could upset your whole system for a few days. This is also a time when you should make quite sure you eat enough fibre.

Pluto in the seventh house

This is a strong position for Sun-sign Taureans in particular. Many people will end a relationship. You could form a new, rewarding business partnership, perhaps with your spouse. New, powerful changes can occur. You may want to make a new start clearing away difficulties between your partner and yourself.

Pluto in the eighth house

This influence has financial overtones. When Pluto is in the eighth house and receives aspects from either Venus or Jupiter, aim to make investments if possible. Alternatively, you might care to do some type of research.

Pluto in the ninth house

When Mercury aspects Pluto, a certain amount of mental strain and tension could build up. Be careful when swotting for examinations: doing masses of revision in the final days may not have the desired result. When Mercury or Jupiter contact Pluto, make a special effort not to drink and drive.

Pluto in the tenth house

Should you feel very fed up, take a few days off and relax; you could make a sudden wrong decision under this influence. Be patient; give yourself time to allow your feelings and impulses to settle – any change you make might prove to be far more drastic than you realize.

Pluto in the eleventh house

Friends could drive you up the wall; if on a committee you may explode with impatience at the frustrating slowness of your colleagues. This is most likely when other "heavy" planets make aspects to Pluto. Don't give up; be patient. At its best, Pluto can make you a real financial wizard at fund-raising.

Pluto in the twelfth house

A tricky position. You must be honest with yourself. Perhaps you have been nursing a grudge or psychological problem for too long. Try to rationalize it. You may find that things will improve when Jupiter makes contact to Pluto. Recognize the fact that you may not be doing yourself much good by keeping everything to yourself.

The Moon

We have so far only used the influence of the Moon in a general way. It has, of course, a very powerful influence on the earth, most obviously on the seas and tides, and on various species of molluscs, insects and animals, including ourselves.

As the earth and the planets are all satellites of the Sun, so the Moon is the earth's only satellite, taking 28 days to travel through all the signs of the Zodiac on its journey round the earth.

The New Moon

The new Moon occurs when the Sun and Moon are in the same sign of the Zodiac – i.e. *in conjunction.* – This happened on November 21, 1987 (see p.102, under *Longitude).*

It gives us renewed energy to start new work, new projects, get around to doing things we have shelved. We set up business meetings or social occasions – sometimes we clean our houses thoroughly. At the time of the new Moon we often write letters or make telephone calls about which we have been procrastinating – readers who work on switchboards receive many more calls and enquiries at this time. All these are ways in which we unconsciously express the young, fresh energy of the New Moon.

Should you find that there is a new Moon on your birthday, the coming 12 months may well be an important period for you – one when you may easily make changes affecting your life for many years to come. Sometimes these changes will relate to your outlook and emotions, perhaps you will deepen a relationship or end it. Maybe you will start a family, or move house. At all events, know that the time is right for vital developments.

The Full Moon

This occurs when the Sun and Moon are *in opposition* (see p.104) – that is, they are in opposite signs of the Zodiac – i.e., Sun in Scorpio, Moon in Taurus (this occurred on November 5, 1987 – see p.102, under *Longitude).*

Again, there is additional energy in the prevailing atmosphere, but the two days or so prior to the full Moon are tense times; it is then that heavy traffic jams tend to occur, people become fractious, mass hysteria can break out where crowds gather. Sadly it is also often the case that violence, assassinations and angry protests are more likely. This is a recurrent pattern, and those of us who are aware of it can at least be careful not to contribute to the tension, and may be able to in some way contain it.

It is fortunately also possible to use the full Moon's energies as positively as one can use those of the new Moon. Provided we consciously control our emotions, we can do much good and exciting work at these tense times. But always remember, however, that we can become overaggressive or easily upset.

Women whose periods occur at the time of the full Moon will sometimes bleed more copiously than usual; if you are a blood donor make donations at this time – the process will be easier and speedier. Conversely, if possible avoid having surgery at the time of the full Moon, since it has been shown that it is more difficult to staunch a blood flow at, and immediately prior to, the full Moon.

Should there be a full Moon on your birthday you probably have an eventful year ahead – the vital influence will definitely colour your year. Changes could be afoot, and in the long term you will find that things will work out well. Remember you may tend to overreact emotionally – perhaps without real reason. Try to control impulsiveness and erratic behaviour. Listen to your intuition, but don't be blinded by it.

The first and third quarters

These times (like the new and full Moons they are often listed in diaries) are slightly tense, but far less potent than the times of the new or full Moon, and you may experience some aggravation. If either occurs on your birthday you could feel unusually restless in the coming 12 months. Be aware that this could happen, and as a counter try to develop new interests or make new friends.

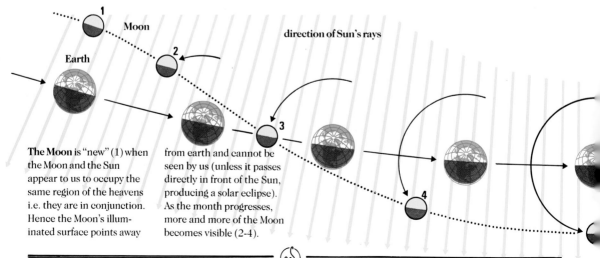

The Moon is "new" (1) when the Moon and the Sun appear to us to occupy the same region of the heavens i.e. they are in conjunction. Hence the Moon's illuminated surface points away from earth and cannot be seen by us (unless it passes directly in front of the Sun, producing a solar eclipse). As the month progresses, more and more of the Moon becomes visible (2-4).

Eclipses

Astrologers have always taken account of eclipses of the Sun and the Moon, although in ancient times these were regarded mainly as omens of doom – but not in modern astrology.

Solar and lunar esclipses are inextricably linked, for an eclipse of the Sun can only occur when the Moon is new, and an eclipse of the Moon can only occur when the Moon is full (see diagram below). Throughout history – particularly before scientists had given any explanation for them – solar eclipses terrified man-kind: the increasing darkness and the eventual disappearance of the sun appalled primitive minds. Astrologers, too, prophesied doom and gloom as an eclipse approached. Many superstitions were added to authentic astrological findings.

Modern astrologers still attach considerable import-ance to eclipses; the difficulty lies in assessing the time-lag between the occurrence of the eclipse and the possible outcome. Some planets seem to have an almost instant effect, while others are notoriously difficult to "time". The Moon is not difficult to time, but the effect of eclipses in particular is often delayed. It can be said that the general effect of the new and full Moon (as described above) are often heightened at the time of an eclipse – so we find more tension when there is a lunar eclipse, and greater activity at the time of a solar eclipse.

As far as individuals are concerned, sound general advice is to avoid planning important events (weddings, house-moving, starting new jobs) at these times, and if possible to allow a few weeks to pass – perhaps until the next new Moon – before fixing the important date.

Should an eclipse occur on your birthday, what we have already said about the new or full Moon occurring on this day will apply even more potently. The 12 months ahead will be a key period of your life. Be circumspect about all decision-making, and try to concentrate on important issues. Don't allow triviali-ties to take up time and energy far more wisely directed in other ways. Try not to act overemotionally or lose your sense of perspective. Listen to, and take, good advice especially if you find yourself needing to make important changes.

These suggestions are also worth remembering if an eclipse of Sun or Moon occurs two weeks before or after your birthday – though the effect will be less potent than on the birthday itself.

The lunar theme

If you get into the habit of looking at your Sun-sign trends for the months ahead, you may find as you refer to your Ephemeris that the New Moon will make a series of aspects to the Sun's position as it was on your day of birth. These do not occur every month or every year; some years may pass without them. (During this time the Moon will be making aspects to the other planets in your full birth-chart). The lunar aspects, when they occur, may affect your life for perhaps five months.

Assume that your birthday is November 21. According to the degree grid on p.102 the Sun was on the 28th degree of Scorpio when you were born. In 1987 there was a New Moon on your birthday.

The New Moon in December 1987 occurred on the 20th. To discover whether this made an aspect with the Sun's position on your birthday, look in the Ephemeris for December 1987 under *Longitude,* and find the position *of the Sun* on that day (ignore the Moon's position, for when it is new it is always in conjunction with the Sun).

Note A series of new Moon aspects to the precise position of the Sun as it was on the day of your birth need not begin on your birthday: they can start on the day of any new Moon in any month, if the Sun on that day is within two degrees of orb of the position of the Sun on your birthday. It will not necessarily follow that the first aspect the new Moon makes to your Sun will be a conjunction (as in our example); it could be any of the aspects listed – i.e., semi-sextile, sextile, square, trine etc. (In this area of astrology we recommend you ignore the sesquare and semi-square, which are more complicated to work out.)

121

At the time of the Full Moon (5), the Moon and the Sun appear to be opposite one another in the heavens. Hence the Moon's entire illuminated surface is visible from earth (unless the Moon and Sun are directly opposite one another, when the earth's shadow produces a lunar eclipse).

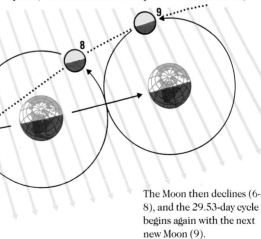

The Moon then declines (6-8), and the 29.53-day cycle begins again with the next new Moon (9).

The Sun's position (and hence the New Moon's position) on December 20th 1987 was 27° Sagittarius – so the new Moon in Sagittarius is *semi-sextile* (see p.104) to your Scorpio Sun.

Astrologers have decided, over the centuries, how nearly exact the aspects must be to have an effect: that is to say, whether or not they are *in orb*. In our example, the aspect the New Moon would make to the Sun would be exact when it stood at 28° of any sign – because the Sun occupied 28°. Scorpio on the day of birth. In the case of the Moon, astrologers agree that the aspect is operative with the Moon within four degrees of the Sun – that is, two degrees on either side of it.

You have now discovered that the new Moon makes a *semi-sextile* aspect to what is called your "natal Sun" on December 20 (see diagram below). But you must look ahead to discover the other aspects it may make during the coming months. So, return to the Ephemeris, turn to January 1988 – and repeat the above process. You will find that the new Moon occurs on January 19: the Sun, on that day, is on Capricorn 28° – again, there is obviously an aspect between it and your natal Sun, this time, because they are two signs apart it is a *sextile* (see p.104).

In February 1988, the new Moon falls on the 17th, on Aquarius 27° – three signs away from your Scorpio Sun. The result is a *square* aspect (see p. 104).

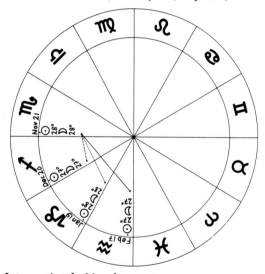

Interpreting the Moon's aspects
The Moon's aspects usually affect one particular sphere of your life. It is difficult to say precisely what this may be, because it will depend on the position of the Moon at the time of your birth, but you will find that when the Moon affects you it will throw one area of your life into focus: perhaps an emotional or psychological problem or a specific aspect of a personal relationship – but perhaps also a more practical area of life, a project just starting, on which you will work intensively during the time covered by the lunar trends. You may start looking for a new

home when the Moon is influencing your life, and complete the deal and move house as the series of aspects ends; or you may work on an intensive study course, or do special research. It is usually the case that whatever is in focus will benefit you for a long period of time.

As a general rule, try to use the Moon's influence by working on it positively and assertively when the aspects are easy – i.e., *conjunction, sextile* and *trine* – and be objective and practical when the aspects are tense or negative – i.e., *square, opposition, quincunx* or *semi-sextile* – though remember that the *semi-sextile* is the weakest of all the aspects.

The Sun's aspects
When you discover that on a cetain day the sun makes an aspect to a planet – a *solar aspect* – refer for the interpretation to *Specific Influences* (pp.125-127). The effect will be identical, but less personal. For instance, for *Sun square Saturn* read under *Saturn's Aspects to the Sun (The Square)*. Those through whose Sun-signs the two planets are travelling may feel depressed or perhaps frustrated, and progress may be slow for them. Use the full interpretations given as a basis for understanding the situation, remembering that the trend is much weaker and less dynamic than when it is a specific influence to the precise position of the Sun on your day of birth.

Aspects of the Moon
We do not normally use *lunar aspects* – other than the New and Full Moon – when looking at monthly astrological trends. They are useful when examining weekly influences, or if you wish to concentrate on one specific day. Remember that, because of the Moon's rapid motion, the lunar aspects only last for a few hours; if you use them, it is advisable to note the precise time when the aspect is exact. It will only be a strong influence for a couple of hours either side of the time stated. The time given in the ephemeris will be Greenwich Mean Time, so make allowances for this by adding or subtracting your time-zone difference.

Mutual aspects
The aspects made by the fast-moving planets – Mercury, Venus and Mars – to each other and to the slow-moving planets – Jupiter, Saturn, Uranus, Neptune and Pluto – are effective for a few days. When using them in interpreting your monthly trends, assume that they will influence your life for about that time. When Jupiter makes an aspect to a planet, its effect will last about a week; in the case of Saturn, 10 days, Uranus, a fortnight, and Neptune and Pluto, a month.

The planet listed first in the list below is the one making the aspect: astrologers always consider that it is the planet nearest the Sun that makes the aspect to the more distant planet, and never the other way around (apart from Specific Influences). Mercury square Pluto, and never Pluto square Mercury. Hence the diminishing number of aspects each planet makes, with Mercury making aspects to all the other planets while Neptune can only make aspects to Pluto.

Ancient astrologers considered some aspects to be "good" while others were "bad": the *conjunction* always being neutral, making its influence according to the qualities of the two planets involved. Modern astrologers divide aspects into "positive" and "negative", remembering that "negative" influences are powerful energizers, and can be used to advantage, as will be seen from the interpretations below.

THE ASPECTS OF MERCURY
Mercury to Venus
Because the orbits of Mercury and Venus fall between Earth and the Sun and can never be more than 76 degrees apart, only the *conjunction, semi-sextile, semi-square* and *sextile* are possible. The *conjunction* and *sextile* are very positive, the *semi-sextile* and *semi-square* are slightly strenuous. Here are excellent times to entertain friends or write letters. If you enjoy creative work or any requiring skilful use of the hands, these are times to embark on a new project. You may feel a certain tension if the negative aspects are operative, but it could just mean exceptional enthusiasm or excitement.

Mercury to Mars
Conjunction, semi-sextile, sextile, trine. These are mentally stimulating. They encourage quick thinking and decisiveness. A good time to put ideas into motion.

Semi-square, square, quincunx, sesquare, opposition. These too are mentally invigorating, but care is needed if impulsiveness or speaking out of turn are not to cause problems. Watch out that nervous tension does not build up.

Mercury to Jupiter
Conjunction, semi-sextile, sextile, trine. Excellent for travelling or for planning holidays – especially abroad. Good for study or test-taking of any kind. Write letters or start your novel! Develop an optimistic outlook.

Semi-square, square, sesquare, quincunx, opposition. As above, but do not exaggerate or overcommit yourself, and watch out for blind optimism.

Mercury to Saturn
Conjunction, semi-sextile, sextile, trine. A good time for long-term planning and serious thought on important matters, but quick results must not be expected.

Semi-square, square, sesquare, quincunx, opposition. Try not to allow dispiriting thoughts to lower your spirits. Consider the long-term but be prepared for some frustration – especially if the aspect is the square or opposition.

Mercury to Uranus
Conjunction, semi-sextile, sextile, trine. You could easily be bursting with new ideas. Beware of eccentric behaviour of any kind.

Semi-square, square, sesquare, quincunx, opposition. Be ready to listen to others' opinions – you could become very stubborn under this influence. Tension might build up and cause headaches. Impulsive changes might seem desirable, but don't rush in.

Mercury to Neptune
Conjunction, semi-sextile, sextile, trine. You may well become inspired and drift into a dreamy mood.

Semi-square, square, sesquare, quincunx, opposition. Although most of the above will apply, forgetfulness could be a problem. Be very careful not to get out of touch with reality or let anyone deceive you.

Mercury to Pluto
Conjunction, semi-sextile, sextile, trine. You may change your mind about a course of action, or change your opinions. If you feel like having a clear out of clutter – do so.

Semi-square, square, sesquare, quincunx, opposition. You may well feel frustration, or that some very annoying incident is blocking your progress. Sit back, let it take its course, and as much as possible try to concentrate on other things.

THE ASPECTS OF VENUS
Venus to Mars
Conjunction, semi-sextile, sextile, trine. A lively influence for your love and sexlife. Time to arrange a memorable date with your lover.

Semi-square, square, sesquare, quincunx, opposition. Also an emphasis on love and sexlife – but don't be overeager, and remember that in your enthusiasm you could cause an upsetting row or quarrel.

Venus to Jupiter
Conjunction, semi-sextile, sextile, trine. You will be in a very generous mood – both emotionally and financially. You should have a lot of fun, but remember, bills run up at this time will eventually drop through your letterbox.

Semi-square, square, sesquare, quincunx, opposition. As above, but you could become very gushing and perhaps put off someone who is less extravert. Don't show off too much – and watch out, you really are likely to overspend.

Venus to Saturn
Conjunction, semi-sextile, sextile, trine. A good time to give serious thought to your relationship, or perhaps to make long-term plans, or even a deeper commitment to your partner.

Semi-square, square, sesquare, quincunx, opposition. You may be feeling fed up, and perhaps have some problems with your relationships. Try to improve communications.

Venus to Uranus

Conjunction, semi-sextile, sextile, trine. Possibility of a new, exciting and dynamic love affair – or equally exciting new interest. Expect the unexpected – especially where your social life is concerned.

Semi-square, square, sesquare, quincunx, opposition. Be careful: there could be quite a build up of tension between you and your partner. Try to keep your cool.

Venus to Neptune

Conjunction, semi-sextile, sextile, trine. A truly romantic influence; it's up to you to make the most of it.

Semi-square, square, sesquare, quincunx, opposition. Be very careful indeed, for you could easily have those rose-coloured spectacles firmly placed on your nose – especially if you have just fallen in love. Try to take a practical attitude about what's going on.

Venus to Pluto

Conjunction, semi-sextile, sextile, trine. A good time for finances. Investments made now should prove profitable.

Semi-square, square, sesquare, quincunx, opposition. Don't be mislead in finance, and don't bottle up emotional problems.

THE ASPECTS OF MARS
Mars to Jupiter

Conjunction, semi-sextile, sextile, trine. If conjunction or trine, you are in a very strong position to influence important people and to push on with plans. Other positive aspects: be energetic and optimistic.

Semi-square, square, sesquare, quincunx, opposition. Although these trends are mainly energizing and positive, be careful not to act prematurely or to assume automatically that the grass is necessarily greener over the hedge!

Mars to Saturn

Conjunction, semi-sextile, sextile, trine. Control your energy-flow and be patient. Expect some delay.

Semi-square, square, sesquare, quincunx, opposition. Frustration and delay will dog your progress, but don't try to force issues. You'll only be wasting energy better used in other directions.

Mars to Uranus

Conjunction, semi-sextile, sextile, trine. You are a live wire at present, but keep your options open and listen to others' opinions.

Semi-square, square, sesquare, quincunx, opposition. You may become very tense and aggressive in argument. Stubbornness could prevent you from getting what you want.

Mars to Neptune

Conjunction, semi-sextile, sextile, trine. Perhaps unexpectedly, life could become attractively colourful and romantic. You might fall into a romantic or nostalgic mood.

Semi-square, square, sesquare, quincunx, opposition. Although life could be fun, be prepared for a minor disappointment – especially if arranging a date or social occasion. Watch out for a touch of food poisoning if eating fish.

Mars to Pluto

Conjunction, semi-sextile, sextile, trine. If you feel like having a blazing row, have one; but keep it short, sharp and to the point – don't bear malice.

Semi-square, square, sesquare, quincunx, opposition. Expect frustration and the inability to move forward in the direction you wish to go. Patience will pay off. Divert your energy into sporting activities, but don't overdo it.

THE ASPECTS OF JUPITER
Jupiter to Saturn

Conjunction, semi-sextile, sextile, trine. (The conjunction is inescapably powerful). Although these aspects often make us feel restless and discontented, they help us eventually to combine the positive extravert areas of our personalities with more introverted traits. We make personal progress while they are operative, usually in relation to the houses they occupy.

Semi-square, square, sesquare, quincunx, opposition. A strong tendency to restlessness could inhibit your progress. Plan your time very carefully and keep to your schedule.

Jupiter to Uranus

Conjunction, semi-sextile, sextile, trine. A lively, exciting and invigorating trend. New developments could occur; don't hesitate to accept them. Above all, stretch your mind.

Semi-square, square, sesquare, quincunx, opposition. Life may become exciting at times. This could lead to a certain strain, tension or irritability. Try to keep calm, and you will get good results.

Jupiter to Neptune

Conjunction, semi-sextile, sextile, trine. You will fall into a quiet and philosophical mood. Don't be surprised if you are accused of being unsociable.

Semi-square, square, sesquare, opposition. It's possible that your imagination is running away with you, especially if you have problems. Try to be practical, and if you feel like opting out, spend some time reading spiritually helpful books.

Jupiter to Pluto

Conjunction, semi-sextile, sextile, trine. This will probably turn out to be a good influence financially. If you are cautious you could make some good investments at this time.

Semi-square, square, sesquare, quincunx, opposition. Be very careful in all financial dealings. Caution is necessary when investing. Keep clear of "get-rich-quick" schemes.

THE ASPECTS OF SATURN

Saturn to Uranus

Conjunction, semi-sextile, sextile, trine. These aspects help us to be practical, ambitious and serious-minded. Those with mechanical skills should express them creatively.

Semi-square, square, sesquare, quincunx, opposition. Some tension and a pessimistic outlook could bother you. Think of past achievements and try to develop original ideas.

Saturn to Neptune

Conjunction, semi-sextile, sextile, trine. You may feel rather unsettled under this influence, but if you can channel your intuition constructively you should get good results. Be practical.

Semi-square, square, sesquare, quincunx, opposition. Confusion and frustration may give you cause for concern. This is a time at which to think constructively and seriously. Keep overidealistic thoughts and impressions at bay.

Saturn to Pluto

Conjunction, semi-sextile, sextile, trine. If you have problems and frustrating difficulties, try not to waste time and energy fighting them. Take a philosophical view and when this trend eases, your difficulties will be resolved almost overnight.

Semi-square, square, sesquare, quincunx, opposition. Very much as above; but watch your health and vitality, since your problems may have an adverse effect on you both psychologically and physically. Take time out to relax.

THE ASPECTS OF URANUS

Uranus to Neptune

Conjunction, semi-sextile, sextile, trine. Combine originality with inspiration and you will get marvellous results, whatever your individual interests.

Semi-square, square, sesquare, quincunx, opposition. You may tend to allow your ideas to get the better of you. Watch out for overemotional reactions to situations which are less dramatic than you think.

Uranus to Pluto

Conjunction, semi-sextile, sextile, trine. A good time for a purge on anything (or anyone) cluttering your life. Speak your mind, get problems off your chest. It is important to control these powerful energies, since you may tend to take overdrastic action.

Semi-square, square, sesquare, quincunx, opposition. Frustration and the knowledge that you cannot take the action you want to take could cause problems. Think through any difficulties very carefully and make a strategic plan. You will instinctively know when the time is right for action.

THE ASPECTS OF NEPTUNE

It is very rare that Neptune makes any other aspect to Pluto than the *sextile,* which is nearly always in orb – so when you find an aspect between these two planets, in the ephemeris you can think of it in the following way: allow the subtlety and inspiration of Neptune and the deep, searching qualities of Pluto to help you resolve any psychological problem, or perhaps explore any compelling interest. Occultism or religion will benefit particularly, but do not become involved with any arcane cult.

Specific Influences

Reading through the interpretations of the trends for the Zodiac signs for a month, you will see that in several of them we have picked out some indications which will affect people born on particular days. These are very powerful, and in essence the sort of interpretations astrologers give individual clients on whose calculated birth-charts they have worked. Once used to referring to the ephemeris, you can apply these simply calculated indications to yourself and your friends; here we tell you how to do this.

Remember that you can – as we have done – insert a few specific influences into your own Sun-sign interpretations – or of course work them out and study them separately.

If you have already read the Moon pages, you will by now know about the "orbs" allowed in aspects (see p.122). We do not allow any orb at all when working on specific influences. But remember that while planetary influences are very easy to "time" *astronomically* (as done here), their *astrological* influences vary. The trend is usually at its most potent when it is astronomically exact – i.e., when, for instance, the planet occupies the same degree of a sign as your Sun (though not necessarily the same one). But the actual length of the astrological influence varies from planet to planet. Some are easy to time – seeming to start and stop precisely when you would expect (Pluto is a good example). Others are much less easy – Saturn, for instance: the effect of one of its aspects may last considerably longer than the time it spends on your Sun degree. Sometimes we feel an influence before it is exact, and it may still hang around for a few weeks afterwards. However, from the point of view of calculation we must use the precise astronomical facts listed in the ephemeris. You will often find that a specific influence can occur, then recur twice more: this is due to the planet's "retrograde" motion (it is marked *R* in the ephemeris, and the letter *D* indicates its return to direct motion), and is caused by the planet's uncertain motion as seen from earth.

From an interpretative point of view you can usually see precisely how the trend will work for you when the planet first hits your Sun degree; it is at its most potent when the planet returns to the position of your Sun for the third and last time. Sometimes a planet will remain on the same degree as your Sun quite long: these trends are specially strong and worth watching for.

Although we are not considering the influence of Mercury, Venus or Mars in the context of specific influences (they move too quickly to be used in this way), should you notice that one of them makes a *conjunction* or *opposition* to your Sun degree, and is *stationary* – that is, remains on that degree – for several days, you will find: Mercury will make you more communicative, Venus more loving or sociable, Mars more energetic (with a *conjunction*) or more hasty and likely to be careless (*opposition*).

In the following interpretations we divide the specific influences into three groups:
1. *conjunction, sextile, trine.*
2. *square, opposition.*
3. *semi-sextile, semi-square, sesquare, quincunx*

The *trine* is the most powerfully positive of the first group, the *conjunction* the most potent – but how positive or negative depends on the planet involved. The *square* and *opposition* are very powerful, while the third group contains minor aspects – though the *quincunx* and *semi-square* are often a source of tension.

The Specific Influences of Jupiter
Jupiter's influences are fairly easy to time, astrologically. The planet occupies a degree of a sign for three or four days, but we usually feel its astrological influence for at least a week, and sometimes what happens during the time when it is working for us specifically will be of lasting benefit.

Conjunction, sextile, trine. These should prove very beneficial (especially the *conjunction,* which will occur only once every 12 years – unless Jupiter returns to the position of your Sun within a couple of months, due to retrograde motion). Push ahead with plans; put your ideas to people who can help bring them fruition. This is an excellent time at which to study or travel. Make investments, take calculated risks, and accept new challenges. Life could well open out for you. Good for finance.

Square and opposition. In many ways these aspects are also positive, but you must be very careful not to become blindly optimistic. Watch out when investing, as a gambling spirit could get the better of you. Rich food and drink might upset you more easily than usual. Read the small print when signing legal documents. Control your sense of drama.

The minor aspects. These work in ways very similar to the *square* and *opposition*, but not so powerfully. Look out for beneficial possibilities, but guard against overdramatization.

The Specific Influences of Saturn
The ancients thought of Saturn as affecting one's destiny – it was "the Hand of Fate". Modern astrologers are less fatalistic, but cannot deny the planet's potent influence, which usually makes for slow but important long-term change, leading eventually to prestige and promotion. Frustration and a general lowering of the spirits can be the result of Saturn's presence, however. It is a difficult planet to time, astrologically: its influence can last for a very long time – especially if it returns to the precise position of your Sun three times, due to retrograde motion.

Conjunction, sextile, trine. You may experience a very important period of your life under this influence – especially if the *conjunction* is working for you. Sometimes we marry, buy a house or make a long-term commitment under its influence. Sometimes we receive promotion which increases our prestige (but may place us out of touch with supportive colleagues). Watch your vitality under this serious but positive influence, for the pressures on you may sap your energy. You are unlikely to make a serious mistake – but know that decisions made now are very likely to affect your long-term future.

Square and opposition. These are heavy trends under which you may experience setbacks and frustration; but with patience you will win through. Your practical approach to problems, backed up by common sense and caution, will help but you could become gloomy. Try to counter this by recognizing that you have over the years achieved much – more perhaps than you realize. In due course any present difficulties will help you to set a more positive future path, since under these heavy trends you are probably gaining much experience – and perhaps self-knowledge.

The minor aspects. It is likely that one sphere of your life will be influenced by the minor influence of Saturn with your Sun. Maybe something will frustrate you, but mostly you will be able to ignore whatever is going on. Under the **quincunx** or **semi-square** you may become low-spirited (a cheering, short break after the influence has eased will help); or if you are tired, your system may be stagnating – so try a course of vitamins. You may feel little or nothing as a result of these minor trends, but don't ignore potential problems; meet them halfway and work on them in a practical way.

The Specific Influences of Uranus
The influences from Uranus will probably work fairly accurately as far as the timing of the trend is concerned. The planet is extremely powerful, and certainly life will be eventful in some way. Irrespective

of the aspect working for you, bear in mind all interpretations – for the unpredictability of the character of the planet's influence insists that almost anything could happen! Dynamic sudden change is a recurring theme.

Conjunction, sextile, trine. These are exciting, invigorating trends, and though they can cause us to act irresponsibly or eccentrically, we often get a new lease of life when Uranus is working for us. Sometimes, in our determination to rejuvenate ourselves, we make silly mistakes – such as overexercising. When under this influence, be prepared for the unexpected. This may be something very exciting or something stressful – even exciting events can cause stress (if, for instance, you suddenly make an exciting trip abroad). Drastic changes very often occur, and sometimes the eventual outcome is to change your personality. These are dynamic influences, and under them it is wise to do anything you have long wanted.

Square and opposition. There will certainly be strain and tension in the prevailing atmosphere, and it will be up to you to be positive. Try to concentrate on interesting and involving work, and break new ground in some way. You may make some kind of new start under this influence. Uranus tends to make you dynamically attractive. If you fall in love under *any* Uranian influence, enjoy the experience but remember it may not last.

The minor aspects. These can prove exciting but strenuous; be prepared for the unexpected, but whatever happens is not likely to be seminally important. Try to keep your cool and relax. The *quincunx* is often the most potent of this group of influences.

The Specific Influences of Neptune

Some people – mostly those very down-to-earth and practical, involved in worldly affairs, interested in making money – feel little or nothing when Neptune works for them, since the planet's influence is extremely subtle. (It seems to work poorly for those with poor dream recall, who say, mistakenly, "No, I never dream.") Some people are affected, whether they recognize the fact or not; and some feel the planet's influence very strongly. Do not be concerned if Neptune seems to have little impact on your life. As you progress with your esoteric interests you should feel it more, and hopefully in a positive way. It is not easy to time a Neptunian influence.

Conjunction, sextile, trine. You may become more sensitive and respond more emotionally under this trend. You could develop natural intuition and imagination, but make an effort to direct these new-found or heightened qualities very positively, otherwise you could waste them. Sometimes religion means more to us, or subjects such as those in this book. In that case, follow up whichever discipline you find most fascinating – progressing from these pages to

continue training under specialist guidance. Under Neptunian aspects, however, beware of cults.

Square and opposition. You may well tend to take the easy way out, to deceive yourself, especially if you have just fallen in love. Face reality, and understand that you may not be seeing your beloved clearly. If worried, be especially careful not to rely on drugs – even medically administered ones – or drink or smoke more than usual.

The minor aspects. The effects are much those of the other Neptunian aspects, though these are strenuous trends which could work positively for you. Read both interpretations and develop an awareness of what is going on; try to use Neptune to advantage.

The Specific Influences of Pluto

Although it is, as far as we know, the most distant planet of the solar system, Pluto is easy to time, astrologically; when its influence is exact astronomically, we always find that its astrological influence is also noticeable. As it passes from our Sun degree, so the influence – whether positive or negative – ceases.

Conjunction, sextile, trine. Something that has been blocking your progress may be focused when Pluto makes one of these specific influences; when it passes on, you will quite suddenly move forward, having resolved your problem or difficulty. Very often, under positive trends people will get to work on psychological problems by starting therapy, for the most common action of Pluto is to bring into the open what has been hidden. Sometimes we are pushed forward, perhaps to have a drastic spring-clean (whether or not it is spring!); we make a fresh start. Even when Pluto works positively we often feel strain, but if you think your progress is non-existent, once Pluto is out of your way your path will be clear and you *will* move forward – especially if the influence is that of a *trine* or *sextile*. Upheavals of some kind usually occur under the *conjunction*; this will only affect Sun-sign Scorpios, since Pluto is in that sign until 1995.

Square and opposition. You may feel shut in, unable to move, with your back against a wall. Be patient and don't try to force issues; be calm and analyse what is actually going on – and your own reactions to it. Things will improve when Pluto moves out of your way. If the planet visits you three times, you will probably get quite a lot of respite between visits in which to concentrate on other spheres of your life. When Pluto finally leaves your Sun degree you should feel purged.

The minor aspects. Like those of Uranus these aspects could work out well or strenuously for you, but far less potently. You may have a problem with the plumbing, or with a machine, or there may be a tax or insurance problem which is annoying. If this does not apply, then perhaps you will clear unwanted items out of your home, or perhaps work on a bothering psychological hangup.

Cards

Card-reading (cartomancy) has perhaps lacked the authority of the Tarot or the I Ching, but it is a well-established and popular form of prediction. Interpretations, preserved orally until not long ago, can vary according to the source. The most widely accepted traditions are used here but, as always, the relationship between querant and cards helps determine the outcome.

A querant consulting the cards is invited to adopt a "client card" – either a King or a Queen to represent himself or herself. A somewhat older man or a woman with very fair hair and blue or grey eyes might take a Diamond King or Queen; a slightly darker or younger blonde will take a Heart; a brown-haired man or woman a Club and a black-haired person with very dark eyes a Spade.

In card-reading, it is usual to use only 32 cards, discarding the twos, threes, fours, fives and sixes. When dealt in a spread, some cards will be inverted. There has been a difficulty with modern packs, since the designs often make it impossible to discover whether a card is inverted or not. It is customary to make a small mark at one end of the *face* of the card to represent its top. The inverting of a card in this system does not denote ill luck; it more often simply has a meaning different from that of the upright card.

Traditional interpretations

There are various traditions associated with the cards: for instance, it is significant if a run of cards of the same suit appears in a reading: Clubs in this context suggest a favourable outlook, Spades the opposite; Hearts comment particularly on love, Diamonds on finance. A run of aces together generally suggests change; Kings, justified optimism; Queens, scandal (though three together, rather than four, imply a happy social occasion); Knaves traditionally imply a more or less rumbustious occasion – anything from a sexual orgy to a noisy public meeting! If most cards are black, the positive effect of the reading is still to come; if red, it has already been achieved.

The same tradition has it that a run of four tens or four nines indicate, respectively, good luck and unexpected events; three tens are a bad omen, three nines a good one; three eights speak of a change in family life (perhaps marriage), four sevens of imminent difficulties and enemies, and three sevens of possible poor health.

In all readings, reversed cards somewhat weaken or delay positive interpretations, and slightly strengthen negative ones. The most widely used interpretations of the cards are presented here.

Cutting the cards

To cut the cards hold them in the right hand, face downwards, and with the left hand lift any number of them away from the others, then placing the pack back together again with the selected cards beneath the others; cards are then dealt from the top or bottom of the whole pack as advised.

How to read the cards

There are many traditional "spreads", some extremely complex, some extremely simple such as the continental system devised to show the events of a week ahead.

The Seven Day enquiry

The querant shuffles the cards and cuts them – always with the left hand, traditionally the mystical hand – into three piles. The reader now takes the top card of each pile and places them, face downward, side by side. The querant shuffles and cuts again, and once more the top three cards are taken and set by the side of the others. The process is repeated five times, resulting in a row of 15 cards.

The card-reader now turns over the two cards at either end of the row, which represent the "climate" of the following day. The right-hand card always takes precedence: if this, for instance, is a spade while the left-hand card is a club, there may be difficulties but they will eventually be overcome. The next two cards represent the day after tomorrow, and so on until you have worked out the "fortunate" and "unfortunate" days of the week ahead. The specific meanings of the cards are not used in this spread. The single card remaining in the middle is used to answer a specific yes/no question put by the querant: *Possibly* (Hearts), *Probably* (Diamonds), *Yes* (Clubs), *No* (Spades).

The Great Star

Perhaps the most impressive of all the spreads is the Great Star, using the 32-card pack.

First, select the card which is to represent the querant (see above), and place it in the middle of the dealing space, face upward; the other cards are also turned face upwards as they are dealt. The cards are shuffled first by the card-reader, then by the querant, and the former then cuts with the left hand. After the cut, 10 cards are dealt, and the 11th is selected as the first of the layout, and placed in position 2 (see diagram overleaf). The remaining 30 cards are placed together as one pack, and again cut by the reader, and the top card of the bottom half of the cut pack is placed at position 3. The cards are cut again, and the bottom card of the top half of the pack is placed at position 4. Now continue to cut, taking cards alternately from the top of the bottom half of the cut pack, and the bottom of the top half – that is to say, from the middle of the cut pack – until you have enough cards to make up the completed spread. When you have chosen each card, the top half of the cut pack should be placed at the bottom of the pack before it is cut again.

To read this elaborate spread, the cards are paired. First, moving anticlockwise around the outer circle, take cards 14 and 16, then 21 and 19, 15 and 17, 20 and 18. Then go to the inner circle, and proceed clockwise, taking cards 10 and 6, 12 and 9, 11 and 7, 13 and 8. The four centre cards are paired 4 with 2 and 5 with 3, and the last card, number 22, stands alone.

THE FOUR SUITS

The commonest method is to use only 32 cards, discarding the twos, threes, fours, fives and sixes. There is a connection between the Tarot suits – Sceptres, Cups, Swords and Pentacles – and Clubs, Hearts, Spades and Diamonds; these in turn have individual qualities:

Hearts

represent maturity, emotions, love, happiness, and the evening. Friendship is indicated by this suit, as well as sexual and romantic love.

Diamonds

represent youth, money matters, luck, springtime, and the morning. Since youth is malleable, diamonds are said to be susceptible to influence from all other cards. They also cover external life, particularly finance.

Clubs

represent adulthood, enterprise, glory, summer, and the afternoon. Business affairs and enterprise can lead to power, particularly over others, fame, acquisitions and creativity.

Spades

represent old age, obstacles, night, enemies and misfortune. The more numerous the Spades in a spread, the more unfortunate – though the effects can be mitigated by other cards.

Hearts	Clubs	Spades	Diamonds

Ace
Good news, love, a house.
inverted: a disappointment, a visit.

King
A generous, loving, helpful fair-haired man.
inverted: betrayal by a lover.

Queen
A generous, loving, fair-haired woman.
inverted: a rival in love, capriciousness.

Knave
An unmarried close friend or lover.
inverted: a dissatisfied lover.

Ten
Good fortune.
inverted: metamorphosis, a birth.

Nine
Success, fulfilment of hopes and dreams.
inverted: temporary failure.

Eight
Invitations, festivities, domestic content.
inverted: rejection, jealousy.

Seven
Contentment, especially in marriage.
inverted: boredom.

Ace
Good fortune, wealth, good news.
inverted: indifferent news, frustrating communication delays.

King
A friendly, honest, dependable dark man.
inverted: difficulty.

Queen
A friendly, comforting dark woman.
inverted: worry.

Knave
A good lover, an athlete.
inverted: loss or lack of confidence.

Ten
Good luck, a long journey, prosperity.
inverted: sea travel, a parting.

Nine
A legacy.
inverted: obstacles.

Eight
A dark lover bringing happiness.
inverted: negative experience.

Seven
Financial success.
inverted: financial failure

Ace
Sexual happiness, fulfillment.
inverted: sorrow, legal troubles.

King
An ambitious, self-seeking man.
inverted: an enemy, trouble on the way.

Queen
A subtle, elderly woman.
inverted: an unfriendly woman bringing conflict and problems.

Knaves
A devious, untrustworthy young man.
inverted: deceit.

Ten
Emotional difficulties, loss.
inverted: minor illness.

Nine
Failure, misfortune.
inverted: the loss of a friend.

Eight
Difficulties with health, troubles.
inverted: denial of love, quarrels.

Seven
A situation worsens.
inverted: an accident, loss of friendship.

Ace
A betrothal, a letter, a ring, money.
inverted: bills.

King
A fair or grey-haired powerful, stubborn man.
inverted: deceit.

Queen
A blonde or elderly woman.
inverted: a flirt or tease, jealousy.

Knave
A man in uniform or messenger.
inverted: a suspicious character.

Ten
Travel, changes, financial matters.
inverted: bad luck

Nine
Worries, a feeling of restlessness.
inverted: family upsets and quarrels.

Eight
Sexual attraction, a short journey.
inverted: sexual inhibition.

Seven
A child, a critic.
inverted: mild success, scandal.

Events indicated by the cards revolve around the King or Queen representing the querant: those directly above it show possible success, those immediately below represent the past. Cards directly to the right of the querant's indicate progress generally towards fulfilment, while those on its left suggest difficulties which may oppose this.

The cards at an angle to the central one are also used, of course: those to the right, above, show helpful influences; those to the left, above, suggest obstructive influences from the past; cards to the right, below, show past accomplishments which will help towards future success; while those to the left, below, represent past difficulties which may still affect the future.

Sample reading

The Great Star deal was made, with the resulting spread. There was a slight preponderance of red cards, indicating that the querant (represented by the King of Clubs) has already achieved much.

The pairings were as follows (R = inverted): **14/16**, the Queen of Diamonds with the Ace of Hearts; **21/19**, the Queen of Clubs and the Ace of Diamonds; 15/17, the seven of Spades and the Queen of Hearts; 20/18, the ten of Spades and the ten of Hearts; 10/6, the seven of Diamonds (R) and the Knave of Clubs; 12/9, the King of Diamonds and the Knave of Hearts; 11/7, the ten of Clubs and the King of Hearts; 13/8, the seven of Clubs and the nine of Diamonds (R); 4/2, the nine of Spades and the ten of Hearts; 5/3, the eight of Spades (R) and the eight of Clubs (R); 22, the Knave of Diamonds.

Interpretation

A loving relationship with a blonde lady is indicated (16/14), but so is a possible sexual approach from a dark woman (21/19). In the past, a generous, fair-haired woman seems to have suffered as the result of a situation (20/18) which perhaps involved that partnership. In the immediate future, good fortune seems linked with travel (20/18).

Criticism will, after some delay, be overcome with the help of a loving partner (10/6); an unmarried,

perhaps fair-haired elderly friend seems connected with past good fortune (12/9, 11/7), while there seems to be some indication of future family problems because of possible financial difficulty (13/8).

A legacy may eventually overcome the financial difficulties (4/2); but care should be taken, for there is a suggestion that quarrels may provoke difficulties with the law (5/3). The final card, 22, the Knave of Diamonds, is a fortunate card, and in the context of financial difficulty seems to suggest that rescue will come through some kind of official intervention.

The Obstacle spread

Not strictly speaking a "spread" at all, this is a very ancient fortune-telling method, and is particularly useful when judging a difficult situation.

With the card representing the querant removed and the pack of 32 cards shuffled and cut, hold it face downwards in your hand. Place the querant's card in the centre of the table, the top card from the pack face upward above it and the second card below it. The third card goes to the left of the querant's, and the fourth to the right. Place the fifth card on top of the querant's, masking it. Now deal eight cards to one side, discarding them, and add another card to each of the five original ones, in the order already given (above, below, left, right, centre). Discard eight more cards, and place the final five cards again in position on top of the others.

Each pile of cards is then read in turn, in the order in which they were dealt, paying attention not to the individual meaning of each card, but to pairs and triplets, to suit colour, and to whether the four high cards (Ace counting high) or the four low ones predominate. The high cards represent the help or intervention of others, the low cards refer to the querant's own efforts. Once more, the cards immediately above the central pile represent the chances of success, those below, the past, those on the right, progress and those on the left, difficulties.

Example

Cards were dealt as above: the top pile consisted of the aces of Hearts and Spades and the King of Spades – all representing the help of others in the situation discussed. The lower pile showed the nine of Spades, ten of Hearts and Queen of Clubs, indicating an element of self-help; but the left-hand pile – nine of Diamonds, Knave of Clubs and Ace of Clubs – and the right hand pile – nine of Clubs, Queen of Spades and Ace of Diamonds – again emphasized others. However, the central and most personal pile showed the eights of Hearts and Diamonds and the seven of Clubs, emphasizing that in the end the querant's own efforts must be dominant in solving the problem.

The spread seems to indicate that success rests on the willingness of others to cooperate; an emphasis on black suits suggests some difficulty – but red predominates throughout the spread as a whole and the three nines provide a strongly positive symbol, so in the end there should be a positive conclusion. In the past, the querant has had a muddled attitude to his problem (one red, one black card) while help was offered by one friend in particular; the difficulties placed in the way of progress by the cards on the left seem to be set up by the others, but the support of friends (on the right), though perhaps far from unanimous, will be helpful. Experiencing some doubt as to the right path forward (there is one black card among the three lower cards in the centre), a sensible decision should be reached, and the fact that Clubs predominate in the reading suggests a positive outcome. The emphasis on black cards indicates that this is still to come.

I Ching

The ancient Chinese book of divination known as the I Ching *("Book of Changes") is one of the Five Classics of Confucius (551-479BC), but its origin goes back far earlier. The trigrams (triple lines) on which the system is based were supposedly discerned on the back of a tortoise by the legendary emperor Fu Hsi in the 24th century BC. The 64 hexagrams (six-line figures) that can be formed from the 8 original trigrams are usually credited to Wen Wang (12th century BC).*

The lines that make up the *I Ching's* trigrams and hexagrams are of two kinds, broken and solid, and each line's composition is determined by the casting of coins (originally stalks of the mystical yarrow plant). Generations of ancient Chinese scholars have provided interpretations of the hexagrams, and these are written in an allusive, cryptic manner that gives scope for the user to interpret its personal significance.

The *I Ching* is not merely a fortune-telling book but a philosophical work expressing a cosmology that unites man and nature in a single system. It has had a very profound impact on Chinese thought. It survived the great book-burning organized by Ch'in Shih Huang in 213BC, and also the Chinese revolution of the present century. Mao Tse-tung consulted it, and its impact in the West has been considerable.

Wen Wang, the Chinese king who probably compiled the present grouping of 64 hexagrams, also started to add explanatory text, a task continued by his son the Duke of Chou. Confucius himself may have elaborated these texts, writing a commentary on each hexagram, and his pupil Pu Shang spread the book's fame. From 400BC onwards the volume of material grew as sages and philosophers added their glosses to the magical prophetic book.

Although not exclusively Taoist, the philosophy underlying the *I Ching* has close affinities with the Taoist belief in the complementary forces of Yin and Yang. This is symbolized by the T'ai Chi sign, a circle divided by a curved line into two portions, one representing the masculine active principle of Yang, the other standing for the female passive principle of Yin. Taoists believe that change is a natural tendency, innate in all things. The universe is in a constant state of flux in which Yin and Yang change into their opposites. This philosophy was elaborated during the third century BC, and in modern times has been much studied in Europe. Its link with the *I Ching* is reflected in the naming of the hexagram's solid (Yang) and broken (Yin) lines.

Each line of the hexagram is capable of change, so that one hexagram may become another by means of some "old" Yin lines becoming "young" Yang lines, and vice versa. It is the stronger lines which are capable of change, and they depend on the numbers chosen by the throwing of coins (see p. 168). The individual lines may be compared to single notes in music, where each has its own pitch and tone, but achieves full significance in its relation to the rest. Thus the *I Ching* explains each separate line, but goes on to give an interpretation of the hexagram as a whole.

In the following pages we concentrate on simplifying this extraordinary and complex book as far as possible, omitting translations of the Chinese texts but offering a guide to the meaning of the verses, and adapting some of the more archaic and abstract imagery for comtemporary use. Study and meditation on the verses which make up the Judgement, the Image, and the Lines, will give the user a reading of the future, and also indicate the wisest course of action.

Western readers may find these verses obscure and difficult to interpret, even with the help of the commentaries. For example, the Judgement accompanying Hexagram 53, *Chien*, reads: *"The maiden is given in marriage. Good fortune. Perseverance furthers."*

This verse relates to ancient Chinese marriage customs, but today we can interpret the Judgement as referring to the user's place in the social order, and the possibility of having to restrain natural feelings in order to get along with colleagues and friends. In the following pages we transcribe the ancient Chinese vision in this way to provide an accessible commentary.

Of all books of oracles, the *I Ching* is the most poetic and inspirational, and the more it is studied the more rewarding it becomes. The following pages represent the slimmest possible introduction to its wonders, and we recommend anyone interested to look further into this extraordinary ancient book.

The Basic Trigrams

Names	Image	Attributes	Family Relationship
CH'IEN: Creativity	heaven	strength	father
K'UN: Receptivity	earth	dedication, yielding	mother
CHEN: Arousal	thunder	incitement, movement	first son
K'AN: The abyss	water	danger	second son
KEN: Immovability	mountain	rest	third son
SUN: Gentleness	wind, wood	penetration	first daughter
LI: Adherence	fire	light-giving	second daughter
TUI: Joyfulness	lake	joy	third daughter
Traditional names given to each trigram, translated from the ancient Chinese.	Heaven, earth and in-between images of nature – symbolic representations of the trigram's qualities.	Description of the qualities given to each hexagram by its combination of lines.	Symbolic indication of the relationship between the two trigrams.

134

Hexagram Table

	Ch'ien	Chen	K'an	Ken	K'un	Sun	Li	Tui
Ch'ien	1	34	5	26	11	9	14	43
Chen	25	51	3	27	24	42	21	17
K'an	6	40	29	4	7	59	64	47
Ken	33	62	39	52	15	53	56	31
K'un	12	16	8	23	2	20	35	45
Sun	44	32	48	18	46	57	50	28
Li	13	55	63	22	36	37	30	49
Tui	10	54	60	41	19	61	38	58

Two trigrams form each hexagram, and permutations of the 8 trigrams make up the 64 hexagrams (left). To find the number of a hexagram, identify the upper trigram (top row) and read down. Then identify the lower trigram (left column) and read across. The number of the hexagram is at the intersection of the two. Thus hexagram 3 (Chun) is upper trigram K'an and lower trigram Chen. In this way you can identify your hexagrams when you come to cast them (see p. 168).

CH'IEN
1. The Creative

Above: *Ch'ien* – Creativity, heaven

Below: *Ch'ien* – Creativity, heaven

Both trigrams in this hexagram are *Ch'ien*, which consists of unbroken lines. Six unbroken lines in one hexagram show great strength and power. This may indicate divine power, but more often suggests creative power and capacity to put thought into action.

The Judgement. The power which is in you must be used in the right way. The six steps represented by the six unbroken lines can lead to great success, but make sure each step is secure before you take the next, and don't tread on people on the way up.

The Image. The verse speaks of time passing ceaselessly, emphasizing the need for endurance. Try to sustain your energy.

The Lines
1: The hidden dragon of your energy is crouched waiting for the right moment to leap out and astound the world. Pace yourself.
2: When the dragon appears, that is when things at last begin to move; take any advice offered by those with more experience than you and, if they are trustworthy, rely on their judgment.
3: As the situation unfolds, the difficulties may appear daunting. Try not to worry and don't let yourself be swept away by popular opinion.
4: The dragon is now airborne but rather uncertain in his flight; you may not be able to decide whether to strike out energetically or to bide your time.
5: Although others will respect and even applaud you, you may feel alone and vulnerable. However, someone will offer valuable help and support.
6: "The arrogant dragon will have cause to repent". Vaulting ambition will result in a quick plunge to earth.

K'UN
2. The Receptive

Above: *K'un* – Receptivity, earth

Below: *K'un* – Receptivity, earth

This hexagram consists completely of broken (yin) lines. The characteristics of this hexagram are therefore those traditionally associated with yin: openness and receptivity.

The Judgement. The Chinese verse uses a metaphor of a sturdy mare to symbolize someone strong and swift but gentle and devoted, ready to carry the weight of responsibility. The message is, "Allow yourself to be led by those you trust."

The Image. The fact that the two trigrams comprising this hexagram both represent earth emphasizes dependability and strength. Earth supports both good and evil. Try to put up with the bad as well as the good things that happen to you.

The Lines
1: An image of cold and darkness, frost and ice, as though the winter is beginning. The outlook is bleak. Learn to interpret early signs of what may be a calamity and prepare yourself for it.
2: The lesson of this line is that by accepting every experience life has to offer, we learn to come to terms with it. Try to be as receptive and yielding as nature and you will be better able to cope with life.
3: Work steadily and quietly; projects will eventually succeed. Premature action leads to regrets.
4: The image of this line is a tied sack, suggesting it is not yet time to let the cat out of the bag. If you reveal your ideas now, other people may oppose them.
5: Discretion is again emphasized. The Chinese lines speak of "a yellow under-garment", indicating something concealed. The colour yellow appears repeatedly throughout the *I Ching* and signifies good fortune.
6: This line suggests arguments and even violence. But few victories are won without injury.

CHUN

3. Difficulty At First

Above: *K'an* – The abyss, water

Below: *Chen* – Arousal, thunder

The Chinese ideogram suggests the effort made by a blade of grass to emerge from the earth – a metaphor indicating a difficult start. The trigrams, thunder and water, indicate a chaotic situation; but thunder clears the air so the situation will improve.

The Judgement. This is a time of growth, but growth brings its own difficulties – so be careful. It is all too easy to damage things in the early stages of their development.

The Image. Further mention of clouds and thunder, and the words "difficulty at the beginning". Perseverance and sound planning will bring the desired result.

The Lines

1: If you come up against a problem, take the time to think your way through. Ask your friends for help and accept their advice critically.

2: Just when problems are weighing you down, something will suddenly happen to break the log jam and set things flowing forward again. You may be suspicious of someone who appears to have been involved in a change in your circumstances. Don't assume he or she is hostile to your interests without firm evidence. On the other hand, don't be too trusting.

3: Don't forge ahead blindly; seek guidance, and if you still can't see a clear way forward, cancel plans.

4: It seems the time for action, but you may be powerless to act. If the opportunity arises, take it even if it means fighting shyness or diffidence. Similarly, if anyone offers help, don't think it is weak to accept.

5: Your motives are misunderstood by others. Be alert and cautious. Try to avoid a row, and make sure that your ideas are clear before pushing ahead. If you work confidently difficulties will vanish.

6: You may need to modify your ideas. Arrogance secures disaster. Be flexible and willing to compromise.

MENG

4. Youthful Folly

Above: *Ken* – Immovability, the mountain

Below: *K'an* – The abyss, water

A spring of water at the foot of a mountain symbolizes youth. The message of the hexagram is that inexperience and folly can be overcome.

The Judgement. Youth and folly are inseparable, but need not spell disaster as long as the young person concerned is willing to seek appropriate advice and is able to absorb it. The entire hexagram highlights the pupil/teacher relationship. A pupil should learn to build up knowledge without repeated instruction. A weak pupil keeps asking the same question; a weak instructor lets himself be a crutch to the pupil.

The Image. A spring finds its way forward, filling every hollow and refusing to stagnate – a metaphor for thoroughness: explore every nook and cranny of a problem or situation before tackling it.

The Lines

1: In dealing with raw youth, you have to lay down the law and point out life's serious elements. Lightheartedness is fine, but discipline is necessary.

2: Learn to suffer fools; be tolerant, don't underestimate people and be prepared to help those weaker than yourself.

3: The Chinese verse draws a parallel between a weak man who gives in to a strong personality, and a girl who throws herself away on the first man she meets. The message is, "Don't trust until you are sure." Similarly don't cave in to another's point of view just because he or she is more adamant than you are.

4: Merely being attracted to something or somebody is not good enough – it takes two to make a partnership. Dreams are all very well, but humiliation awaits those who do not proceed from a practical base.

5: A blunt truth may hurt, but you should still pay attention to it. Don't cut yourself off from others, and don't make mountains out of molehills.

6: Sometimes a foolish action needs to be reprimanded to avoid a repetition, if you have to administer punishment, do so with justice and mercy. If you are the one receiving punishment, do so with humility provided you recognize that it is deserved.

HSU

5. Waiting

Above: *K'an* – The abyss, water

Below: *Ch'ien* – Creativity, heaven

The combination of the two trigrams suggests creativity which needs to be nurtured. *K'an* represents external danger, while *Ch'ien* emphasizes inner strength. The message is that the strong, wise person

SUNG
6. Conflict

Above: *Ch'ien* – Creativity, heaven

Below: *K'an* – The abyss, water

preserves his inner strength while biding his time and waiting for danger to pass.

The Judgement. To "cross the great water" as the Chinese verse puts it, means to travel or overcome obstacles, and you will not only need physical strength but inner confidence; that will only come if you are clear about your objectives.

The Image. The Chinese verse encourages you to eat, drink and be merry. Keep body and mind well fed, and wait patiently for the right time to take action when the situation reveals itself.

The Lines

1: The Chinese verse speaks of "waiting in the meadow". Something is about to happen, there is a stirring in the air. Carry on as usual; don't waste your strength trying to guess what is around the next corner.

2: It may seem as though danger lies ahead; your ground seems less firm. Remain calm, don't blame others if your life becomes unsettled. If they speak ill of you, bide your time, don't take action yet.

3: The sand now turns to mud, perhaps signalling premature action. Enemies take advantage of your vulnerable position and prevent you from reaching the safety of the river bank, that is, from attaining your goals. As long as you recognize your vulnerable position and take it seriously you should be able to overcome difficulties.

4: The image of this line confirms the seriousness of the situation. You may seem to be entirely isolated in a position from which it is impossible to extricate yourself. If this is the case, do not make matters worse by desperately floundering about – you will only aggravate the problem.

5: The Chinese verse says, "Perseverance brings good fortune". Even when things appear at their worst, there will be glimpses of light in the darkness, and it is up to you to make your way forward and finally emerge into the sunlight.

6: This line symbolizes disaster: "One falls into the pit." But although you may not succeed in avoiding calamity, "uninvited guests" arrive, bringing good fortune. You may be slow to recognize that they have come to offer help.

Water flows downward, but heaven stretches upward so there is clearly disparity here. Similarly, *Ch'ien* seems to indicate strength and *K'an* danger: another possible conflict. Overall the impression given by this hexagram is unsettling.

The Judgement. You probably feel that you are entirely in the right and that other people are unreasonable to obstruct your wishes. Even if this is true, it is unwise to assert your opinion so strongly that you become inflexible. The Chinese verse says, "It does not further one to cross the great water." In other words, you would be ill-advised to set out on any great adventure or project just yet. The time is not ripe.

The Image. Conflict may seem inevitable, but it can be avoided provided that you look carefully at all options and are perfectly aware both of your own duty and of what other people owe you. It is important to examine every aspect of the situation. Make sure you fully understand all the circumstances before you decide to make a move.

The Lines

1: Avoid extremes. You may be forced into an argument but there should be no real problem provided you are willing to make allowances and even re-think your position.

2: You may be out of your depth; retreat before it is too late. Don't be drawn into a battle you are bound to lose, and remember that a conflict may harm others as well as yourself. It would be unfair to involve bystanders just because you are too proud to accept a temporary setback.

3: Don't sell yourself short, resist any action that involves you in compromise or self-sacrifice.

4: You may feel aggressive and, if your opponent is weaker than you, you are likely to win. But consider carefully – are you really in the right? If not, your victory will be physical but not moral and the conflict indicated by the title of this hexagram will indicate your resultant conflict of conscience.

5: Someone sits in judgment. If you are in the right, you will not be judged harshly.

6: The conflict ends, and if you have persevered you will come out on top. But the battle is not over; the hexagram suggests that the attack will continue.

137

shih

7. The Army

Above: *K'un* – Receptivity, earth

Below: *K'an* – The abyss, water

The earth retains water as a dam holds back a lake. In the same way discipline is used to restrain waywardness. The strong line of this hexagram is the second (the only solid line) and it represents a commander, but since it is in the lower trigram the commander is in turn subject to a higher authority.

The Judgement. The lesson of this hexagram is that we all need discipline, but the best discipline comes from within. A leader wishing to wage war has to be sure that his followers understand the reasons for it; otherwise the army will not have the necessary determination to succeed.

The Image. The lesson is that military power cannot be achieved without the tacit agreement of the people. Decisions made on other people's behalf are not advisable without their approval.

The Lines
1: Order is essential. If there is to be a struggle it must be in a just cause. Obedient soldiers need careful organization if the battle is to be won.
2: The strong line represents a trusted leader. He must be trusted in turn by *his* leader. Communication and cooperation towards a common goal. Honours must be shared among the team that secured them.
3: The strange, somewhat bleak image of this line, "Maybe there are corpses in that wagon", seems to indicate that things are not as they seem. An unworthy person has assumed authority and may cause harm.
4: If faced with defeat, beat a timely retreat.
5: An invasion is in progress; oppose it but be disciplined – don't allow the situation to become chaotic.
6: Success, victory. But don't relax your guard, remain strong and maintain control. Over-generosity could be fatal. You can afford to be generous materially, but not with power.

pi

8. Alliance

Above: *K'an* – The abyss, water

Below: *K'un* – Receptivity, earth

All rivers eventually flow into the sea, where the waters are united. We have one strong line in the fifth place, holding the others together, and symbolizing a leader supported by others who reflect his attitude.

The Judgement. Unity brings success, but it is usually necessary to have a central figure around whom to unite. You may see yourself as this figure, but before you assume the role, be convinced of your aptitude for the task. If you find yourself wanting, give support instead to a leader near to your own viewpoint but better equipped for the task. Act now, timing is all. The bonds of a union are sealed at an early stage and latecomers will be unable to identify as closely with it.

The Image. The verse speaks of kings of old establishing friendly relations with their barons. Ancient China was united as a nation because its various rulers held together on principle, despite petty disagreements. It is important that all members of a group or society should identify closely with it.

The Lines
1: Sincerity is the basis of a sound relationship. Truth, according to the Chinese verse, is like a bowl full of earth; the contents are important, not the container. Don't trust appearances or empty phrases.
2: Take note of instructions, but remain independent rather than trying to curry favour by doing what you think others want you to do.
3: It may well be that you have to spend much of your time in the company of people who aren't at all sympathetic to your way of thinking. This is often inevitable, but preserve your integrity; march to the rhythm of your own drum.
4: Again, don't be led astray. But if you are in contact with someone you trust and admire, don't hesitate to show your support.
5: Caution is not always a virtue. You should know when to "run your luck", and also when to listen to good advice. Promotion may be round the corner.
6: Get things right from the start. A wrong turning will lead into a labyrinth of confusion and ultimate failure.

hsiao ch'u

9. Small Is Beautiful

Above: *Sun* – Gentleness, wind

Below: *Ch'ien* – Creativity, heaven

This hexagram says that small is not only beautiful, but powerful. Five solid lines are restrained by a broken fourth line, which questions the power of the others; the small undermines the power of the great.

The Judgement. The image here is said to be based on the example of King Wen, who restrained the tyrannical Chou Hsin by gentle persuasion. Success can be clearly seen in the distance, but there are certain obstacles before we reach it. These will only be overcome by quiet but firm tactics – the iron hand in the velvet glove.

The Image. Wind drives clouds across the sky, but as this is only moving air its effects are temporary. Sometimes you may feel that your efforts are making no impression, but don't be discouraged.

The Lines

1: If you meet an obstruction that seems impassable, look for another route.

2: Take notice of other people's errors; don't expose yourself to the same dangers. Retreat and consolidate before looking for new ways forward.

3: Oblivious to problems you blunder forward and are disappointed and frustrated.

4: When asked your opinion and advice you may find that an honest answer leads to a very difficult situation. However, this is unavoidable; you must be honest and say what you think.

5: Loyalty can take the form of blind devotion or active encouragement and help. The latter is the best course, and your involvement will be recognized.

6: Success is now firmly in prospect as the result of many small deeds, but you will need to be cautious; if one domino falls, the others may well be knocked over, so take one step at a time.

Lü
10. Ethics

Above: *Ch'ien* – Creativity, heaven

Below: *Tui* – Joyfulness, a lake

This quite simply represents ethics – proper conduct. The trigrams indicate a family relationship, the father above and the younger daughter below. They symbolize convention or tradition.

The Judgement. The verse speaks of a man stepping on a tiger's tail – symbolically the weak are forced into contact with the strong. If you find yourself in such a situation, tread carefully.

The Image. The Chinese name for this hexagram is "stepping", and relates to social order; the strong (physically, socially or financially) should not tread on the weak. People should be judged according to their personal worth, not their status.

The Lines

1: We are all free to follow our own star provided we do not obstruct other people. This line emphasizes modesty: overweening ambition brings dissatisfaction. Strive to be good at your job and you will be rewarded.

2: The symbol is of a solitary wise man. Try to ignore material concerns and concentrate on finding and being true to yourself.

3: "A one-eyed man is able to see," says the Chinese verse, but his vision is partial. The message is to recognize your limitations.

4: Again, the imagery of this line refers to a man stepping on a tiger's tail, but this time suggests that danger may be respectfully courted for the right motives, provided one is cautious. Press forward now and success should result.

5: Provided you are fully aware of the danger, it is reasonable to stand your ground. Full knowledge of the situation will make it safe for you to press forward to success.

6: Whatever the problem was, it is now resolved one way or another; in order to judge how you have come through, think back on your conduct up to now. If it has been good, then a satisfactory outcome is assured.

T'AI

11. Peace

Above: *K'un* – Receptivity, earth

Below: *Ch'ien* – Creativity, heaven

The position of the trigrams *Ch'ien* and *K'un* convey the **Judgement**: heaven and creativity placed below earth suggests that your physical nature is now under the control and guidance of your spiritual nature.

The Image. Happiness, progress and prosperity are indicated, but complete relaxation at this stage would be a mistake.

The Lines

1: The Chinese verse says, "The grass is pulled up, its roots come also." In the same way, when things go well people tend to stick together, and your success or failure will inevitably affect colleagues and friends.

2: Try not to be impatient with people slower or apparently less intelligent than yourself. Be prepared to undertake particularly difficult tasks yourself; you are in a strong position to cope with them at the moment. Preserve your independence.

3: Life moves in cycles, and good times are invariably followed by bad. As long as you remember this you will avoid the trap of complacency and be prepared for all eventualities.

4: If you find yourself unable to move forward because some project is delayed, don't be impatient. Treat everyone with equal politeness and sensitivity.

5: This line refers to the ancient Chinese king Ch'eng T'ang who, giving his daughter in marriage, ordered her to obey her husband despite her superior lineage. Remember it is sometimes necessary to subordinate yourself to others whom you may consider in some way inferior. You will then realize that harmony between people of all kinds is what really matters.

6: If disaster occurs, recognize it for what it is; don't try to ignore it, but don't magnify it either. Approach it with due humility and consider your share of the blame.

p'i

12. Stagnation

Above: *Ch'ien* – Creativity, heaven

Below: *K'un* – Receptivity, earth

The combination of these two images suggests earth sinking away while heaven stands aloof and unattainable. A time of stagnation, lack of progress.

The Judgement. A time of confusion. Those who hold great influence over your life appear unsympathetic. Don't provoke argument or friction. Continue to play your part faithfully and well.

The Image. This is not the time to press forward with any plans of your own; even if it seems possible that you could bring off a coup, you are strongly advised to delay action.

The Lines

1: Hold back for the time being and take the line of least resistance; harbour your energies for a later effort which will be far more likely to achieve success.

2: If things are at a standstill, don't think that you can push your superiors into action by flattery. The truth is that you will have to accept a period of quiet and apparent stagnation before things begin to move again.

3: People who are at the moment in control of affairs, may be having some doubts about their own efficiency, but it is too late for them to change. Be on your guard against possible disaster.

4: Things should soon begin to move; what is needed is someone to take control properly in the future. This may or may not be you. Whoever takes control should be driven by the demands of the situation and not blind self-assurance.

5: Caution. Confucius warns that there is always danger when we are too sure of ourselves.

6: End of stagnation. Improvement. Sustained effort brings good fortune.

T'UNG JEN

13. Comradeship

Above: *Ch'ien* – Creativity, heaven

Below: *Li* – Adherence, fire

Fire rises towards heaven, hence the image is one of union, fellowship. Union strengthens, but the hexagram has one weak and broken line, indicating the necessary flexible element in any relationship which is capable of swaying even the strongest alliance.

The Judgement. The Judgement stresses social harmony which can only be attained if members of a society are not motivated exclusively by self-interest. A first-rate, strong-minded leader is needed to guide the group openly towards unselfish goals – a shared goal with which members can identify is even more unifying than shared perspectives.

The Image. Organization is underlined. However admirable the intention of a group, however similar their attitudes, strong leadership is essential.

The Lines

1: The first line contains the idea of "fellowship at the gate", which means that union should ideally take place at an early stage, when the idea or ambition is germinating, thus enabling the group to plan its campaign of action. The organization must be open and outward-looking.

2: Try to prevent divisions developing which will weaken the thrust of the organization or group. Factions too often spend their energy working against other groups rather than for the common good, and therefore contain an element of selfishness which is ultimately destructive.

3: Pettiness alienates an individual from the group and its interests.

4: The end of discord is in sight, and although there are still difficulties to be overcome; their very persistence will bring the group closer together in an effort to surmount them.

5: Two people are indicated who share a common goal, but who are separated by the very different circumstances of their lives. If they are determined they will succeed in reducing the distance between them.

6: A final doubt: you may feel at one in fellowship with others, but apart from the shared interest of support-ing a mutual cause, can you really say that you are in the company of friends? If not, you are not to blame; so, provided you are happy to give your support, be content with your achievement.

TA YU

14. Rich Possession

Above: *Li* – Adherence, fire

Below: *Ch'ien* – Creativity, heaven

Fire from heaven. This hexagram is said to indicate a modest person who has achieved a high position by means of humility and gentle persistence.

The Judgement. The time is very favourable for anyone wanting to take a step forward. There is a strong indication of material success, but success achieved by unselfish persistence and without causing any harm to others.

The Image. Once you have obtained success, be it of wealth or status, the power it gives you should not be abused. The sun shines upon both the just and the unjust person; learn to see your unworthier actions or ambitions clearly; suppress them and endeavour to act fairly and generously.

The Lines

1: You should not be ashamed of any talent or possessions which have come your way by inheritance or accident; the important thing is to be conscious of any difficulties that may arise out of the situation, and not to waste either material or spiritual gifts.

2: The image is of a large wagon able to carry a heavy load, and the suggestion is that you should be mobile – never stand still. Those who are either self-satisfied or burdened by inhibition will encounter difficulty. Accept any help that is offered.

3: Regard your possessions as held in trust for the general good; hugging to yourself wealth of any kind, even spiritual wealth, is petty and reprehensible. Generosity is a sign of greatness.

4: If you have to keep the company of the rich, powerful and unscrupulous, remember that they may be exercising a bad influence on you. Material possessions are of no value unless they can be used for others' benefit as well.

5: The situation is very favourable: those who seem attached to you are sincerely so because you have been sincere in your dealings with them. But don't rest on your laurels; people expect you to be consistent and to live according to your own high standards.

6) Goodness is rewarded.

CH'IEN

15. Modesty

Above: *K'un* – Receptivity, earth

Below: *Ken* – Immovability, the mountain

Modesty is an admirable quality and indicates an ordered mind and calm spirit. A modest person deserves to be treated with honour and respect.

The Judgement. All circumstances are subject to change. A modest person is much better equipped to cope with sudden changes in fortune and is therefore less likely to be disappointed in life. The ancient Chinese upheld modesty as one of the greatest virtues.

The Image. Once at the top of the mountain, you forget the effort climbing it. Similarly, a successful person can easily lose sight of his origins. The modest person will always remember his past struggles and will then be more sympathetic in his treatment of others.

The Lines

1: The greater the task before you, the more important it is to try to simplify it and your approach to it. Someone who has a naturally modest attitude tends to rationalize problems and as a result solve them quietly and easily.

2: Truly modest behaviour is its own recommendation. You can influence others to greater effect by good example rather than by dogmatism.

3: The single solid line in the hexagram indicates those accomplishments which have established your reputation and earned you respect. If you are over-impressed with yourself, however, you will quickly find your influence waning and support from others will be less forthcoming.

4: The intermediary can be more important than the person above or below. In this position one must earn the respect of a superior, but respect in turn the talents of someone more junior. The modesty stressed throughout this hexagram does not mean blind adherence to rules; you must be willing to take responsibility for interpreting rules and even breaking them when the need arises.

5: Sometimes the most modest person is forced to take action. On such occasions, it is important to maintain a balanced attitude. Examine all the angles carefully.

6: The entire hexagram stresses the value of modesty, not always a notable Western characteristic. The final line stresses that modesty is not a sign of weakness but self-awareness.

YÜ

16. Awareness

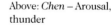

Above: *Chen* – Arousal, thunder

Below: *K'un* – Receptivity, earth

One trigram indicates movement while the other indicates passivity. The whole hexagram suggests either balance or natural uninhibited exuberance.

The Judgement. The indication here is of a natural leader. A successful leader must always be aware of the needs of his followers, otherwise he will not be able to count on their enthusiastic support.

The Image. A thunderstorm clears the atmosphere and releases tension. The Chinese verse mentions music as a valuable means of relaxation through its combination of discipline and emotion. There is also reference to religious reverence and sacrifice, suggesting that true repose needs a spiritual dimension.

The Lines

1: The urge to boast should be suppressed. Even too much enthusiasm for an idea can give the impression of self-satisfaction and arrogance.

2: Don't be deceived by illusion. The enthusiasm of others can obscure the true situation. Be alert.

3: He who hesitates is lost, so seize the moment and

142

act upon it. On the other hand, this line also hints at a leader and suggests "looking upward" to someone with more self-confidence and knowledge.

4: If you are confident, sure of your position and certain that you are doing the right thing, you will be able to persuade others to follow your lead.

5: Delay. This may not have an entirely negative effect, however, for it will force you to think harder and not expect instant results.

6: If your enthusiasm for an idea proves ill-founded, you can still save the situation as long as you recognize the truth and change course.

sui

17. Following

Above: *Tui* – Joyfulness, a lake

Below: *Chen* – Arousal, thunder

The relationship between the two trigrams is that of the youngest daughter, *Tui*, and the eldest son, *Chen*. Note that *Tui* is above *Chen*: the elder defers to the younger. Be receptive to help from all quarters.

The Judgement. Flexibility is stressed: intransigence or cunning will only provoke antagonism. Confidence that you are right will ensure that others accept your word and follow you.

The Image. The importance of flexibility is underlined a second time. If you are in a difficult situation, find time for relaxation and contemplation. Don't be disheartened if things seem to go slightly wrong.

The Lines

1: The solid first line followed by two broken lines suggests that you must persuade others according to your perception of right and wrong, while remaining receptive to their ideas.

2: Choose your friends carefully. Time wasted with the wrong people is time you could have spent with valuable friends.

3: However enjoyable, the company of weak or confused people must be set aside if you are to develop.

4: If you allow yourself to be surrounded by people who spend their time puffing your ego, eventually you will come to need them as props, and by then it will be too late to make your own way, especially when that way is unpopular.

5: You must have a personal star to follow, an idea or an ideal in which you believe and towards which you can make progress.

6: In ancient China, men who had served the kings well were given a place in the royal temple of ancestors

and regarded as one of the family. If you feel you have done enough, that you need some rest, think again – you may forfeit your position.

ku

18. Rebuilding Of Ruins

Above: *Ken* – Immovability, the mountain

Below: *Sun* – Gentleness, wind

Ku is the Chinese character representing a bowl full of worms, and indicates decay. The hexagram represents guilt and its message demands a sense of shame which leads to rebuilding and recantation.

The Judgement. You can rebuild what you have spoiled and indeed this is an excellent time to start doing so; seize the moment energetically and don't be put off by the size of the task ahead of you. However, the hexagram urges a little thought; you need to know what is wrong before you can start putting it right.

The Image. If the problem is one which involves others, make sure they understand the situation and are in argeement with the steps you intend to take. If they are hesitant, you may have to modify your plans to get the backing you need.

The Lines

1: Consider whether your refusal to change with the times or alter your attitude and opinions may be unrealistic. There is still time to change.

2: Try to ensure that you don't do more damage in trying to put things straight than you did while the rot was setting in. Deal gently with everyone concerned.

3: Don't rush in. A gentle approach is the right one, however enthusiastic you may feel, if emotions and egos are not to be bruised.

4: If you simply sit still and watch things fall to pieces around you, you will end up being blamed and humiliated. Weakness is culpable when only positive action can prevent ruin.

5: Perhaps the ruin around you is the result of years of apathy on the part of others who could have prevented the calamity. It may be that you lack the power to set things right on your own, in which case gather others around you who are prepared to work and rebuild.

6: Some men and women feel the need to set themselves apart, preferring solitude, and occasionally their moral stature is such that they become an example to mankind like the sages of ancient China. But make sure such a strong reaction is appropriate; it is more likely that your practical help is needed and you should involve yourself.

LIN

19. Morality

Above: *K'un* – Receptivity, earth

Below: *Tui* – Joyfulness, a lake

One ancient Chinese meaning of *Lin* is "becoming great". Growth is further suggested by the images of the trigrams – joy is ascending and growing just as the light of the sun grow when spring approaches.

The Judgement. Optimism and the steady growth of hope, the approach of spring after a hard winter. However, you must seize the propitious moment and make sure you use every minute of your time in the right way. Circumstances may change.

The Image. The image is of a patient teacher. If someone is trying to teach you something, accept the lesson and try to build on it. If you are the teacher, pass on your knowledge without condescension.

The Lines

1: Things are now beginning to move, but don't let enthusiasm obscure your judgment; make sure they haven't taken off in the wrong direction.
2: The man or woman who leads a movement must realize that everything has a natural curve of accomplishment: having reached its peak it must decline.
3: Things never go so well that you can afford to fall asleep at the wheel! If you suddenly find you have taken a wrong turning, don't be afraid to reverse and set yourself on the right track again. Carelessness could prove particularly dangerous if you are dealing with other people.
4: Favour from above. Someone in a responsible position, who is receptive to the suggestions of his subordinates, may be prepared to encourage their progress.
5: If you have to engage others to help you, be cautious in selecting them; but once you have made your choice, give them freedom of action, allow them to take responsibility.
6: The Chinese verse urges a "great-hearted approach"; be generous with your time and wisdom.

KUAN

20. Contemplation

Above: *Sun* – Gentleness, wind

Below: *K'un* – Receptivity, earth

The shape of the hexagram suggests an ancient Chinese gate or watch tower, which traditionally stood on a hilltop; everyone around could see it and orientate themselves by it. So the governing idea of *Kuan* is, set a public example, and also follow it.

The Judgement. Someone in an exposed position must give particular thought to his or her behaviour, and the Judgement suggests the need for careful contemplation. The Chinese verse has religious undertones and indicates the importance of faith as well as deep thought.

The Image. The verse speaks of the Chinese sages' custom of travelling around the country to impart wisdom. There will always be people who can see and understand more than you; their presence is of great value and their example should be followed.

The Lines

1: Words of wisdom need to be carefully considered. A superior intellect should be able to recognize the difference between good advice and bad. An inferior mind, however, needs direction and should not be blamed for inability to understand.
2: The Chinese line refers to a glimpse through the crack in a door, that is, having a partial view. Don't accept limited information, and take every opportunity to frustrate those who try to restrict it.
3: Careful self-analysis facilitates decision-making. Never rely on too little information.
4: If someone appears with a thorough command of the situation, treat him or her with great respect and don't try to take advantage.
5: If you are at the top of any particular organization, always make yourself available for questioning; be as open as possible; self-examination should be regular but not egotistical. Look beyond your own motives to the effect your actions may have on others. If those effects are damaging, change your ways.
6: Here is an entirely admirable person who has removed every personal element of egotism or self-satisfaction from public life.

shih ho

21. Biting Through

Above: *Li* – Adherence, fire

Below: *Chen* – Arousal, thunder

The Chinese hexagram resembles a mouth holding a stick between its teeth (the solid line in the fourth place), so that it cannot close unless the stick is bitten through. The hexagram originally referred to the way in which the law triumphs over crime, but today may be taken as meaning elimination of obstacles.

The Judgement. When you encounter obstacles, act quickly before too much damage is done, but be clear that you are adopting the right method.

The Image. The clear view of a situation referred to in the Judgement will result in a balanced outlook and thoughtful action.

The Lines

1: Punishment or loss: a first offence attracts a milder punishment than a second. The Chinese say that if you merely put someone's toes in the stocks, the example set should be strong enough to prevent a repetition of the offence.

2: Sometimes the offence is so slight that the effort to chastise it is scarcely noticeable: don't over-react; in such a case, make sure the punishment fits the crime.

3: It is no use threatening punishment if you are seen as someone whose will is not equal to the task of carrying it out. Administering punishment is sometimes as difficult as receiving it.

4: This line speaks of sturdy weapons: these are needed to overcome strong opposition. Make sure you know just what you are up against, and you will succeed.

5: Although inclined to be impartial, you will need to

make a decision and take a firm stand.

6: The first line refers to a first offender, the last to a hardened one. This time the image is of a person with his neck in the stocks. His ears are covered, indicating deafness to warning. Conflict, loss of responsibility.

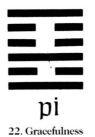

pi

22. Gracefulness

Above: *Ken* – Immovability, the mountain

Below: *Li* – Adherence, fire

The combined images of the two trigrams indicate a flame leaping, so that its light illuminates a mountain: an image which suggests that every situation must have an element of beauty and order.

The Judgement. Above all, this hexagram represents the world of beauty and art. However, the Judgement points out that beauty is not essential to success: what is pretty on the outside may not be good inside.

The Image. Your concern with beauty and form is all very well, but do not expect it to resolve all your problems for you.

The Lines

1: The artist, like the artisan, must learn his art: poetry and pictures cannot be made without much background study and application. Don't think you can relax and depend on instinct to resolve any problem; work at it.

2: The Chinese verse speaks of a man cultivating a beard and indicates a certain vanity – undue importance attached to superficial concerns. Concentrate on what your idea means and what it will accomplish, and only then devote time to embellishing it and making it acceptable to people who might be put off by an untrimmed, direct approach.

3: Sustained effort. It is easy to relax once an idea has been thought out and you have begun to act on it. Don't rely on things to move ahead under their own impetus.

4: The Chinese lines speak of a white horse – an image of purity or simplicity. Get to the root of problems, especially if a relationship is concerned.

5: Never be ashamed to consult friends for fear that you may be thought to be wasting their time. True friends don't react in that way, and provided you genuinely want their advice, will be happy to give it.

6: Having stripped the question down to bare essentials, the answer will seem so obvious you will wonder why you ever had to ask yourself the question. As in art, it is the central idea that is important – everything else is trimming – true form is what matters.

po

23. Disintegration

Above: *Ken* – Immovability, the mountain

Below: *K'un* – Receptivity, earth

FU

24. The Turning Point

Above: *K'un* – Receptivity, earth

Below: *Chen* – Arousal, thunder

Rising up from beneath, the weak forms of the broken Yin lines attack the solid top line, undermining it so that there is danger of disintegration and collapse. The image associated with this hexagram is that of a house with its roof falling in.

The Judgement. Instability, dissent, disruption. It is a bad time to argue or resist. Be careful not to antagonize anyone.

The Image. Consider whether you are at fault: if people or circumstances seem to go against you, maybe it is with good reason. Reassess your situation in order to rectify it.

The Lines

1: An unstable situation which cannot be helped. Sabotage from below. Don't listen to gossip.
2: Danger increases confusion. Opt for the easiest route out. It may not be admirable but in this case it is advisable.
3: If you find yourself surrounded by people you mistrust, lose no time in cutting yourself loose from them. This will at least make your standpoint clear. There is perhaps one person who seems entirely trustworthy. Lean on him or her.
4: The Chinese verse says plainly and unequivocally, "misfortune", which may come without warning; and it does not seem that there is anything you can do but accept the situation.
5: At last a light appears at the end of the tunnel and, as you make your way towards it, past misfortunes seem less grievous.
6: Having reached the bottom, there is nowhere to go but up, and now that the worst is past you will find that all is not lost. The Chinese verse points out that the superior man is strengthened by misfortune; only an inferior man allows his world to be shattered.

The hexagram represents the winter solstice, broken at last by the coming of light; a new era, success, opportunity.

The Judgement. The hexagram signifies the coming of light after a period of darkness, a natural recovery after a difficult time. The recovery is not brought about by force but by gentle resignation and acceptance. The theme is of death and rebirth, the natural cycle of life. The single line at the beginning represents the turning point: sunrise, spring.

The Image. New Year in ancient China was not only a time of celebration, but a time to pause for reflection before new vigour and activity. To repair a quarrel, allow time for thought and reconciliation. If recovering from an illness, a period of rest is important.

The Lines

1: Occasionally, everyone makes mistakes; the important thing is to recognize them before too much damage has been done. If you do not realize when you have taken a false step, you may go so far down the wrong road that there is no prospect of turning back.
2: Admission of error is never easy; make the decision now and act on it immediately. If possible, follow the example of someone you admire.
3: It may be too late to retrace your steps after a hasty action. Damage may not be permanent but minor irritation may result, so don't be impetuous.

4: If you make a decision on moral grounds, and find yourself completely alone, don't be swayed by the actions of those around you. Stick to your guns provided you are convinced that you are right.

5: Always be prepared to explain your actions. If you recognize that you have been in the wrong, resolve to change your ways; it is best to confess and make it quite clear that you understand where you took a wrong turning.

6: If you see an opportunity and don't seize it, it may be lost. Obstinacy often makes it extremely difficult to say or do the right thing at the right moment. If the opportunity is not taken, it may be a very long time before another presents itself, and misfortune may follow.

2: Every action should be natural and spontaneous.

3: One man's gain is invariably another man's loss. You may feel reluctant to benefit from another person's expense but you have no choice; if the moment is not seized and used, no good will come to anyone.

4: "To thine own self be true, and it shall follow as the night the day, thou can'st not then be false to any man." These lines from *Hamlet* effectively capture the *I Ching's* message in this line.

5: Don't struggle against fate, adopt a simple approach to whatever life brings. Even bad fortune has a lesson to teach.

6: If the time is not right for action, all effort is fruitless; wait for the appropriate moment to come.

WU WANG

25. Surprise

Above: *Ch'ien* – Creativity, heaven

Below: *Chen* – Arousal, thunder

TA Ch'u

26. Restrained Power

Above: *Ken* – Immovability, the mountain

Below: *Ch'ien* – Creativity, heaven

147

The person who preserves innocence and has no ulterior motives is blameless provided all his actions follow natural law. The strong lines of heaven have their influence upon the weaker lower trigram. The first line suggests something unexpected and unusual.

The Judgement. Innocence is man's natural state. Truly innocent people are instinctively drawn towards goodness. They are not motivated by self-interest or prejudice. Try and follow your instinct to decide between good and bad.

The Image. The young buds that sprout forth in the spring are fresh and innocent, and the best people display a similar quality. They can distinguish good from bad, the right time to act from the wrong one.

The Lines

1: "Innocent behaviour brings forth good", the Chinese verse says. Innocence brings out the best in people. Always try to act naturally.

A powerful hexagram. Creativity is stressed, but to achieve its potential it needs to be controlled, directed and nurtured (spiritually or physically).

The Judgement. This hexagram stresses the importance of consistent inner strength. To maintain a position of power, energy needs to be sustained. The imagery suggests that a demanding task lies ahead, possibly one in which you will use your talents for the public good. Do not hesitate to grasp responsibility.

The Image. "Heaven within the mountain" hints at buried treasure – at some hidden strength within you. Study of the past may help to increase wisdom.

The Lines

1: An obstacle holds you back, and if you attempt to force a way forward, you will only make matters worse. Danger is at hand.

2: Everything is at a complete standstill – there is nothing you can do to ease the situation. Conserve your strength and wait for change.

3: An opening occurs and things begin to move, perhaps as a result of someone else's initiative. Be cautious and alert for danger. Eventual progress.

4: Try to see trouble approaching and protect yourself; it can do you damage.

5: Danger can be overcome by careful tactics rather than brute force. Try to anticipate problems.

6: Obstructions should now be out of the way, and the energy you have had to suppress can now be released and directed towards success.

i

27. Nourishment

Above: *Ken* – Immovability, the mountain

Below: *Chen* – Arousal, thunder

The shape of the hexagram resembles an open mouth, conveying nourishment. The lower half is said to represent a desire for corporal nourishment while the upper half indicates spiritual food.

The Judgement. The central idea is extended to nourishment of others. The way we love is often a revealing indication of haracter. Some are concerned only with themselves, while others seem entirely forgetful of self, devoting much time to charity and care for those less fortunate than themselves.

The Image. This is a hexagram suggesting moderation in all things: not only in the food one consumes but in the words one speaks – for words can, like food, prove indigestible.

The Lines

1: The Chinese verse contains an image of the "magic tortoise", which had the power to live on air. The suggestion is that you should not envy those who appear better off than yourself – be content with what you have. Envy and grumbling only arouse contempt.

2: Complete dependence brings misery. Over a long period of time it can be enervating and destructive. Self-reliance may be hard but bestows self-respect.

3: Sensual pleasure lasts only for a moment, but the *I Ching* stresses that true nourishment is spiritual.

4: The ideal life pattern is difficult enough to achieve and even more difficult to sustain. If you surround yourself with like-minded people, you will encourage one another towards attaining a common goal.

5: If you know what sort of a life you want to lead, and are sure that it is the right life for you, you still need the help and assistance of like-minded friends.

6: Finally, a solid line which represents the highest peak of personal achievement. At this point you are in

a position to nourish others as well as yourself; this is a great responsibility but one that should be welcomed. Enjoy the freedom to take the lead in events, to undertake difficult and strenuous tasks; even if you fail, which is unlikely – happiness lies that way.

TA KUO

28. Complacency

Above: *Tui* – Joyfulness, a lake

Below: *Sun* – Gentleness, wind

The images of these trigrams suggest a peaceful atmosphere of contentment, but weak lines at the top and bottom indicate a potentially disastrous complacency.

The Judgement. You may have taken on more than you can handle, a weight too heavy for your shoulders. Try to think deeply and clearly and consider the gentlest but firmest way out.

The Image. The image is of a flood rising above the tree tops – a remarkable but temporary event, for the waters will drop, and as long as the trees stand firm things will return to normal. So the message is, remain steadfast.

The Lines

1: The chief emphasis of this line is on thorough preparation. Adopt a cautious approach to decisions.

2: The Chinese verse speaks of an elderly man taking a young wife and of new growth and hope; the best solution may be to take a new starting-point.

3: Impetuous behaviour brings misfortune.

4: A responsible and cautious approach, and moral support from others bring success. However, be considerate: selfishness leads to disaster.

5: Look for new alliances which can not only be supportive but refreshing. An individual approach will be exhausting and inadequate.

6: Sacrifice. The image is of a swimmer whose head vanishes beneath the water, suggesting a valiant but ineffectual approach.

K'AN
29. Water

Above and below: *K'an* –
The abyss, water

Two trigrams suggesting water – water in motion which may indicate vacillation. The depth of water also suggests danger.

The Judgement. Continual danger is suggested here. However this can be dealt with by adopting the correct attitude to it. The flow of water is seldom impeded by obstacles in its course; it simply adapts itself by flowing down, through, or around them. The message is, confront all difficulties head on, grasp and understand them. Your natural reaction will then be the right one.

The prospect of danger keeps the mind alert.

The Image. The Chinese image draws a parallel between water and virtue and suggests that virtue should stream constantly through our lives. Keep to the actions and attitudes which you know to be right.

The Lines
1: The constant presence of danger could harden you and render you insensitive. This is a negative attitude; disaster results.
2: When disaster occurs, don't panic or allow yourself to be overwhelmed by it. Recovery will be gradual.
3: You find yourself in an abyss. All options seems equally dangerous. Wait; struggle is pointless. Consider your position carefully before choosing.
4: Apply common sense at all times and particularly in times of danger. It is important to maintain a balanced attitude, to see the situation in perspective and remain calm.
5: Here the line of least resistance is recommended as the best course of action. The Chinese verse points out that water, confined to a ravine, need only rise to the lowest edge of it in order to escape; similarly, in times of difficulty there is no need to exert more force or argument than the occasion demands. Search for the easiest route out and don't hesitate to take it. Once out of danger, don't look back.
6: Finally, consider whether it is your fault that you are trapped in a difficult situation. If so, remedy your faults before trying to extricate yourself, otherwise you will be like a convict trying to escape over a wall in a full set of chains.

Li
30. Fire

Above and below: *Li* –
Adherence, fire

The shape of this hexagram suggests a grate within whose bars bright flames flicker. The attributes of *Li* are fire and clinging; a brilliant fire is only sustained by that to which it clings; it has no real form of its own and is constrained by the burning object.

The Judgement. Fire needs to be fed or it will die. In the same way, a dedicated man must cling to what he feels is right. A cow, symbol of docility, is mentioned in the verse, showing the need for gentle perseverance.

The Image. The image is of a man using fire to illuminate the dark corners of the world. Goodness shines out like a flame.

The Lines
1: As the sun rises, so humans rise from the unconsciousness of sleep and plunge into activity. But don't allow yourself to be swept along by custom or daily routine.
2: The image of this line is the mid-day sun, symbolizing harmony, balance and success.
3: At nightfall we are reminded that life is only a temporary gift and that change, (a recurring theme in the *I Ching*), is a constant feature. Live for the present.
4: The Chinese verse says: "Sudden fire which flares and dies is forgotten." This image warns against sudden passion which can blind judgment. It suggests constancy and clear vision.
5: Sudden fire soon extinguishes itself. Do not throw yourself so whole-heartedly into something that at the moment of accomplishment you find you have burnt yourself out.
6: Root out faults and check weaknesses. Everyone has faults; awareness of them reduces the risk of error. Set yourself realistic goals.

149

hsien

31. Stimulation

Above: *Tui* – Joyfulness, a lake

Below: *Ken* – Immovability, the mountain

Tui represents the youngest daughter or young woman and *Ken*, the youngest son or young man – a strong and a weak party, a complementary pair.

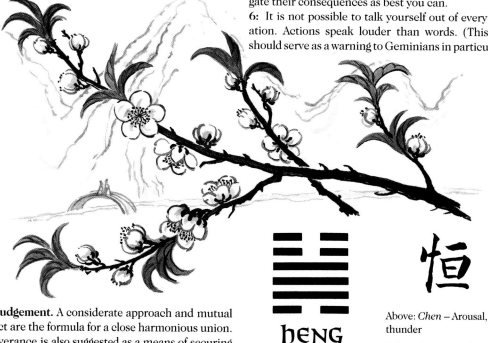

The Judgement. A considerate approach and mutual respect are the formula for a close harmonious union. Perseverance is also suggested as a means of securing success.

The Image. Misplaced confidence leads to error. A humble approach will be more successful. If you think you know all there is to know, it is highly probable you are mistaken. Be prepared to listen to others and accept their advice. The strong sometimes need to yield to the weak.

The Lines

1: Check the temptation to do something you know is wrong. It is easy to take a superficial approach, but some situations demand thoroughness.

2: This line supports the first, pointing out the danger that follows from an inappropriate approach; a first move in the wrong direction takes on its own impetus and drags you further on than you would wish to go.

3: Freedom can only be measured with respect to restriction: without discipline you cannot be entirely free. Accept the first temptation that comes your way and you may well find yourself enslaved by it. Always pause until you are sure that your instinct is natural, good and wise.

4: Most men and women are fallible. They often follow their hearts rather than their heads and court disaster. The heart's assurance should always be questioned; be calm and fix your mind on your real desire. It is also wrong to influence or manipulate others to make decisions that are not in their interests.

5: Determined action is suggested but this line refers to the unconscious mind which will influence you whatever your conscious aims or decisions. However, this does not release you from blame if you behave badly. Learn to recognize unsound instincts and mitigate their consequences as best you can.

6: It is not possible to talk yourself out of every situation. Actions speak louder than words. (This line should serve as a warning to Geminians in particular.)

heng

32. Endurance

恒

Above: *Chen* – Arousal, thunder

Below: *Sun* – Gentleness, wind

Permanence in partnership. Traditionally this hexagram was linked to marriage; generally it refers to a strong partnership in which one party is active, the other passive (thunder and wind). It may also refer to a business partnership.

The Judgement. An enduring partnership must not stand still but develop and move forward, each partner in step with the other, moving at the same pace and sharing a common goal.

The Image. The strong suggestion is that you should be flexible of opinion and attitude; receptive not only to your own instincts but those of partners and friends as well. Your personal standard of good and bad naturally influences your actions. The Chinese verse urges constancy. Adapt to changing circumstances while adhering to your personal standards.

The Lines

1: Don't demand too much from a partner at the beginning of a relationship. A relationship, like anything worthwhile, demands careful nurturing and thought.

2: Blinding ambition should be avoided. This advice is also appropriate with regard to relationships.

3: Do not allow the expectations of the outside world to interfere with your own view of life. External pressures on you can have distressing results if you begin to feel obliged to submit to them. Give good advice an ear, but in the end the decision must be your own.

4: Your ambitions should be realistic; otherwise, however persistently you forge ahead, contentment will elude you.

5: This line is specifically concerned with ancient Chinese tradition and suggests that, in a partnership, the woman should be a conservative influence while the man should be adventurous. The message can be updated to suggest that in any partnership there should be a balance; one partner should be passive and exercise a calming influence over the other.

6: Continual restlessness encourages misfortune. There is little point in rushing unless you have worked out your route.

TUN

33. Retreat

Above: *Ch'ien* – Creativity, heaven

Below: *Ken* – Receptivity, the mountain

The central idea of this hexagram is of a retreat from evil, a retreat made in caution rather than fear. The dark hand of winter is about to descend over the landscape. Retire indoors to comfort and security.

The Judgement. The enemy seems to have won a victory. In the face of overwhelming hostility, a wise person withdraws. This does not mean running away in panic but effecting a deliberate strategic retreat.

The Image. The actions of an antagonist, or perhaps the worst side of your nature, should be dealt with firmly. Inner calm is important.

The Lines

1: If you feel too close to the situation which is threatening you or your peace of mind, it may be preferable to delay reaction.

2: The line refers to the colour yellow, indicative of moderation, balance and duty. It suggests that you should stand by what you know to be right.

3: Compromise is often necessary, however undesirable it may seem. This is undoubtedly an uneasy and

threatening time; but there is nothing you can do at the moment but acquiesce.

4: Retreat gracefully. The fact that you have to lose ground may not mean that you have to lose face, nor that your convictions have necessarily been shattered.

5: It is time for a discussion. Provided you have chosen the right moment to retreat and conducted it carefully, with due regard for others, you should soon be able to establish yourself anew.

6: The path seems clear and you can proceed without regrets. Now things should begin to return to normal and you will feel secure in the knowledge that you have made a right decision.

TA CHUANG

34. Power

Above: *Chen* – Arousal, thunder

Below: *Ch'ien* – Creativity, heaven

The attributes of this hexagram provide an image of powerful ascendancy. It is also associated with the Spring, a time of renewed strength in nature.

The Judgement. Great power needs to be directed by a sound sense of justice. A position of power is easily abused and can also generate an impatient attitude which incurs mistakes. If you are aware of these two weaknesses and counteract their influence, this will be a time of great advancement.

The Image. Great strength is again emphasized, but you must be sure of your aims and sure that those aims are good. Avoid any action which is not in harmony with the established order.

The Lines

1: A position of power is easily abused if not treated with sensitivity. Avoid the temptation to use your power rashly and override the wishes of others.

2: Steady advance, no resistance. This may give you a false sense of security. Remind yourself that your actions also have consequences for other people.

3: Only the inferior man uses power thoughtlessly for his own ends. Another warning against thrusting forward without considering the consequences. The Chinese line conveys this in an image: "A goat butts against a hedge and gets his horns entangled."

4: Power need not be flaunted. Quiet, steady work brings the best results.

5: Success is its own reward. Once at the top there is no need to boast of one's accomplishment.

6: Another reminder not to go too far: Restlessness, arrogance and blind ambition are negative qualities.

chin

35. Progress

Above: *Li* – Adherence, fire

Below: *Kun* – Receptivity, earth

The combined attributes of the trigrams indicate sun rising over the earth, the spreading of light. This hexagram therefore indicates leisurely progress.

The Judgement. The central idea is of a person not born to power; someone who seems just like everyone else and who has a modest attitude, but is able to command respect and bring people together.

The Image. As the sun rises, its light spreads further and further, illuminating the darkest corners of the landscape. The image likens man's inner goodness to the rising sun: at times it may be clouded, but pure goodness eventually shines out for all to see.

The Lines

1: Stride forward cheerfully. Maintain the courage of your convictions and ignore attempts to undermine your confidence. Perseverance brings good fortune.
2: Poor communication and delayed progress. Continue to persevere. An unexpected contact may relieve the situation and foreshadow great happiness.
3: Don't worry if at the moment you feel unable to cope with your life alone. Provided you gather the right sort of support from those around you, you will continue to make good progress.
4: Greed overreaches itself and leads to disaster. Proceed modestly. Others may seem to be racing ahead and making considerable material gains. Don't allow envy to lure you into dishonest ways. Underhand dealings will almost certainly be exposed.
5: If you find yourself in a position of power, don't be tempted to use it for personal advantage. You may feel that you are not making enough progress, but quiet, measured actions are often best in such a situation

and you will be building a sound base for the future.
6: Strong action is justifiable if others are hindering you and you feel confident that your plans are best. But it is dangerous unless you are completely sure of your ground. Beware of ill-founded prejudice concerning people you don't know well and who don't know you.

MiNG i

36. Sunset

Above: *K'un* – Receptivity, earth

Below: *Li* – Adherence, fire

A flame sinks beneath the earth, symbolizing sunset. In Chinese, *Ming I* literally means "wounding of the bright thing", and there are many references here to hurtfulness and injury.

The Judgement. A passive approach may be the best way to combat enemies. Allow them to think they are in control, preserve your integrity. Sometimes you have to hide your motives to succeed.

The Image. Caution. Again make no outward sign of your inner hostility – this would only attract antagonism and perhaps violence. Keep your own council.

The Lines

1: You may have to put up with a certain amount of antagonism from others. It is a difficult time, but if you stick to your principles, you will win through.
2: Obstacles are again underlined but they are only obstructions and not insurmountable. If in doubt follow the dictates of duty.
3: Unexpectedly fate seems to play into your hands (the Chinese verse speaks of the sudden capture of an antagonist.) Don't assume that this means your troubles are over. Obstacles will diminish, but hard work is required to remove or transform them.
4: If things are going wrong, it might be better to leave the sinking ship while there is still time.

5: If you cannot get out of an uncomfortable situation, the way to survive is to cling to your inner convictions and behave cautiously.

6: Darkness seems to cover the earth but the Chinese verse reminds you of the principle of change: as Yin changes to Yang, darkness eventually turns to light.

CHIA JEN

37. Family

Above: *Sun* – Gentleness, wind

Below: *Li* – Adherence, fire

This hexagram represents the family – a strong family unit which is strengthened and held together by the two strong lines at the top and bottom. It may not literally mean a family, but any group of people held together by strong bonds.

The Judgement. Loyalty and love between husband and wife hold the family together and represent authority; if each member is strong the unit can withstand adversity. A set of common standards or principles characterize this small unit.

The Image. Influence within the family circle must be based on a recognizable moral system, but theories have no force unless they are backed up by action. If your children do not have an example to follow, words are worthless.

The Lines

1: Children must grow up within a family hierarchy, recognizing their place within it. It is no good suddenly becoming aware of this when they are old enough to reason – it will then be too late. Discipline is sometimes hard to impose but it is absolutely necessary.

2: Weaker members of the family or group need to be guided by the will of the stronger.

3: Discipline is one thing, severity another; make sure that there is a balance. Allow a certain amount of freedom. However, the *I Ching* insists that in the final analysis too much discipline is preferable to too little.

4: The family income needs to be well managed. This line repeats the message indicated throughout – responsibilities need to be taken seriously.

5: The image is of a father or king who cares for his people: a rich man whose actions are unselfish. He is concerned for the general good of his subjects.

6: The ruler of the house or the leader of any enterprise must be prepared to assume responsibility for other, perhaps weaker, people around him. Don't shy away from responsibility. Allow your own moral standards to guide you.

kuei

38. Argument

Above: *Li* – Adherence, fire

Below: *Tui* – Joyfulness, a lake

Water and fire, the attributes of the two trigrams, are two strong elements; one can never completely dominate the other. This hexagram therefore emphasizes disagreement or disunity. The Chinese verse portrays *Li* as the second daughter and *Tui* as the youngest. Both are married to different men and living in the same house – sparks fly.

The Judgement. It is almost impossible to accomplish a major project in collaboration with someone else if there is strong disagreement between you; try not to come to blows. There is always room for a measure of agreement when two people are prepared to reason, and this small base must be built upon. The Chinese suggest that opposition takes energy which can be more usefully spent in a constructive argument.

The Image. Fire and water are natural antagonists. They have equal force, so if you are involved in a conflict of some sort you can be sure that your opponents will not succeed in changing your nature, even if they win the argument.

The Lines

1: "If you lose your horse, do not follow, it will return by itself." If an argument occurs and the person with whom you are in conflict is a close friend, you will not necessarily jeopardize the friendship. According to the law of change, which the *I Ching* says governs all things, a difficult situation will eventually remedy itself.

2: If a real break has occurred formal meetings will only provoke further hostility. Try to meet in friendly surroundings. A compromise may be necessary.

3: Even if the world seems to be against you, it is still important to stick to your principles. Cling to what you know and trust.

4: It is possible to respect others' judgments without sharing their opinion. This sort of conflict can be stimulating, increase understanding and bring good results.

5: Be prepared to recognize an ally and enlist his or her support. If someone offers help, accept it graciously.

6: Opposition reaches a peak, then suddenly changes character. Here circumstances change because of another person's involvement; this may be a former friend, someone whom you have perhaps misjudged.

chien

39. Obstruction

Above: *K'an* – The abyss, water

Below: *Ken* – Immovability, the mountain

The attributes of these trigrams combine to give a hexagram that suggests danger. However, the fact that the danger is visible indicates that all is not lost. A danger whose presence is visible can be overcome.

The Judgement. If you cannot see a way forward, confide in someone with experience who can advise you. In order to escape from your predicament some difficult and perhaps dangerous moves must be made, but provided you are strong-willed success is assured.

The Image. There is no point in despair; your fate is in your own hands. Consider what mistakes or wrong turnings led you to your present unfortunate position.

The Lines

1: Don't start to climb the cliff immediately, nor lower yourself blindly into the chasm. Consider all options carefully and proceed cautiously.

2: The situation is rather like that of a soldier ordered to advance into danger. Duty may dictate a difficult course to follow; rise to the challenge or abdicate responsibility.

3: This line encourages a responsible approach. Before making any moves bear in mind the consequences your actions may have for other people – dependents such as family or employees. In view of your responsibilities it may be wise to defer action.

4: The message of this line echoes those above, it would be stupid to plunge into any kind of action which cannot hope to succeed without support. Look around you, there may be someone in sight with the necessary experience to advise and support you.

5: You may not need to be led by anyone, but you may well need a team you can lead, whose support and help will enable you to climb out of difficulties.

6: The obstruction indicated throughout this hexagram may not simply refer to difficulties facing you, but those facing other people. Be conscious of the problems of those around you. Offer a helping hand; provided your offer is sincere you may find that kindness to others is the source of your own final recovery.

chieh

40. Deliverance

Above: *Chen* – Arousal, thunder

Below: *K'an* – The abyss, water

This hexagram marks the beginning of the end – a movement towards recovery.

The Judgement. The suggestion of this verse is that you are now on the path to success. Proceed slowly, responding to new situations as they present themselves, and you will secure success. Hastiness or over-ambitious goals could set you back.

The Image. The Chinese verse speaks of rolling thunder followed by rain – the calm after the storm. A sudden shock or outburst of anger concerning a task improperly done. The *I Ching* encourages forgiveness in these circumstances. "The superior man forgives error and deals compassionately with wrong doing."

The Lines

1: If you are recovering from a difficult situation, relax for a while to recover your strength and decide on your next move.

2: Keep your goal in sight, and don't be put off by the petty ambitions or plots of others.

3: Overconfidence courts disaster. Confucius pointed out that carelessness invites robbery; similarly, unless you are entirely in control of your life, others will find it easy to disrupt it.

4: Success also attracts hangers-on who may at first be useful but later cling on like limpets long after they have ceased to be of any assistance. Discard them, or you will suffer for your lack of judgement.

5: The break with unworthy or unhelpful people must be complete. Don't allow yourself to be trapped into too much sympathy for them.

6: An unworthy person in a position of power has to be demoted before progress can be made.

SUN

41. Shrinking

Above: *Ken* – Immovability, the mountain

Below: *Tui* – Joyfulness, a lake

The attributes of the two trigrams (water beneath a mountain) combine to give a hexagram which denotes instability. When water undermines the foundations of a house there is a danger of collapse. Here the image is used to suggest hidden danger.

The Judgement. In times of trouble, others will understand and may well be able to offer useful aid. Look at the problem simply and approach it directly. Do not try to disguise the truth.

The Image. While cheerfulness is excellent, there is no point pretending to be light-hearted. Better to remain silent and develop inner strength.

The Lines

1: No matter how much energy your own preoccupations consume, retain some to offer to others worse off; nor should you be too proud to accept help from those who appear less successful than you.

2: It is wrong to expect you to neglect your own problems in order to support someone else; kow-towing to others is not the way to earn their respect.

3: "Three people walk together and lose one." Two's company, three's a crowd. But everyone needs a confidant, and in the end will find the right person.

4: One may have friends who seem extremely close and supportive but your faults can alienate them. The more you can eliminate such faults, the closer your friends or lovers will be.

5: The Chinese verse speaks of tortoises. These were considered a sign of good fortune.

6: Success can be contagious. Admire and emulate those who secure success yet remain unselfish.

42. Increase

Above: *Sun* – Gentleness, wind

Below: *Chen* – Arousal, thunder

This hexagram is said by Wilhelm to be central to the whole philosophy of the *I Ching*. The general message offered is that true leadership is also servitude.

The Judgement. Leaders who are seen to make sacrifices for the good of their employees are trusted and respected, receiving their support no matter how difficult it maybe to give. If they demand sacrifices of their subjects, these will not be begrudged.

The Image. One of the most important qualities is self-knowledge – recognition of what is good in one's nature, deserving encouragement, and what is bad, needing control. When you see admirable qualities in others, imitate them and make them your own.

The Lines

1: If you receive a sudden and perhaps unexpected bonus, be it money or promotion, use it to achieve something which would have been impossible.

2: A time of good fortune. Recognize goodness in others and strive to attain it yourself. Always be receptive to the best in other people. Make the most of any opportunities that come your way.

3: There are certain times when everything just seems to go right no matter what the odds. This is one of them. Consolidate your position by maintaining high standards.

4: There is always a place for a clear-sighted person who can act as a go-between to reconcile opposing forces. It may be that you can serve in such a capacity or you may need to search for such a person to act on your behalf.

5: Unsolicited kindness attracts a deeper gratitude than a favour which had to be prompted.

6: Good fortune falters. Be thoughtful. Confucius studying this hexagram added this message: The important thing is to think before you speak and certainly before you act; for if you do not persuade those closest to you to back you up, your enemies can close in with ease.

KUAI

43. Resolution

Above: *Tui* – Joyfulness, a lake

Below: *Ch'ien* – Creativity, heaven

KOU

44. Contact

Above: *Ch'ien* – Creativity, heaven

Below: *Sun* – Gentleness, wind

The attributes of the two trigrams suggest force that wells up from below under great pressure, eventually breaking through like water through a dam.

The Judgement. An unworthy person in a position of great power halts progress. A single fault can destroy a man. Recognition of faults and weaknesses is the only way to combat them.

The Image. Just as the rising water will eventually burst a dam, if you hug your possessions to yourself and concentrate only on gathering more, you run the risk of losing them all. A wise man keeps what is necessary and supports charitable causes with the rest.

The Lines

1: The first step in any enterprise is often the most difficult. Don't rush in when opposition starts to mount; take the measure of it and equivocate until you are sure of your own power.

2: The Chinese verse suggests: Try to anticipate problems; listen for what you cannot yet hear, watch out for what is not yet in sight, and arm yourself.

This hexagram suggests strength undermined by a single weakness; the power of Yin to shake Yang.

The Judgement. The Chinese verse speaks of a powerful maiden and is a warning against deceptive appearances. Partnerships may be advantageous provided the motives of each party are in harmony.

The Image. In the Chinese verse, wind blows under heaven carrying whatever is confided to it, as when someone in command sends out a general instruction to workers or colleagues. The influence of authority

and sound judgment should be all-pervasive.

The Lines

1: If you recognize a weak spot in your character or your theories, deal with it right away; if you ignore it, it may well develop into a major flaw.

2: There is no need to be heavy-handed in dealing with weaker elements: it is important, however, not to allow them to infect other people.

3: It is all too easy to ignore problems but they should be dealt with immediately: a clear view of the danger will enable you to prevent it from developing.

4: Remember that if you decide to weed out weak people – of whatever kind – you will also be alienating them and destroy any hope of calling upon them for help to accomplish something positive. When in a vulnerable position it may be to your advantage to tolerate them until you can afford to dispense with them.

5: This line suggests that if you are seen to be upright

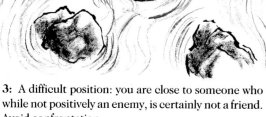

3: A difficult position: you are close to someone who while not positively an enemy, is certainly not a friend. Avoid confrontation.

4: There seem to be insuperable obstacles at present. You may have adopted the wrong approach. Relax.

5: The Chinese lines point out that the only thing to do with weeds is dig them up completely; be thorough when rooting out problems or they will reappear.

6: Persevere. You appear to have won, but there may be one more battle to fight. Remain vigilant.

and strong, just and truthful, others will inevitably be attracted to follow your example.

6: Occasionally, people who recognize and understand the base motives of many of their fellow humans become discontented with the world and withdraw from it. There is nothing wrong with this attitude if it is truly held; but it is a pity to allow it to develop into bitterness which is self-destructive. The disapproval of those whom we despise is unimportant.

TS'UI

45. Togetherness

Above: *Tui* – Joyfulness, a lake
Below: *K'un* – Receptivity, earth

The two trigrams suggest a lake held by the earth, symbolizing a complementary pair and the togetherness of the title.

The Judgement. This hexagram insists on the value of harmony between men. If they are to survive, there must be a leader and a common sense of identity.

The Image. The image warns that in large gatherings of people there is inevitably discord, perhaps over possessions. No large group is invulnerable to attack; remain on your guard.

The Lines

1: A leader is necessary. There may be considerable dissension, but when the right leader appears, he or she will be instantly recognized; as the verse puts it: "One handshake and we smile again."

2: Crowd-consciousness can be destructive (as in mob violence) but, if properly led and directed towards good, will continue on the right path.

3: You may feel like an outsider, denied entry into a group with whose ideals you strongly identify. Someone influential will initiate you if you persevere.

4: The leader must be seen to work for the good of all; as long as it is clear that he is not personally ambitious, he may be trusted.

5: People may be drawn to the group for superficial reasons, but every effort should be made so that curiosity develops into commitment.

6: If you feel hard done by, a humble attitude may persuade others that you are right, and that they should accept you or your point of view.

SHENG

46. Ascension

Above: *K'un* – Receptivity, earth
Below: *Sun* – Gentleness, wind

This hexagram suggests effort to make a success of something, and the eventual attainment of your objective as a result of that effort.

The Judgement. There seems to be no obstacle to success provided you achieve your ambitions sensibly and adopt the right attitude. It is a very good time for tackling any project. Apply all your energy.

The Image. "Wood growing up through the earth symbolizes ascensions." As plants grow towards the light, so your project will also grow and prosper if you devote time and energy to nurturing it.

The Lines

1: The first line is broken, symbolizing a weak start at the beginning of a project. Have confidence.

2: Someone who appears unprepossessing may make a valuable contribution.

3: Just as a deserted city can be entered without fear of opposition, so it will be easy to achieve your goals without major obstacles. But proceed now in case obstacles develop later.

4: This line tells how King Wen gave his trusted servants a place on his sacred mountain, and suggests achievement and favour. There is also a spiritual element so it will be satisfying emotionally and spiritually as well as materially.

5: Do not allow success to sap your energy or ambition; slow steady progress must be maintained.

6: Don't exhaust yourself. Set enough time aside for relaxation and planning; otherwise the fight to climb ever higher will sap energy you need to maintain your position and continue forward.

K'UN

47. Difficulty

Above: *Tui* – Joyfulness, a lake

Below: *K'an* – The abyss, water

This is one of the most pessimistic hexagrams of the *I Ching*; the water has been drained from the lake so it can offer no more sustenance.

The Judgement. At least from the bottom there is nowhere to go but up. The wise man is resilient and will use misfortune as a spur towards better things

rather than immerse himself in depression. It is important not to exhaust yourself entirely.

The Image. The Chinese verse speaks of a lake without water. The wise man wastes no time setting forth to try and remedy the situation. "The superior man knows his life depends on persevering in his way."

The Lines

1: The first step out of difficulty is to come to terms with it emotionally. The verse pictures a man sitting under a leafless tree and sinking into deep depression. Dwelling on a hopeless situation only makes it seem worse. Try to think positively.

2: Although life may be rich, one can still lose conviction of its value. In such a case, the trouble is obviously within oneself and so is the solution: "patience of spirit" is what the Chinese recommend.

3: Confucius said of this line that to allow yourself to be defeated by minor setbacks is disgraceful. Keep problems in perspective.

4: Opposition can be overcome provided you do not allow others to interfere.

5: Gradually the end of the tunnel approaches and those who have opposed your plans show signs of coming round to your point of view.

6: You will soon emerge into the light, but full recovery depends on your resolution. Don't allow the shadow of past failure to hang over you, and have no

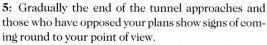

ChinG

48. The Well

Above: *Sun* – Gentleness, wind

Below: *Kan* – The abyss, water

regrets. The image associated with this hexagram is of a well into which a wooden bucket is sunk to bring up water, symbolizing a quest for nourishment.

The Judgement. For the ancient Chinese, the well stood for the depths of tradition and history from which the best lessons were drawn. A well was also seen to represent the eternal springs of human nature.

The Image. Just as plants soak up water, so the best people draw upon wisdom's wells to enrich their lives.

The Lines

1: Water from a muddy well is of little value: wisdom from the wrong source will gain you nothing.

2: If you undervalue or neglect your talents, like water in an unused well, they will stagnate and eventually dry up. Watch out for bad influences.

3: This line also points out that an unused well is useless. Here it refers to someone else. You may have failed to recognize someone else's abilities.

4: Sometimes it is necessary to work on a well. While the work is being done, the water cannot be used. The implication is that you may sometimes have to devote time to others. However this will eventually be to the greater benefit of all.

5: A stagnant well is no use to anyone; just as the water needs to be continually refreshed by a living spring, so you must always be open to new ideas.

6: A well should be available to everyone; so should your resources, both physical and mental. The more water you draw from the well, the more water runs into it. Similarly the more you use your mind for the benefit of society as a whole, the sharper and more comprehensive will be your understanding.

KO

Above: *Tui* – Joyfulness, a lake

49. Revolution

Below: *Li* – Adherence, fire

The family relationship of these two trigrams is that of two daughters. The younger one is above, which accounts for the associations of this hexagram with insubordination. Like fire and water, the two trigrams are uneasy companions. The Chinese character *Ko* means an animal's fur. Fur moults every year and is replaced. This emphasizes the central idea of the *I Ching* – constant change.

The Judgement. The annual replacement of an animal's fur is compared to revolution. A very special and entirely selfless person is needed to lead such a movement, someone who is able to respond to popular feeling and restrain it when necessary.

The Image. "The superior man makes a calendar, marking the order of the seasons." In other words, a wise person understands that change governs all life and is able to anticipate when events are about to turn.

The Lines

1: The image presented here is that of a yellow cow, the cow being a calm, unexcitable animal, and yellow being the colour of peaceful balance and continuity. So you are advised to approach problems quietly and not make any radical moves.

2: If a quiet approach has no effect, stronger action may be necessary. Timing is very important to success. Make careful preparations and plan every move.

3: Before starting any kind of revolution, be sure that it is appropriate. Both excessive violence and excessive caution can bring disaster.

4: Revolution or change should be brought about for a good cause. The leader must be convinced he is right or his campaign will be ineffectual.

5: Even after you have achieved your ends, be prepared to be flexible. The Chinese verse extends the image of an animal changing coats to suit the climate – you must be prepared to adapt.

6: Small subtle changes rather than major upheaval will be effective. A successful revolution relies on a carefully planned system of reform.

TING

Above: *Li* – Adherence, fire

Below: *Sun* – Gentleness, wind

50. The Cauldron

The two trigrams combine to give a hexagram whose shape suggests an old-fashioned Chinese bronze *ting* or cauldron from which the head of a family would serve guests. It symbolizes sustenance, both physical and emotional.

The Judgement. In this positive hexagram, the judgement indicates a civilized culture founded on a sensible, instinctive and practical understanding of life.

The Image. The cauldron may contain food but fire is needed to make it palatable. The Chinese compare fire to fate, understanding of which gives a constructive approach to life; balancing free will and fate bestows proper understanding of how to live.

159

The Lines

1: Perseverance and the right motives bring success, but unselfishness is necessary. The Chinese verse has the image of the *ting* turned upside down and cleaned, symbolizing the need to remove stale ideas before making a new start.

2: When involved in a good cause, one can afford to ignore pettiness and jealousy. It is important to have the necessary ambition to attain goals.

3: The Chinese image is of a *ting* whose handle is broken so that it cannot be lifted to serve the food which is in it. It is like a person who has much to offer but is prevented in one way or another from being of service. This is only a temporary setback.

4: Someone who when faced with a specific task fails to attack it with sufficient vigour, or asks help from the wrong people, encounters problems. Confucius spoke of a weak person in a place of honour, an ignorant person with over-ambitious plans, someone of limited power but great responsibility – all recipes for disaster.

5: An approachable and modest person will always find it possible to persuade first-rate people to assist, but must retain their respect once the job is done.

6: A final splendid image of the *ting* with handles of jade – it is beautiful, strong and very valuable, symbolizing the utmost good fortune.

CHEN
51. Arousal

Above and below: *Chen* –
Arousal, thunder

KEN
52. The Mountain

Above and below: *Ken* –
Immovability, the mountain

Both trigrams have a strong line in the third place indicating mounting force from below. They combine to give a hexagram suggesting shock and even terror.

The Judgement. The ancient Chinese verse speaks of shock in the sense of religious experience; the sort of deep shock one experiences after the sudden apprehension of God. This is followed by rejoicing. The Judgement serves as a reminder that fear is quickly followed by a sense of relief.

The Image. A sudden shock can sharpen the mind and stimulate progress. Arousal of fear provokes you to examine your innermost motives.

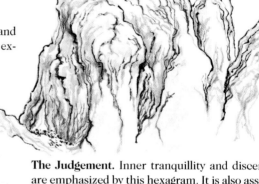

The Lines
1: A sudden shock temporarily sets you at a disadvantage, especially if it occurs in the context of work, but recovery and a feeling of relief soon follow.
2: The shock may come from a loss of material possessions or of position. Don't grieve over the loss but use what remains as a basis for rebuilding.
3: You cannot anticipate the shocks dealt by fate, but if you allow their effects to overwhelm you, you will not recover. Respond quickly.
4: The most dangerous position to be in is one where there is no possibility for manoeuvre. Never allow yourself to become inflexible.
5: If the problem is not a single shocking event but a series of them, the important thing is to maintain your balance. Don't allow yourself to be overwhelmed by the sudden onslaught and don't panic.
6: When in a state of shock, it is impossible to see things clearly, so avoid making any important decisions. Don't allow friends to force you into taking any kind of action for a time. Composure and stillness now will save agony later. As the Chinese verse puts it: "Present action will be disastrous."

Another case of a double trigram: *Ken* above *Ken*, mountain on mountain, representing stillness. Wilhelm interprets the hexagram as centring on "the problem of achieving a quiet heart".

The Judgement. Inner tranquillity and discernment are emphasized by this hexagram. It is also associated with meditation, balance, thoughtfulness and calm; the inner assurance and strength which make a wrong move impossible.

The Image. Problem-solving requires considerable concentration, so don't allow yourself to be distracted.

The Lines
1: Think about a situation thoroughly before becoming embroiled in it, for it is then easiest to see it clearly without the glosses placed upon it by other people or the complexities which may later obscure the truth.
2: This line holds a warning: sometimes one is swept along behind a stronger person to whom, or to whose actions, one is very firmly tied – either emotionally or materially. It may be impossible to save him or her from disaster: but maybe you could save yourself.
3: The Chinese verse encourages meditation and points out that you must not expect instant, remarkable results from it.
4: When one tries to "treat" a problem or mitigate a disaster through meditation, progress may be slow but perseverance will bring success.
5: This line urges complete silence or very great reserve. Not only will you be less likely to offend, but when you *do* declare yourself others will take much

more notice of what you say.

6: Having calmly examined and subdued your own personal worry, you will find your attitude to greater problems is equally calm and assured.

uncertainty should only be temporary.

6: The wild goose now soars to the heights; when you have achieved your ambition, you will impress others while feeling free and in command.

chien

53. Steady Progress

Above: *Sun* – Gentleness, wind

Below: *Ken* – Immovability, the mountain

kuei mei

54. The Bride

Above: *Chen* – Arousal, thunder

Below: *Tui* – Joyfulness, a lake

The combination of the two trigrams gives a vision of a tree growing on a mountainside, which has developed the deep roots necessary to enable it to maintain its secure position. The hexagram refers to a strong one-to-one personal relationship.

The Judgement. Here is a warning against haste, either in the development of a relationship or in any other circumstance.

The Image. Persuading others to come round to your opinion can take time. A sudden argument or speech can ignite a spark, but for a lasting effect slow, thorough persuasion, based on conviction drawn from experience, is more convincing.

The Lines

1: In every one of the six Chinese verses accompanying the lines there is an allusion to the wild goose, said to represent fidelity. Here it symbolizes a single person taking his or her first, tentative steps in life; learn a lesson from each setback and steady progress will follow.

2: Progress. Self-confidence and the willingness to share good fortune rather than hugging it to yourself.

3: A warning against sudden change. Allow things to develop at their own pace. Energy should be spent in consolidating your present position.

4: The Chinese image for this line is of a wild goose trying to land in a tree, symbolizing the difficulty experienced by someone caught in an inappropriate, perhaps perilous situation. Concentrate on an aspect of the problem which you can grasp.

5: No "high place" seems entirely safe; you may feel isolated or vulnerable to attack. However, this kind of

Chen above *Tui*, the eldest son above the youngest daughter, and a suggestion of a happy marriage between a girl and an older, more experienced man.

The Judgement. This is above all the hexagram of true love. The verse speaks of respect and a sense of duty as the formula for a successful relationship.

The Image. A relationship should not rely merely on affection and mutual enjoyment, but on a thoughtful caring attitude between the partners.

The Lines

1: The verse is about a girl who becomes a man's mistress under the eye of a loving wife. We may take this as the image of someone who enters our circle in an inferior position – an employee, perhaps – who must be tactfully taught his or her place.

2: Loyalty is stressed to a partner who has been unfaithful. The basic idea is of clinging to an ideal.

3: The image of this line indicates someone who, unable to find conventional happiness, has to settle for less and may compromise.

4: This verse pictures a girl who is disappointed in love but eventually finds "the partner intended for her". Virtue triumphs in the end.

5: A girl's family gives her in marriage when it chooses, and insists on her obedience. This emphasizes the virtue of modesty; inauspicious beginnings may lead to considerable happiness.

6: In a complex verse based on ancient Chinese religious practices we are told that without inner discipline, concern and a degree of hard work, any partnership will fail. Avoid a flippant attitude.

161

FENG

55. Abundance

Above: *Chen* – Arousal, thunder

Below: *Li* – Adherence, fire

Chen stands above *Li*, suggesting not so much a fulfilled, happy person, as one who has become too self-confident; the abundance has negative connotations.

The Judgement. Both in the life of a civilization and that of an individual, times of great happiness and fulfilment are all too brief. While things are good, therefore, it is important to make the most of them, not in fear that such a happy time will end, but in order to celebrate life at its best.

The Image. The Image relates to the two trigrams and emphasizes justice – *Li* provides the light by which we can search out the truth of a situation, and *Chen* the application of justice in the light of the facts.

The Lines

1: Here is an indication of a special and successful partnership in which two people perfectly complement each other and can work together over a considerable period of time with vigour and application. It would be a mistake to ignore the opportunities such a partnership can provide.

2: If there is disturbance and difficulty due to the interference of someone whose position is stronger than

your own, cling to what seems to you to be the essential truth of the situation, and bide your time.

3: You may find it very difficult indeed to grasp just what is going on: the verse speaks of a "total eclipse". Rather than fighting in the dark, wait for the light.

4: The darkness recedes and things begin to become clear.

5: Here is a picture of a wise ruler ready to accept advice from those who offer it. You may be the person to whom good counsel is given, or the one to advise others. In either position the exchange will prove advantageous.

6: Obstinate disregard of good advice will result in downfall and confusion, as will selfishness.

LÜ

56. Isolation

Above: *Li* – Adherence, fire

Below: *Ken* – Immovability, the mountain

Li and *Ken* are said to be two trigrams which are irreconcilable, and fly from each other. Thus each is isolated and fragmented.

The Judgement. If you find yourself isolated, do not allow it to make you impatient or ill-tempered; consider whether the reason for your isolation might be your own lack of patience or sympathy with others. Seek out the company of those you wish to emulate.

The Image. The Chinese verse speaks of dry grass on fire; the flames do not last, but run quickly over the surface of the earth. It warns you, if engaged in quarrel or litigation, not to be detained in such irritating matters for longer than is absolutely necessary. Having won or lost, forget the whole thing.

The Lines

1: While being friendly, be neither condescending nor ingratiating. If you make too obvious an effort to be included in an already close circle of friends, you may well be rebuffed. A quiet demonstration of sympathy will be far more successful.

2: More insistence that you should not be too pushy or flamboyant, especially when dealing with people you don't know well. Quiet self-confidence is attractive. There is a suggestion that travel will be important to success.

3: A suggestion that someone will be obstructive and disruptive, and put you in a difficult and even dangerous position – perhaps because you have momentarily lost control. Others offer little help, so be careful where you place your trust.

4: A certain amount of insecurity is still indicated, though circumstances may have improved somewhat.

5: Success, particularly in a new job, or perhaps promotion to a new position. Although slightly intimidated at first by the unfamiliarity of the situation, you should fulfil expectations.

6: A warning: carelessness could result in loss. Remember that a certain seriousness should inform you in practical matters if you are not to jeopardize your security.

with a particular religious sacrifice where three types of animal were offered. Its message is, use all the resources at your disposal.

5: Having recognized a problem and acted to resolve it, you should then try to arrange things so that they don't recur. This will call for firm and decisive action.

6: If you are unable to take the proper action to set things right, the fact that you have understood the situation will be of considerable help; be content to ride out the storm.

SUN

57. Gentleness

Above and below: *Sun* – Gentleness, wind

TUI

58. Joy

Above and below: *Tui* – Joyfulness, a lake

A double trigram, *Sun* indicates a gentle wind which sweeps over a whole landscape, warming and refreshing everything in it. The hexagram suggests thoroughness: sound judgment and insight.

The Judgement. Here is a suggestion of someone working in the background, away from the limelight, achieving results that surprise people simply because they are achieved without ostentation. Nevertheless, considerable hard work is needed to identify objectives and attain them.

The Image. The lightest wind can wear away the surface of stone over a long period of time; it works by sheer persistence, rather than a show of force. The same applies when you want to influence other people: a sudden shock will frighten and upset, but quiet insistence persuades.

The Lines

1: Gentleness does not mean indecision. Do not be bemused by your problems, however numerous. Single out the most pressing, and deal with them, at a single stroke if possible; you will find that once you start this process, the impetus will carry you forward.

2: It is important to get to the root of difficulties and not just skim the surface, otherwise the problem will only raise its head again. Sometimes it is difficult to trace the source of a particular problem; but it is well worth persevering, for you can then deal with the matter conclusively.

3: As you dig down to the root of a problem you may find that there are many reasons for it. Don't allow this to confuse you, and don't spend too long on detailed analysis. Forthright action is continually advised by this hexagram.

4: This line is associated in ancient Chinese custom

Both trigrams symbolize a lake and offer joy. The two strong lines which form the base of each trigram indicate that a firm decisive morality must lie at the bottom of every happy life.

The Judgement. "Joy" does not mean a burst of happiness but something much deeper and more lasting. True joy reflects a balanced attitude to life.

The Image. The joining of two lakes represents the joy of sharing knowledge.

The Lines

1: The inmost joy of the heart arises from recognition of all that is highest and best in the human spirit, and determination not to be led astray.

2: A warning against "low pleasures": examine your conscience. Resist the temptations offered by those who are perhaps less rigorous in their understanding and pursuit of inner contentment.

3: Idle diversions, although pleasant, are self-indulgent and worthless. They are usually sought by those who have no inner resources: nature abhors a vacuum, so when your life is empty it is tempting to fill it with meaningless distractions.

4: A warning against passion. Enjoyment should be measured and relaxed rather than excited and febrile. Sometimes only experience can teach this lesson. A wise person will be self-disciplined enough to avoid the problem completely.

5: The wise person recognizes danger when it approaches, and avoids it. Don't allow apparent happiness to obscure your better judgement.

6: It is remarkably easy to be seduced by pleasure, especially if it has tempted you for some time. Having once given in, it is all too easy to spiral downwards to disaster.

hUAN

59. Dispersion

Above: *Sun* – Gentleness, wind

Below: *K'an* – The abyss, water

Wind (*Sun*) blowing over water (*K'an*) whips it up into froth and spray, so that even the strongest current's power is sapped.

2: Do not allow yourself to be embittered, however much people or circumstances seem to be against you. The fault may be with you.

3: You may feel completely overwhelmed by the amount of work you have to do. It is important to cut out all distractions and devote your energies to the task for as long as is necessary.

4: A view from the top of the hill is better than one from halfway up; similarly, your own personal view is better than one which is confused by the advice or opinion of many other people. Do not allow others to influence you, however much you may admire and trust their judgment.

The Judgement. This hexagram is not only a symbol of dispersed energy, but it also indicates too much self-involvement and egotism. Egotism divides hearts. In ancient China this was dissolved by religious ritual. The verse stresses the value of harmony and selfless cooperation.

The Image. The Chinese verse speaks of ice melted by the balmy winds of spring; the symbolism is intended to draw a parallel with the hard hearts of men melted by a general movement towards the good. The specific impetus is a religious one, but religion means many things to many people, and a general consensus of right action for right reasons can be equally admired and sought.

The Lines

1: The time to resolve disagreements is at the very earliest opportunity. Before misunderstandings take root, act firmly to explore, understand and end them.

5: The Chinese verse speaks of the crisis of an illness, when things may swing either way – towards death or recovery. Similarly there are times in our daily lives when a really momentous decision must be made, requiring the utmost energy, or a sudden, brilliant stroke of intuition. If this is such a time for you, the auguries are good.

6: The dispersion of danger. You should be able to avoid danger and help those around you do the same. The outlook is good.

chieh

60. Limitation

Above: *K'an* – The abyss, water

Below: *Tui* – Joyfulness, a lake

Both trigrams are concerned with water. Above is *K'an*, also symbolizing the abyss, while below is *Tui*, representing joy, as well as a lake; so between them they suggest some limit must be set if the whole of creation is not to be swamped. The overall idea is not so much of limitation as a restraint of ambition or energy – discipline as a regulator.

The Judgement. Limitation in the shape of discipline increases power, as the aperture of a fountain increases the height of the jet. However, discipline must not become inhibition, or ambitions will seem unattainable; nor must it be too lax, or they will never be attained. Even discipline must be limited.

The Image. Again, discipline is emphasized, this time in respect of how one establishes and maintains it. Accepting certain limitations enables us to develop full strength within those limitations – and having done so, new boundaries may be marked out.

The Lines
1: Confucius urges caution in all things, especially in

the development of new ideas. This line suggests that, by confining our ambition to what we know we can achieve, we foster our energy and are ready to set new goals.
2: However, when action is needed we must act. Remain tentative as long as the situation is not clear; pounce when the time is right. A lost opportunity may never recur.
3: Learn from experience. Having missed one bus, make sure you catch the next.
4: Don't waste energy trying to flout natural laws, and only exert your strength to attain the attainable. Be ambitious but try and achieve your ambitions by natural means.
5: You cannot insist on applying to others discipline which you are not prepared to accept yourself. If you set a good example, you can reasonably expect that others should at least respect, and may emulate you.
6: Severe discipline which is imposed over a long period will be opposed, and eventually rejected completely. Remember the suggestion made in Line 5.

ChUNG FU

61. Truth

Above: *Sun* – Gentleness, wind

Below: *Tui* – Joyfulness, a lake

Sun stands above *Tui*, and as it blows over the surface it disturbs the calm – as when our unconscious discloses to us hidden emotions or motives. This is one of the hexagrams which makes the *I Ching* so attractive to Jungian psychologists, for it represents the inmost truth which we are scarcely capable of revealing even to ourselves.

The Judgement. Learn to recognize your own motives and acknowledge how difficult it is to recognize those of other people. Beware of snap judgments. First impressions, however, have value, for in these moments you rely on your instinctive judgment to assert itself. The most diverse people can have common springs of natural feeling.

The Image. The highest and most admired form of justice in ancient China was founded on understanding of the reasons for the offence, however heinous, and a readiness to exercise mercy. Natural justice attracted such regard that the most hardened criminal accepted the law.

The Lines
1: Success can be inhibited by false friends and by your own deviousness. Be frank and open; when others know you as well as you know yourself, you will receive wholehearted support.
2: This line refers to a sense of righteousness. Even those whom you would expect to despise what they take to be weakness, are convinced by idealistic aims which are forcibly and clearly expressed.
3: However excellent your friends and associates, and whatever the benefit you get from leaning on them, if you rely utterly on them you will come to grief, for no other person can live your life for you. This is a time when you should make your own choice.
4: In the midst of friends and loved ones, you must still have your own vision of what your life is about and how you feel you should live it; it is *your* goal that must be kept in mind.
5: It is a good time, but whether it remains so depends upon one person (you, or another?) who must hold the reins firmly and not allow things to get out of hand.
6: Success, at the moment, is possible but not marked; you should certainly not start crowing until there is something to crow about.

165

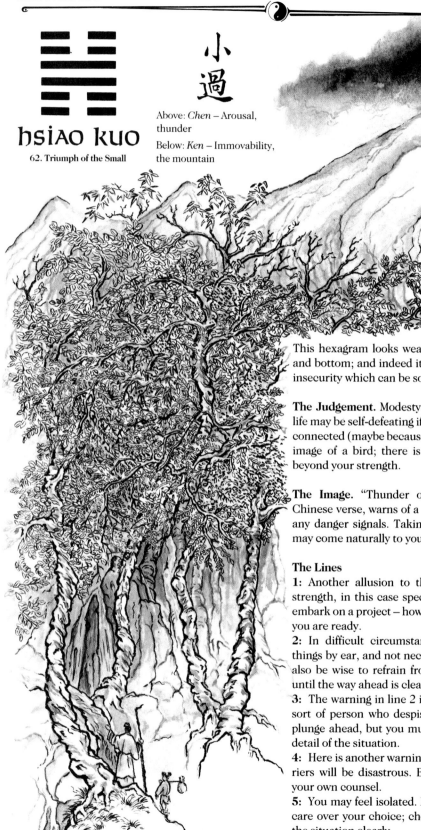

hsiao kuo

62. Triumph of the Small

小過

Above: *Chen* – Arousal, thunder

Below: *Ken* – Immovability, the mountain

This hexagram looks weak, with broken lines at top and bottom; and indeed it indicates a general state of insecurity which can be somewhat worrying.

The Judgement. Modesty and a tentative attitude to life may be self-defeating if excessive. The hexagram is connected (maybe because of its appearance) with the image of a bird; there is a warning against soaring beyond your strength.

The Image. "Thunder on the mountain", in the Chinese verse, warns of a distant threat. Take note of any danger signals. Taking the side of the underdog may come naturally to you, and will be rewarding.

The Lines
1: Another allusion to the bird which out-flies its strength, in this case specifically warning you not to embark on a project – however well it promises – until you are ready.
2: In difficult circumstances, be prepared to play things by ear, and not necessarily by the book. It may also be wise to refrain from action for a while; wait until the way ahead is clearer.
3: The warning in line 2 is repeated: you may be the sort of person who despises caution, and prefers to plunge ahead, but you must take note of every small detail of the situation.
4: Here is another warning. Any attempt to crash barriers will be disastrous. Be inwardly firm, and keep your own counsel.
5: You may feel isolated. If you need assistance, take care over your choice; choose someone who can see the situation clearly.
6: Small things and small people obstruct your ambitions. You will have to tolerate this for a while; wait, circumstances are on their side.

chi chi

63. Fullness

Above: *K'an* – The abyss, water

Below: *Li* – Adherence, fire

This hexagram denotes success and harmony: a peak moment, fullness or completion; but according to the *I Ching* notion of change, "fullness" must wane.

The Judgement. The situation is propitious; only small details remain to be arranged, otherwise circumstances move forward under their own momentum. However, it would be a mistake not to keep a watchful eye on those small details.

The Image. The Chinese verse depicts a kettle boiling over a fire; this means not only heat and energy, but tension. You should be ready to take action.

The Lines

1: When things begin to go well, the forward movement can sometimes speed up rather more quickly than one expects, and matters can get out of control. Keep one hand on the brake.

2: Those who have up to now supported you may become critical. Don't respond with anger.

3: Plans for any enterprise should include a policy of consolidation. Keep an eye on your financial situation, or any area, even psychological, where you need to top up your resources.

4: Though the overall situation may be relaxed and pleasant, it is always possible for sudden small difficulties to arise. Never ignore such minor difficulties, which may be the symptoms of bigger storms ahead.

5: Keep your life as simple as possible. If you allow your projects to break into flower without pruning them they will be susceptible to disease.

6: A final warning: don't be confined by past experience, and beware of self-satisfaction. Always be prepared to consider new ways forward.

wei chi

64. Before Completion

Above: *Li* – Adherence, fire

Below: *K'an* – The abyss, water

This hexagram signifies movement towards the completion of a venture, a thought, a personality. *Li* stands above *K'an* in a rather unbalanced structure of broken and unbroken lines – which Wilhelm likens to spring, a time of hope when summer is promised, but its nature is so far unknown.

The Judgement. There is a promise of success, but great care is needed; you must tread carefully and calculate the results of every step.

The Image. While fire mounts upward, water sinks – obviously there are going to be difficulties in reconciling these two movements; so it is necessary to study your situation with great care, and perhaps apply new solutions to any problem. Above all, make quite sure where you stand.

The Lines

1: "There is a tide in the affairs of men, Which taken at the flood leads on to fortune." Watch for the moment when the tide turns, and take it. Be absolutely sure of your timing, however, or disaster may follow.

2: This is probably not a time for action but there is no reason why you should be preparing yourself for the moment when the time *is* right. Try to see your target clearly, and to calculate precisely the amount of strength you need, and how best to organize and use it to maximum advantage.

3: When the time does come, seize it. You will know, instinctively, when to make your move. If you feel you are not yet ready, better lose the moment than let things go forward prematurely.

4: Once you have started to move forward, press on steadily and do not entertain any doubts. With self-confidence you are set for success, and should attain it.

5: This line is the symbol of complete success. If things have to some extent disintegrated because of the efforts you have had to make or the methods you have used to attain your position, set your mind to remedying the situation.

6: Celebrate your success; but don't lose control. The moment of success can too often be a moment of relaxation which allows the first seeds of dissolution to be sown. Be watchful.

The *I Ching* ends, then, with an image of success in the last of the 64 hexagrams. However, the message is, as always, related to the attitude of the reader. Very characteristically, it cautions against self-satisfaction or the suggestion that one can ever completely relax. As T. S. Elliot put it, "In my end is my beginning"; the cycle of life goes on.

How to interpret the *I Ching*

Though the interpretation of the text which traditionally accompanies the *I Ching* hexagrams is difficult and needs much practice (which is why we present a simplified system here), arriving at the appropriate hexagram for your purpose is very simple. It involves the use of three coins. Of course it would be very nice if you could use ancient Chinese coins, such as would have been used traditionally – round, with a square hole in the centre, and four figures on one side of each. But of course these are not easy to come by, and the oracle works perfectly well with ordinary copper coins – pennies or dimes.

However, as with your Tarot pack or your runes, you should make the coins very personal to you: wash them well, and keep them about you for some time, storing them always in the same box, or perhaps a wash-leather bag, and using them only when you are casting the *I Ching*.

When you are ready, find a reasonably quiet place where you can feel relaxed, take the three coins and hold them for a moment in your hands, concentrating your mind on the question you want to ask, and, still thinking of your question – addressing it to the oracles, as it were – cast the coins down onto a flat surface.

Make a note of the way the coins fall: two heads and a tail, two tails and a head, or whatever, and note down the resulting score (see below). When you have cast them six times you are ready to draw your hexagram.

This consists, of course, of two trigrams, one above the other. Look these up on the Hexagram Table (p. 134), and cross-referencing them, find your hexagram (for instance, trigram *K'un* at the top and trigram *Li* at the bottom make hexagram 36, *Ming I*).

Referring to the interpretation of this hexagram apply it to your problem. Then go to your original hexagram, re-draw it turning the "changing" lines (if any) into their opposites, and consult the new hexagram.

For instance, you may originally have hexagram 36, *Ming I*, but with lines 5 and 6 (the top two lines) marked as Old Yin, which means that they are "changing". Redrawing the hexagram with lines 5 and 6 solid instead of broken, look again at Table X: the bottom trigram is still *Li*, but the top trigram has now turned from *K'un* into *Sun,* so when you cross-reference them you arrive at hexagram 37, *Chia Jen.*

One of the most fascinating things about consulting the *I Ching* is that although there are many hexagrams which will have little or nothing to say about your particular query, you will find that almost invariably the coins "choose" one with an apposite comment.

Sample reading

A querant who was deceiving his wife put the question "How may I best end the deception and get back to a proper relationship".

The thrown coins totalled 6, 9, 7, 8, 8, 7 – which, reading from the bottom, produced hexagram number 18, *Ku – Rebuilding of Ruins.* This shows the situation as it is, and its implications. Because the first line,

---

Casting the coins

If the coin falls heads or (Chinese coin) on the four-faced side, it is considered Yang, counts 3 and indicates an unbroken line; if tails, it is Yin, counts 2 and indicates a broken line. But that is not all, for some lines will be Young Yang or Young Yin and remain constant, while others are Old Yang and Old Yin and will change, carrying you on beyond the hexagram you have "chosen" (which comments on the situation as it is at present) to another (which will indicate the resolution of your problem). The principle is based on the ancient Chinese philosophy of T'ai Chi, which holds that when a force reaches its climax and becomes "old", it changes to its opposite.

When you are drawing your hexagram, it is a good idea to mark the old (changing) lines with a little circle or cross, which will make it easier for you to construct the hexagram. Now count up your score and draw your hexagram, always starting from the bottom.

Score of 6
means Old Yin and is indicated by a **changing** broken line:

Score of 7
means Young Yang and is indicated by an unchanging unbroken line:

Score of 8
means Young Yin and is indicated by an unchanging broken line:

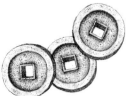

Score of 9
means Old Yang and is indicated by a **changing** unbroken line:

Ku

Pi

produced by a score of 6, is Old Yin it changes to Yang, and the second line, produced by 9, is Old Yang, it changes to Yin, giving a second hexagram, number 22, *Gracefulness*, which indicates the eventual outcome of the situation. In "reading" the advice of the book, think carefully about the interpretation, and omit anything that seems to have no bearing on the matter (but be careful: the significance of the metaphors and advice reveals itself at a later stage – it is always valuable to dwell on the message of the *I Ching* at length).

Considering *Ku* first: the top trigram is *Ken* and the lower one *Sun*: the symbol for a mountain, immovability, over that for wind, gentleness. The hexagram emphasizes the feeling of guilt which animates the querant at present. The Judgement shows that it will be possible for him to rebuild the relationship he has injured, and that the present is a good time at which to do so. But his approach to the subject should be thoroughly thought out; he should dig to the root of the problem before dealing decisively with it. The Image adds that he needs the cooperation of the other people concerned if the situation is to be remedied without too much damage. Line 1 points out that intractability is one source of the problem; he has lacked the impetus towards change. Line 2 warns again that he should deal gently with everyone concerned. Line 3 also urges a gentle approach; line 4 underlines the fact that he should act now if things are not to fall apart. Line 5 advises the querant to draw strength from those around him if he feels incapable of solving the problem alone; line 6 adds the warning that though he may think himself capable of dealing with it by self-control, he should not rely on this. He should not, at all events, simply detach himself from the situation and assume that good intentions alone will resolve it.

Turning then to 22, *Pi, Gracefulness*, we find an in-dication of the outcome: the mountain now stands above *Li*, representing flame, light, hope. The Judgement and the Image both speak about beauty (and the querant is indeed concerned with the arts), making the point that this is incompatible with the life he has been leading. The lines point out that just as art must be worked at, so must human relationships. Line 3 warns that energy will be needed, and line 4 counsels simplicity, stressing the necessity to get down to essentials; line 5 points out that friends will remain important. Line 6, perhaps most important of all, indicates that the querant really knows the solution himself, and has known it all along; the *I Ching* never shrinks from pointing out the foolishness of man!

As with every reading of the *I Ching*, some elements of the suggestions offered seem immaterial, and comparing the interpretation above with those on pps. 143-5 for the two hexagrams concerned, you will see that we have both selected and slightly changed them. The ability to see what is material and what is not sharpens with familiarity; the querant above recognized the elements of his situation in the *Ku* reading, and saw a clear way forward in that for *Pi*; as usual, there seemed a strong connection between the first and second hexagrams, *Pi* continuing the line of commentary begun in *Ku*, and suggesting that the theme of retreat and withdrawal at first suggested must necessarily lead to change; but, rather than an over-sudden grasp at a quick solution, caution and calm, patience, quiet consideration, conviction without stubbornness, and thought rather than talk would lead to a resolution of the problem.

Though this is to some extent advice rather than prediction, *Pi* offers a glimpse of the future, though a future dependent on one's own action and free will – more satisfactory in most people's eyes than a future dependent entirely on fate.

169

Phrenology & Physiognomy

Unlike most of the other systems in this book, physiognomy (the study of people's faces to read their character) and phrenology (the study of the bumps and hollows of the skull) are now almost entirely neglected, despite a history, for physiognomy at least, as long as those of many other methods of divination.

A study of the lines and character of the face and the bumps of the head was never, of course, used to predict future events. Yet is was claimed that they could represent so clearly the character of their owners that to some extent they were predictive, showing later developments of character (much as palmistry not only indicates character but also future changes of temperament).

Phrenology

It was in 1796 that Dr Franz Joseph Gall (1758-1828), a brain anatomist and physiologist working in Vienna, devised his celebrated system of phrenology, based on the theory that each mental faculty of the brain was localized, and that the size of the region where it was seated had a noticeable effect on the conformation of the human skull. So, inspecting bumps on its surface, the phrenologist could assess the personality and ability of a subject – and to some extent predict the course his or her future emotional life would take, based on an understanding of the psyche.

For a while, other scientific discoveries supported Gall's view: Pierre Flourens (1794-1867) experimented on animals and confirmed that certain areas of the brain were indeed essential to certain functions (though he found their localization less precise than Gall); then Paul Broca (1824-80) was the first to discover the speech centre in the left cerebral hemisphere of the brain, and Fritsch and Hitzig stimulated various areas of the brain electrically, and succeeded in localizing certain centres. In Britain, George Combe did much to popularize Gall's ideas.

Though the 20th century has seen the almost complete destruction of Gall's theory, phrenology has still not entirely vanished from the world of physiological psychology, though today practised chiefly by eccentrics. And after all, while the emotion and mental faculties of a foetus are being formed, its skull is soft and malleable; the idea that its final, hard conformation may be partly influenced by the shape of the brain beneath need not be outrageously unacceptable. Modern neurology has related mental functions to specific brain areas. Only those who are able to believe that scientists already know everything about the earliest stages of human life, might reject phrenology altogether.

Physiognomy

The first modern textbook of physiognomy was probably *De Humana Physiognomia*, written by Giambattista della Porta (1535-1615), finally published in Italian in Padua in 1672. In that work he quoted many earlier authorities, claiming for example that the Pythagoreans, c.500BC, had insisted that no-one should be accepted as a student unless their physical appearance suggested an ability to learn. Nature constructed the body, they believed, in proportion to the properties of the soul – a belief held also by Plato and Aristotle.

From the earliest times there was a strong association between physiognomy and astrology: the lines of the forehead, for instance, were allied to the six known planets and the Moon, and were said to affect the personality of the person concerned according to the strength and depth of the line observed. Astrologers for many centuries also took account of "the marks of the body", and it was said that by studying the birth chart, a good astrologer could tell precisely where on the body of a client a mole or moles were likely to be found – indeed, some would perform this trick to prove how accurate they could be!

Though physiognomy is now for the most part dismissed by serious predictors and scientists alike, its popularity is understandable, for we do make judgements of character on sight, and mistaken though we may often be, those impressions are remarkably difficult to shake off. One difficulty in trying to compare faces is that we tend to remember them in a very rough and ready fashion: as the police discover when a witness tries to describe a criminal, we file away in our memory only a short-hand sketch of a face, which depends on our recollection of its obvious features – we often find it difficult to recognize a close friend if he covers his eyes, nose and mouth. A close study of the human face means paying attention to each separate feature, as well as to the whole. Whether, given that, it is ever possible to say that one facial characteristic indicates intelligence and another dullness, is highly arguable – though even modern man has sometimes thought so: it was Proust who said that "if the eyes are often the organ through which the intelligence shines, the nose is generally the organ which most readily publishes stupidity".

Physiognomy: How to do it

John Casper Lavater remains the most famous expositor of physiognomy, and the following interpretations are mainly based on his researches. The most complete translation of his work comprises a book of over 500 pages (*Essays on Physiognomy,* 1840). Here are some of his main conclusions.

The forehead

Lavater believed the proportions of the forehead showed "the propensity, degree of power, thought and sensibility" of a person. The texture of the skin and its wrinkles reflected the passions and the present state of mind, while the bones beneath the forehead indicated "the application of power".

The ideal forehead should be clear-skinned and in proportion to the rest of the face i.e. one-third of its length. It should be oval at the top, free of wrinkles when relaxed, but falling into them when in thought.

Longer: proportionately, the more intelligent but less active the person.
Shorter: a firm and more decisive person.
Curved: proportionately, the more tender the person.
Completely perpendicular: lack of intelligence. But if gently curving as it reaches the hairline this person has "a capacity for cold, profound thought".

Retreating: wit and acuity.
Projecting: immaturity and weakness.
Well-arched: (chiefly in women) thoughtfulness and perspicuity.
Small, wrinkly, short, shiny: weakness and lack of imagination and emotion.
Knotty bumps: vigour, firmness and passion.
Divided into two arches: clear, sound understanding.

Perpendicular wrinkles: "application and power"
Horizontal or broken wrinkles: carelessness and lethargy.
Perpendicular wrinkles between eyebrows: special intelligence in men, and (Lavater says) "when found in women it is difficult to find any more discreet and sensible".
Without wrinkles: persons who are "cold, malign, suspicious, severe, selfish, censorious, conceited, mean and seldom forgive".
Perfectly regular: without hollows or bumps, perfectly smooth and featureless, shows a lack of intelligence and ideas.
Oblique lines: suspicious mind.
Parallel lines: very intelligent, wise, rational people.

The eyes

Lavater believed blue eyes to be "generally more significant of weakness, effeminacy and yielding" than brown or black eyes. On the other hand blue-eyed people are calm and cheerful in temperament. Very clear blue eyes usually indicate people who are given to suspicion and jealousy. Brown eyes show a choleric nature, while green eyes show ardour and courage. Small, black, sparkling eyes indicate cunning.

Arch beneath the eyebrow: if perfectly round, indicates goodness and tenderness, sometimes timidity.
Perfectly horizontal eyelid: denotes a subtle, acute, able person.
Wide, open eyes: show courage and rashness
Long, sharp, horizontal corners: an indication of genius, especially if the eyelids are thick-skinned.
Large, open, transparent: quick discernment, elegance and taste, irritability, pride and "a most violent love of the opposite sex."
Deep-sunk, small, dull blue eyes: beneath a bony forehead, show a proud, suspicious, harsh and cold-hearted nature.

The eyebrows

Lavater said that, in general, "clear, thick, roof-shaped, overshadowing eyebrows which have a wild, luxurious bushiness are always a sign of a sound, manly mature understanding; seldom of original genius; never of volatile, aerial, amorous tenderness and spirituality."

Horizontal: understanding, coldness of heart and a capacity for framing plans.
Regularly arched: characterize, in a man, a degree of femininity.
Horizontal and regularly arched: excellent balance.
Wild, unruly: a wild and perplexed mind, unless the hair is especially soft, which suggests sensuality.
Firm, well-shaped: "manly, mature understanding, profound wisdom and a true and unerring perception."
Meeting above the nose: found in open, honest people, but may indicate "a troubled heart."
Weak, small eyebrows: with sparse hair, especially combined with long eyelashes, shows a weak constitution but usually a high degree of sensuality.
Angular, strong and thick: fire and creativity.
Close to the eyes: depth of character and firmness.

The chin

Projecting: a positive person
Retreating: a negative person.
Dimpled: someone with cool understanding.
Pointed: a sign of intelligence and quickness of mind.
Soft, fat or double: someone who enjoys their food, but is also wise and discreet.
Long, bony, broad, thick: only found in rude, harsh, proud and violent people.

(Right) *"The spirit of projecting – want of wisdom – brutal boasting wrinkle the countenance."*

(Left) *"The image of bloodthirsty cruelty, unfeeling, without a trait of humanity"*

"The face of a censorious and severe man from whom no mercy should be expected, whose piercing eyes will penetrate men's thoughts but who will say little himself. His eyebrows indicate a deep and original thinker."

"Fine sensibility and excellent taste shine from his features, suggesting a writer who would extol the beauties of nature or the joys of friendship, as shown by the lips or the eyebrows. Science will not appeal . . ."

The nose

A beautiful nose, Lavater affirmed, is always a sign of a beautiful nature. Its length should equal that of the forehead, be gently indented at the top, where it should broaden slightly; its end should be neither hard nor fleshy, and it should be neither very pointed nor very round. Where it meets the arch of the eyebone, it should be at least half an inch broad. The nostrils should be pointed at the top and round at the base.

A small nose: its owner is better at thinking than acting, at listening than speaking.
Arched near forehead: someone born to command.
Rectilinear: a well-balanced personality; people possessing a broad nose are always in some way extraordinary.
Small nostrils: timidity.
Flared nostrils: someone who is sensitive, but "may easily degenerate into sensuality."
Turned up at the tip: someone inclined to pleasure – benevolent and talented, but perhaps jealous.
Turned-down: a coldhearted, sarcastic, ill-humoured person.
Arched at top: voluptuousness will certainly be marked.
Wrinkled: denotes someone truly good.

The mouth

If the mouth is as wide as the eyes, this shows dullness or stupidity. A projecting lower lip is also a mark of stupidity and rudeness or avarice. Disproportion between upper and lower lip shows folly.

Firm lips: firm character.
Weak, loose lips: weak character.
Well-defined, large: one who loves pleasure, but are never seen in men and women of evil nature.
Thin: much concern with order and appearance, can indicate vanity and even malice.
Fleshy: a person much given to indolence and sensuality.
Mild, overhanging upper lip: a "good" person.

Teeth

Small, short teeth: especially if discoloured, show weakness of character.
Long teeth: "are certain signs of weakness and faint-heartedness."
White, clean, well-arranged: visible but not projecting, a good, honest person.
Upper gum: if visible when a person speaks this is a sign of coldness of temperament.

Phrenology: How to do it

Gall divided the skull into three major areas, and subdivided these into other larger and smaller sections, greater or lesser size and prominence indicating (he claimed) the degree to which the individual possessed the emotional or mental characteristics ruled by the faculty which lay beneath the skull at those points. His theories were later elaborated by Johann Kaspar Spurzheim, at one time his assistant (1776-1832) and by American psychologists and phrenologists, and the finally accepted "phrenological head" contained 42 divisions: the intellectual faculties were alleged to reside at the front of the skull, the instincts at the back, and the moral faculties at the top.

"Reading" a head becomes easy only with practice: at first, only the major "bumps", called "faculties" or organs by phrenologists, will be obvious; but with experience it becomes possible to compare the size of the smaller "bumps". A thick, plentiful head of hair is admittedly not a great help, and the larger the number of relatively bald friends one can muster, the quicker one's progress!

The Bumps

1. Language. A bulging eye, or a bulge showing just the below the eye, shows a talent for languages.

2. Configuration. Slight bumps at the sides of the nose, which make the eyes seem wide apart, indicate a keen appreciation of form and configuration; a total absence of such bumps means you can't draw at all.

3. Proportion. Just above (2), a bump here indicates a feeling for visual proportion.

4. Weight. Good judgement of weight; a large bump here indicates a love of heights.

5. Colour. Love and good judgement of colour values. Absence: colour-blindness.

6. Planning. Shows good planning ability, neatness; absence means untidiness and lack of thought.

7. Mathematics. The last bump of this line, beyond the line of eyes, indicates mathematical ability; lack of one indicates at best, incompetence and at worst innumeracy.

8. Observation. Immediately above and between the eyes, this bump, if well-developed, shows excellent powers of observation.

9. Locality. The bump of locality (higher than (8) and each side of it) shows a love of travel, of new and unfamiliar places; if really prominent, the urge to explore.

10. History. A love of the past and a capacity to remember it; if very prominent, the tendency to bore people by over elabortion of facts.

11. Analysis. Good analytical powers and the ability to muster arguments.

12. Judgement. Especially of people; excellent ability to evaluate others; if too large, hypercritical; if absent, a lack of discrimination.

13. Sympathy. A sympathetic disposition; humane and kindly. Too large, easily imposed on.

14. Veneration. Respect for society and its rules, also perhaps for religion: if overdeveloped, subservient.

15. Self-satisfaction. The size is relative to possible conceit and arrogance, but also to firmness.

16. Self-esteem. This bump, if prominent, emphasizes the individual's determination to be successful; a large bump can indicate conceit and arrogance, but if almost lacking, suggests lack of confidence and feebleness.

17. Fame. Somewhat similar to (16), this bump indicates a desire for fame, popularity and determina-tion to achieve it; large, it can assert too great a degree of self-importance.

18. Integrity. A consciousness of moral values and conviction of one's own probity. Stressed, an inability to see others' point of view.

19. Aspirations. Optimism and forward-looking ambition; a determination to be happy. Lacking, an indication of pessimism.

20. Spirituality. An indication of psychic and religious ability.

21. The Stage. A bump said to be common in actors; otherwise, indicates a talent for mimicry and self-dramatization.

22. Social grace. Indicates the talent to make oneself agreeable in any company.

23. Thought. A suggestion of intellectualism and rational thought; absence would indicate lack of judgement.

24. Time. An acute consciousness of the passing of time, memory for dates, a sense of rhythm.

25. Laughter. An indication of wit, humour, and enjoyment of good times; a large bump of laughter can mark a practical joker; lack of this bump indicates lack of humour, an inability to enjoy oneself.

26. Artistic Sense. The bump of artistic ability, either as creator or appreciator; the mark of the poet. If lacking, vulgarity.

27. Greatness. An appreciation of great things, sweeping gestures, the sublime in human creativity.

28. Caution. A cautious disposition, avoiding risks; a sitter-on-the-fence – if the bump is well-developed, to the extent of never making up one's mind.

29. Concentration. The ability to concentrate on a subject continuously: well-developed, a disposition to be finicky and repetitive.

30. Friendship. The capacity for friendship, the love of friends and the need for their company; gregariousness. Absence, the inability to make friends.

31. Home. The love of home as a physical place; also patriotism.

32. Parenthood. Affection of parents for children and vice versa; also love of animals. Too prominent, this bump indicates excessive possessiveness.

33. Love. The indication of single-minded, constant faithful love.

34. Sex. Erotic love in all forms; the larger, the more pronounced.

174

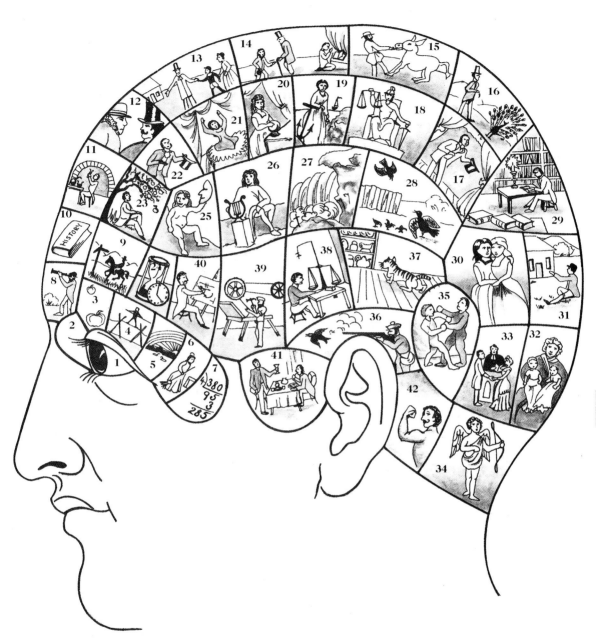

35. Argument. Indicates the degree of courage and combativeness in one's nature – with a large bump, a hot temper and argumentativeness, even to the extent of physically fighting.

36. Severity. This bump indicates a strong, enduring nature, efficient and even ruthless; a large bump sug-

gests vindictiveness, perhaps cruelty.

37. Secretiveness. At best, tact and trustworthiness; but a large bump here indicates possible deceit and secret plotting.

38. Acquisition. Love of property and wealth, and the wish to acquire them.

39. Mechanics. Mechanical ability, engineering, design.

40. Planning. This bump indicates the ability to plan in detail, to be systematic in carrying out plans.

41. Appetite. An indication of physical appetite; a well-developed bump suggests the gourmet, an over-

developed one the glutton.

42. Vitality. An indication of the subject's vitality, energy-level and general health – but too well-developed suggests hypochondria.

175

176

Graphology

Graphology – the study of handwriting to reveal character – developed later than most of the other techniques described here. This is mainly because it is dependent on a wide degree of literacy, which even in the West was unusual until comparatively recently. However, as the ability to write increased, it became clear that each individual's "hand" was unique. When read with knowledge, it offers a detailed profile of the personality, and hence a chance to predict future trends.

In the ancient Greek and Roman worlds, there seems to have been the beginning of an approach to systematized graphology: Julius Caesar's meticulous autograph and his style of setting out a page were noted by Suetonius. The Chinese, too, were aware of the characteristics of their calligraphic style and its relationship to personality.

In medieval Europe most of the writing was done by monkish scribes who wrote in a very decorated, formal style which left little room for character-revealing personal idiosyncracies. It was not until 1622 that the first notable book on graphology was published – Camillo Baldo's *The Means of Knowing the Habits and Qualities of a Writer by his Letters*. However, Baldo's interest failed to ignite that of other scholars, until Lavater included an essay on graphology in his *Physiognomical Fragments* (1776). This was a very basic work, stating that "if the handwriting looks harmonious, it is easy to say something about the harmonious character of the writer."

Modern graphology

The study of handwriting as a key indicator of personality really began towards the end of the 19th century in Germany, when the physician George Preyer and the psychiatrist George Meyer concentrated on interpretation rather than the previous bland statements that a particular graphological characteristic indicated a particular personality trait. Dr Ludwig Klages further defined the new approach to the subject with the foundation in 1886 of the first graphological society examining what he called "the personal motive" in handwriting.

Since the turn of the century steady work has continued in the field with contributions by, amongst others, the Swiss Dr Max Pulver (a criminologist), the American Louise Rice, founder of the American Graphological Society in 1927, and the Harvard psychologists Gordon W Allport and Philip Vernon. By the 1970s, graphology was being taught in South American and European universities.

In a paper published in 1933 (*Studies of Expressive Movements*), Allport and Vernon summarized the modern attitude to graphology:

Handwriting provides material that is less artificial than [data from psychological] tests, and more convenient for analysis; and since it can be studied at leisure, it is superior to facial expression, gesture and gait, which are so fleeting and difficult to record . . . No one who has considered carefully the experimental and theoretical work on handwriting seems to deny the a priori case for graphology . . . It seems to be intricately woven with deep-lying determinants of conduct. Graphic movement is, therefore, expressive movement. If our thesis is correct that expressive acts are not specific and unrelated to one another, then handwriting itself will show consistencies with other expressions of personality.

As a predictive tool, graphology is of general rather than specific use. No sample of handwriting will reveal what is going to happen tomorrow, but it may help employers to gauge the potential of prospective employees, counsellors to assess the compatibility of partners in an emotional relationship, paediatricians to suggest possible careers for young people, or psychologists to evaluate areas of a parent/child relationship. It can tell us about our own physical and mental health even before we are aware of it by revealing, say, tension and anxiety in a tightening up of the autograph.

Graphology predicts how people will act in the future by reading their personality as expressed in their handwriting. Graphologists claim, in fact, that the handwriting is a mirror of the character. Their art or science is extremely complex, and in the following pages we can offer little more than a primer; but sufficient information is provided for the reader to make a start on what is a fascinating and persuasive field of study.

The zones

One of the most important indications for graphologists is the placing of the hand-writing within three *zones* – middle, upper and lower. When learning to write, many people use lined note-paper and are taught to space their letters so that they sit on a middle line with the upper loops reaching an upper line and the lower loops a lower one. If you bear this in mind, the three zones will immediately become apparent.

To graphologists, the middle zone is the one containing the "small" letters *a, c, e, i, m, n, o, r, s, u, v, w*, and *x*: the letters *b, d, h, k, l*, and *t* enter the upper zone; the letters *g, j, p, q, y* and (sometimes) *z* enter the lower; and the letter *f* enters all three zones. Capital letters are of course another matter and will be dealt with below.

The formation of letters lying in the *middle zone* relates to the character of the writer and his self-awareness. When these sit

comfortably within their zone, steady upon the line, they may indicate a steady personality. If they occasionally fall above or below their zone they show a tendency for the writer to be easily influenced; if they seem to have little or no relation to their zone, not only straying outside it but also varying in size, this may indicate someone not fully confident of his own identity – it is often seen in the writing of adolescents. If middle zone letters are larger than those going above or below, a practical and down-to-earth person may be indicated.

The *upper zone* is concerned with thought, artistic temperament and spiritual development. The heavier the emphasis on this zone, the more marked the movement away from earth to air, from the real to the ideal.

The *lower zone* is thoroughly materialistic, but also concerns itself with instinct and emotion – including sexual emotion.

Handwriting in which middle-zone letters rise into the upper zone therefore suggests an aspiration towards the intellectual or spiritual. Letters which remain in the middle zone suggest an average, middle-of-the-road lifestyle and character. If there is an emphasis towards the lower zone, with, say, very heavy loops to the *g*s or *y*s, you may expect a sensual, earthy character.

Graphology: Preparing the ground

The essential piece of equipment you will need here is a magnifying glass of about 2 × magnification. However a second glass of 4 × is very useful, and you will also need a ruler marked out in millimetres.

As with other disciplines, it is important from the beginning to keep notes and establish files. Begin by keeping handwritten letters and their envelopes – but we should point out that some graphologists disqualify envelopes on the grounds that we sometimes (but not always!) make our handwriting artificially neat when addressing letters.

It is best to mount each letter in a looseleaf file, with a plain sheet opposite it on which you can write a summary of the known characteristics of the writer. Note their age, sex, marital status, occupation, temperament, hobbies – anything which establishes their identity.

You can group the samples together according to the similarity of their writing rather than their characters – for instance, all very small handwriting could be kept together. You will find that as your collection of samples mounts, you will be able to gauge automatically how each example should be filed. As the collection builds up, make notes to add to the personality summary opposite each sample. Gradually you will be able to attempt an interpretation of the writing of people unknown to you.

Interpretation

As regards size of handwriting, the general rule is that lower-case or "small" (i.e. not capital) letters are considered average in size if about 3mm in height. With practice you will not need to measure the letter size – your eye will tell you into which category they fall – but at first it may be useful to rule two lines 3mm apart on a piece of tracing paper, which you can place over the handwriting to help you evaluate its size.

Categories of size are necessarily very rough; but in general large handwriting is held to indicate the extravert, confident type, while small writing may suggest an introverted, thoughtful, perhaps academic person, with a greater ability to concentrate on detail. Handwriting of average size may suggest a balanced character. It does seem that small writing indicates the thinker, and large handwriting the doer; but small handwriting may also mark an over-modest person, perhaps with an inferiority complex, while a large "hand" may suggest someone self-important and boastful. However, to graphologists the formation of letters, together with other information, may overrule and will certainly modify indications suggested by the mere size of the writing.

Slant

The upright letters are seldom completely vertical in handwriting; most examples slant either to right or left. Graphologists find the direction and degree of the slant important in interpretation,

students with this graphological characteristic.

The lines

You can sometimes only judge the straightness of the lines of a sample when it is written on plain unlined

for it relates closely to the emotional balance of the writer.

The degree of inclination of the slant should not usually be more than 45° from the vertical; more than this is extreme (see diagram above).

In general, the slant is more often to the right, or forward, than to the left, or backward. There is something to be said for regarding average writing as having a slight forward slant. Most schools seem to turn out

paper, although there are extreme cases when the writer will simply ignore the ruled lines. Sometimes an entire piece of writing will slant determinedly uphill or downhill. If you are uncertain, turn the page upside down; the writing will betray its natural sense of direction when divorced from meaning.

Uphill writing tends to denote the optimistic and ambitious;
downhill writing indicates the pessimistic and depress-

ive;
straight firm lines suggest a well-balanced, straightforward person.

Pressure

The popularity of the ballpoint pen has posed problems for graphologists in the judging of *pressure* – the signs of pressure exerted by a nib pen vary to some extent from those of a ballpoint. You will learn to discriminate through practice – studying the back of the paper may help, if it is fairly thin. In general, an even pressure denotes health and wellbeing; uneven pressure may indicate ill-health or imbalance within the personality. Heavy pressure is fairly common, suggesting a sensual, energetic nature, whereas extremely light pressure, the mark of a sensitive, critical nature, is comparatively rare; it may also indicate a lack of vitality.

Connections

One of the first things a graphologist looks at is *connections* – the way in which we join, or fail to join, the letters of our words together. Connections fall into four groups: *garlands, angularities, arcades* and *threads*. Writing in which almost every letter of every word is connected to the next denotes a rational mind; those who do not use fully joined-up writing are often intuitive and even psychic. But remember that

it is common to break a word when dotting an *i* or crossing a *t*; ignore these when evaluating an autograph for connections.

The *garland* type of connection, flowing and smooth, indicates an easygoing, sympathetic, friendly personality, someone who is probably optimistic and sincere; in an extreme form it can be an indication of an over-feminine or sentimental nature.

Angular connections, spiky and assertive, denote someone firm and decisive, orderly and thorough, with a nature that is based on reason rather than emotion – at worst callous, intolerant and aggressive.

The *arcade* connection seems often hesitant and unsure, and can illustrate a personality in which there is a strong element of formality, secretiveness and pride; someone independent, trustworthy, but perhaps shy, with a strong sense of tradition, who may be naturally suspicious.

Finally, the people who connect their letters together with a mere *thread* – a wavering line – are far from the indecisive type; though perhaps nervous and emotional, they tend to be versatile, adaptable and instinctive, collecting impressions and evaluating them thoughtfully.

179

Garland

Angularity

Arcade

Thread

Beginnings and Endings

Graphologists pay particular attention to the way in which we begin and end each letter – the *initials* and *terminals*. We are taught to begin and end each letter with a careful stroke which is the way we join one letter to the next. As we grow up, the initials tend to drop away, and the terminals change, sometimes dramatically, becoming less a means of joining the letters together than a gesture of self-expression.

Initials: First, look to see if there *is* an initial stroke – the difference between (1) and (2). An absence of an introductory stroke generally means that the writer is

self-assured and without doubts about identity; forthright, though open to the opinion of others. If there is an initial stroke, ask yourself how prominent it is. A long stroke (3) can indicate pride, but without self-assurance, and perhaps with less confidence than one might expect. A stroke which begins below its zone

and travels upwards (4) can indicate a hasty temper.
Terminals: Some letters show the terminal stroke more than others: *e* and *o*, in particular. A very short terminal (1) suggests carefulness with money and affection – even stinginess. A really abrupt terminal (look at the *ys* – (2) rather than (3)) denotes a rude person.

A long, graceful terminal (4) suggests the opposite – generosity (both financial and emotional) and a sense of humour. The higher the tail of a long terminal the more marked the generous instinct. If it tends to curl inwards (5), this could suggest that the emotional instinct may be turned in on itself and become egoism.

Loops

Letters with loops falling either into the upper or lower zone are important: upward loops are an index of spirituality and idealism, lower ones of the writer's physical characteristics.

Upper loops: The *larger* the loops of the *l*, *h*, *b*, and *k*, the more imaginative and idealistic the writer; if the lines of the writing go uphill, this characteristic is strengthened. If a loop is found in the writer's *ds* and *ts* (6) there is a suggestion of a need for attention.

Lower loops: A *wide* loop (7) shows physical robust-

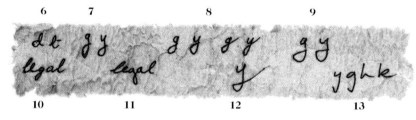

ness, especially if considerable pressure is involved; if it *slants* to the left (8) there is a strong element of mother love; a loop which is *wide* towards its bottom (9) shows a well-developed sex drive.

If upper and lower loops seem *equally well-*

developed (10), the personality itself is well-balanced – soundest when the loops are not so large as to unbalance the autograph in general. Handwriting in which the loops seem to *slope* in different directions (11) reveals emotional imbalance. A loop with a *flourish*

(12) suggests a showy, even conceited, individual. Loopletters with *lines* rather than loops (13) denote determination, perhaps obstinacy, especially with heavy downstrokes. Very *short loops* may indicate lack of imagination (upper) or of physical strength (lower).

Dotting the I's

There is disagreement among graphologists about the importance of the placing of the dot associated with the letter *i*. Dr Irene Marcuse, for instance, a distinguished graphologist, says that the dots above the *is* are "merely additions to the letters". The furthest she will go is to suggest that if well-centred, the writer is "punctual and exact", if placed high, they suggest "idealism and optimism", if ahead of the letter, impulsiveness, and if behind it, procrastination. Other

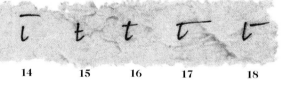

experts in general agree with Dr Marcuse, merely adding glosses of their own. For present purposes, her rough guideline can be accepted as sufficient.

Crossing the T's

T-bars, however, are a different matter – everyone agrees that they are an

important guide to the writer's temperament. A *short* t-bar shows lack of confidence and an unwillingness to accept responsibility; an *absence* of t-bars (and perhaps of i-dots, too) can indicate someone impulsive to the point of declining to accept responsibility – or absent-minded. A *high* t-bar

(14), floating above the letter, suggests shortness of temper. A very *low* t-bar (15) suggests caution, lack of self-confidence, maybe proneness to depression. Relatively well-proportioned t-bars in the "correct" position (16) reflect a moderate, conventional personality; particularly *long* t-bars (17) show leadership, enterprise, dynamism. If the bar is not connected to the *t* itself (18), it suggests that while enterprise is still shown, there is also a certain degree of impatience.

Capital letters

The plainer the form of capital letters, the better-educated the writer tends to be – and not only in the sense of formal education. Highly decorated capital letters betray showy, self-dramatizing, ignorant people. Plain letters (which may be unconventional in form, but are economically formed and without decoration), suggest assurance and self-confidence. Capitals in proportion to the other letters – neither too large nor

19   20   21   22

too small – denote a person with an excellent sense of proportion.

Large capitals are generally a mark of opinionated people with a tendency to social climbing and egoism. *Small* capitals, however,

can be a mark of enviable modesty and simplicity, but also of self-negation and lack of confidence.

The "I"

The way we denote ourself – the "I" in our writing – is

sometimes given too much importance, but usually contributes something to an assessment of character. A small *I* suggests modesty – but look at the loops: an open loop (19) shows a degree of confidence, a closed one (20) obstinacy. A small, closed *I* (21) suggests an inferiority complex, while a simple vertical stroke (22) denotes self-assurance and a logical mind. An *I* which leans backwards may indicate over-reliance on others.

Composition on the page

Spacing: We consider two ways in which the words in an autograph are spaced: the horizontal – or the spaces between the words – and the vertical – or the spaces between the lines. Balanced spacing, both horizontally and vertically, shows education and a well-organized, sensitive and cultured mind. Cramped horizontal spacing betrays a disorganized mind, and sprawling horizontal spacing disorganized thought and inhibition. Cramped vertical spacing, with the lower loops of one line overlaying the upper loops of the following one, can show sexual inhibition. Make allowances for the mood of the writer, however – and this applies to other facets of graphology.

Layout: The "design" of a letter can also say much about the writer. A sprawling, disorganized letter reflects a mind similarly messy – though perhaps, as we have already suggested, it is only temporarily so because of haste.

The *left-hand margin* is important however, because we choose it (the right-hand margin may be

regulated by the words themselves). A wide left-hand margin shows considerable reading, and is usually a mark of education (though if too self-conscious it can reflect snobbishness). The narrower the left-hand margin, the greater the degree of caution, care, even perhaps meanness. An irregular margin, narrowing or widening towards the bottom, usually signifies carelessness or perhaps tiredness.

The *right-hand margin*, when wide – as wide perhaps as the left-hand one – is a mark of shyness and inhibition. A margin so narrow as to be virtually nonexistent shows vitality and haste.

Upper and lower margins are less revealing, but a wide upper margin may denote respect towards the recipient of a letter, while a narrow one is more informal. A wide lower margin (if it does not simply mark the end of the letter, of course) can also indicate respect, if not a desire to impress. A narrow lower margin may tend to be left by someone who is naturally verbose, has a lot to say, and is eager to communicate.

181

Signature

Every graphologist agrees that the calligraphy of the autograph signature is distinct from handwriting in general. It is not safe to take the signature only as a reliable guide to character, although the prevalence of typewriters and word processors sometimes means that the signature is the only personal mark the writer makes on paper.

It can safely be said that we develop our signature fairly carefully as we grow up: most children write their name unnumerable times on various pieces of paper, gradually evolving a signature they like, and which they eventually adopt as a

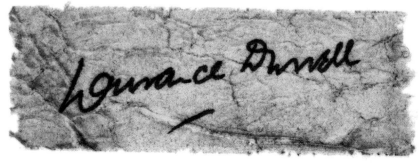

mark as personal as their palm-print. It rarely varies throughout life.

It is obvious that an over-large signature suggests pride, and an over-small one, modesty. If the signature is larger than the ordinary writing, it indicates self-confidence – though there is

a difference between a signature large enough to be readily legible and one over-large and flamboyant. If the signature is smaller than the usual handwriting, the writer may be modest but again there is a difference between modesty and servility.

A signature with a *back-*

ward slope suggests someone in some way repressed.

A firm horizontal line beneath the name denotes someone who will stand no nonsense and is capable of taking responsibility. An ornate underlining indicates showiness and a tendency to play for effect.

Dreaming

Dreams are universal, and have always been regarded as important. From the earliest times to the present day, they have been seen as messages, whether from gods, as was once believed, or from our own unconscious minds, as is now widely thought to be the case. Interpretation of dreams is a question of decoding the message so that it makes sense to you. Whether or not they are "prophetic", they can certainly tell us a lot about how we should approach the future.

Dreams were once thought to be divine messages, and to this day they still contain a mysterious, often uncanny quality. This may be because they are essentially messages from our unconscious to our conscious selves, expressed in a coded, symbolic form particular to the dreamer. They may be referring to our innermost desires and fears, or commenting on everyday events, fulfilling wishes or jumbling together disparate thoughts and fancies. And because they frequently look forward to the future, the dream "message" may indeed have a prophetic quality.

Small impressions, noted in the course of our waking existence but not registered by the waking mind, may form the basis of a prophetic dream. For example, a person may unconsciously note a small defect in the brake pedal of a vehicle, but dismiss it from his or her mind. The worry will emerge, perhaps, in the form of an accident dream – and subsequently an accident arising from the fault may well occur. The same sequence of events may herald an illness; unconscious awareness of a symptom is translated into a dream that warns the dreamer of a real problem.

The earliest dream book goes back to ancient Egypt, some 1,300 years before Christ. The Greeks, too, believed that dreams were divine messages, with particular reference to disease; they set aside sacred places where the "incubation" of dreams could be induced, suggesting a cure for the dreamer's ailments. In addition to the treatment of illness, the Greeks believed that dreams "are infused into men for their advantage and instruction".

Many cultures, such as that of the Australian aborigines, set great store by dreams. In common with other people, they believe that dreams are concerned with the adventures of the soul when it leaves the body during sleep. Naturally, these often have a prophetic quality. The researches of Freud and Jung make great use of dreams, and provide much of the basis for modern dream therapy. Terminology and interpretation of dreams vary enormously, but a belief in the significance of dreams is constant.

Some apparently prophetic dreams may carry unconscious warnings. But what about dreams affecting other people? The popular press frequently comes up with examples of, say, the death of a prominent individual being foreseen by dreamers. However, sceptics will point out that, given the prevalence of dreaming, some of these "prophetic" dreams must by the law of averages "come true". Several people claim to have dreamed of the assassination of President Kennedy on November 22 1963. But how many people dreamt of his assassination on days when it failed to occur? Nevertheless, there are still a number of spectacular examples of predictive dreams that do not easily respond to these explanations.

How to recall and analyse your dreams

Some readers may think that they never dream, and that they are therefore excluded from the fascinating possibility of being able to glimpse the future in this way. But this is not really so. Thousands of experiments in dream laboratories, under controlled conditions, have proved beyond doubt that everyone dreams, not once but several times during a normal night's sleep. The fact is that many people rarely recall their dreams, and some never do. The latter are those who "never dream"! You can prove this for yourself. The very fact that you *want* to remember your dreams may start a change of pattern. So begin by telling yourself firmly, just before you go to sleep, that you will be dreaming and will remember at least one of your dreams. When you go to bed, keep a pencil and paper by your bedside. On waking, lie still for a moment, then reach for the pencil and paper and write a word or two that will summarize the theme of the dream. It is important to record just how you felt when dreaming – frightened or confident, elated or bored, stimulated or without emotion. When you get up, transcribe these notes as fully as possible into a larger notebook; you may find that, while writing, you

will remember more details. Your dream recall will get better with practice. After making notes for a night or two, you will remember more and more clearly.

As we have pointed out, most psychologists believe that dreams are messages from our unconscious to our conscious selves; we are talking to ourselves about our problems, reminding ourselves of events and emotions submerged and forgotten. Dreams can be enormously helpful when we have an important decision to make, and can really help to solve problems. Kekulé's famous discovery of the benzine molecule during a dream is only one example.

Many of the most impressive predictive dreams seem to be about other people rather than yourself. If you have had a worrying dream about a friend, it is worth checking up to reassure yourself, but be careful not to be alarmist.

A dream about yourself will reflect your general attitude as well as the nature of the dream. As we have seen, a dream of a motor accident could indicate an unconscious awareness of some mechanical defect. But you should never lose sight of the fact that dreams work in symbols, so it could very well mean that your unconscious thinks you are heading for disaster at home or work, and the dream may have nothing to do with your car. Such predictive dreams may be a crystallization of your own attitude to future events – as warnings or information.

One of the best examples of dreams as warnings concerned the Duke of Portland, who helped organize the coronation of King Edward VII in 1902. He recalled the following dream just before the ceremony:

The state coach had to pass through the arch at the Horse Guards on the way to Westminster Abbey. I dreamed that it stuck in the arch, and that some of the Life Guards on duty were compelled to hew off the crown upon the coach before it could be freed. When I told the Crown Equerry, Colonel Ewart, he laughed and said, "What do dreams matter?" "At all events," I replied, "let us have the coach and the arch measured." So this was done and to my astonishment, we found that the arch was nearly two feet too low to allow the coach to pass through.

Of course, it is possible that Portland had subconsciously noticed the height of the coach relative to the arch, but the arch would originally have admitted the coach – only recently had road works lifted the surface to a higher level. Whatever the explanation for that dream, it was useful; noting such dreams is obviously worthwhile.

One way in which dreams can help is in medical diagnosis. If you dream part of your body is in pain, it is worth noting the fact. There may be a simple explanation: if you dream that your foot is painful and wake to find it in a cramp, you can discount it. But if you dream you are suffering from pain in a healthy limb, or of any illness of which there is no sign, it will be worth consulting your doctor. It is now recognized that the body can signal in sleep an illness not yet sufficiently advanced to be noticeable when awake.

Dream Symbols

The study of dreams is fascinating and can reveal much of your state of mind and feelings. Interpreting them is not easy, for events experienced in dreams are hardly ever what they seem. We can appear in our dreams as something else – we could be the telephone ringing (we have an urgent message for someone), or a boat running ashore (into danger). So examine everything you remember and apply them in some way to your life. We have no space here for a complete dictionary of dream symbols but we can look at some themes which almost everyone sometimes experiences, and suggest ways they may apply to your future – usually in the form of action you might take to change or mitigate situations.

If your dream recurs regularly, note it carefully each time, recording any difference from previous versions – the differences will often provide clues to your progress in tackling the problems represented by the dream. You will instinctively "know" when a dream is important and you will remember it much more vividly. Remember, even experienced psychoanalysts can only help discover the key to your dreams; only *you* can decide what they mean.

It seems probable that the great majority of predictive dreams are sparked off by an unconscious awareness of a situation, based on observations actually made but no longer recalled to the conscious mind. On the other hand, there are well-authenticated instances of unaccountably prophetic dreams: Lincoln's vision of his own coffin, shortly before his assassination, and Bishop Lanyi's dream of Archduke Franz Ferdinand's murder in 1914 are two of the best known.

People tend to worry particularly about dreams of disasters, and wonder whether their dreams may be precognitive; but you should never forget that dreams work in symbols, and it is very rare indeed for one to literally "come true". As the noted dream researcher Ann Faraday has pointed out in *The Dream Game:* "For every uncanny story that gets written up in the press, there are thousands of equally vivid dreams about friends dying, air crashes, floods, war breaking out, or presidents being assassinated, which are never literally fulfilled."

Only by systematically recording your dreams, in the way we have suggested, will you able to establish their predictive quality for yourself. Remember, everybody dreams. If you take the trouble to recall and examine your dream life, you will open up a fascinating world which will prove enormously rewarding, whether or not it enables you to glimpse future events.

Weather
Dreams of the weather almost always relate to our attitude to life – as it is now or as we think it may become. A dream of a storm may relate to a disagreement in waking life – and our dream often tells us what our true attitude to it really is. You may have either sheltered in a corner or strode on, braving the elements. Consider your waking action closely – such a dream may encourage you to take a firm line.

Pursuit
Dreams in which we are being chased are common. Occasionally we are doing the chasing – but it is the former type of dream which is often worrying or frightening. Consider whether someone, or something, is pursuing you, and what they might represent. If your pursuer is gaining on you, you may be failing to come to grips with a problem. If you are doing the chasing, this could be a positive sign – you are in control.

Landscape
The setting of your dream adventures often indicates the area in your life on which the dream concentrates. If wandering through particularly beautiful countryside, this may suggest that you relax and enjoy life more; a rough craggy landscape may suggest problems at home or work. Your attitude to the landscape is important; does it frighten or delight you?

Animals, birds
The kind of animal or bird in your dreams, and its context, can be so various that it is difficult for anyone else to suggest what it may mean. Dreams of animals are often puns; a man who dreams of a wolf, for example, may be planning a seduction. Think particularly of your basic "animal" instincts and how they are being satisfied.

Food and Drink
If on a diet, your dream may have an obvious connotation: starving men often dream about delicious meals. If this is not the case, consider the nature of the food you are eating and how you are eating it. Were you entertaining friends in your dream meal? If so, have you something important to share with them?

Travel

Dreams of aircraft or cars crashing or ships sinking just before a journey may often be due to tension – although if very detailed, examine them more seriously. Exploring strange landscapes in your dreams can suggest you are ready to undergo some new experience. Dreaming of travelling without a ticket often relates to a feeling of inadequacy.

Disasters

Dreams of disaster are among the most common of prophetic dreams. Some dreams clearly merit action: if you dream that the brakes of your car have failed, it is worth checking – you may have unconsciously noticed something wrong. But remember that for every apparently prophetic dream of disaster, thousands of others are never fulfilled.

Crowds

Dreams involving crowds can refer to many areas of our personalities; they often involve claustrophobia. Crowds can also represent "the establishment" – government, employers, even the family. The mood of the dream will be very important in understanding it.

Sex

Freud saw sex in almost every dream symbol; this attitude is now criticized. Overtly sexual dreams should be enjoyed for themselves. If frightening or violent, try to relate them to what you feel about sex in waking life. Recurrent dreams of sexual violence suggests you should consult a therapist. Try not to be worried by "disgusting" sexual dreams; unconscious needs are often expressed like this. Remember that no-one places disgusting images in our dreams except ourselves and they have a purpose. If, for example, a heterosexual has a homosexual dream, it is a reminder that to some extent we are all bisexual and may relate to some unkind or chauvinistic attitude we should reconsider. It does not necessarily predict a change in our sexual inclinations.

Nudity

The embarrassing dream of being without one's clothes in public normally relates to insecurity. What attitude do the people in the dream take to you? If they are aghast, then think again before revealing yourself too freely to them in your waking life. Do you feel "exposed" in some way, or are you apprehensive that too much is about to be revealed of your private life?

Water

Water symbolizes our unconscious, and any dream involving the sea, in particular, might be suggesting that you pay more attention to a lingering psychological problem. If you are swimming, how strongly? This may indicate how you are dealing with a problem. If you are washing yourself, perhaps the idea of cleansing suggests re-examining an attitude.

Birth and Death

Dreams of death often upset people. The evidence is that they do not signify physical death but change – often positive change. To dream of your own death probably means that you are about to undergo considerable psychological change, which your unconscious has noticed before you have. The death of someone else often signifies the same and you may be able to help them considerably. It is rare to dream of the death of an enemy: one indication of the positivity of such dreams. Birth dreams have much the same significance – often referring to the birth of a new project.

Fire

Fire represents energy – so what the fire is attacking is significant; it may suggest more vigorous application to some problem, or indeed that someone is attacking you. Fire also has a sexual significance, so it may imply that you are about to become violently attracted to someone. A dream of walking unscathed through fire obviously suggests needless worry about some problem which is not as fierce as you suppose – but an uncomfortably hot fire may suggest withdrawal from some situation.

185

Flying

Almost every textbook relates dreams of flying to sexuality, and there is often a sexual implication – though usually one of simple pleasure. But the pleasure may be in being high enough to see over an entire landscape; or perhaps you are a bird of prey – or the victim of one, which may say much about your job and your attitudes to colleagues. Dreaming of effortless flight often signals the wish to be free of everyday problems.

Biorhythms

All life on earth has, since its inception, been governed by, and responded to, the natural cycles that influence us all, whether from within our bodies or from external sources. But beneath these self-evident rhythms beat thousands of others, more or less well known.

Every woman will have been familiar since puberty with her body's menstrual cycle. But the bodies of all human beings have their own cycles – from the beating of the heart (about 76 times every minute) to the 128-day life cycle of a red blood cell. Besides all these, there exist three other discernible rhythms – biorhythms, which we now know affect our present and future lives with inescapable power.

The physician Hippocrates 2,000 years ago noticed that human beings appeared subject to good and bad days irrespective of their general state of health, and that medical therapy was more or less effective depending on when it was administered. There matters rested until the end of the last century, when two of the three biorhythms were discovered. In 1904

Dr Hermann Swoboda, professor of psychology at Vienna University published the results of his research over the previous decade, titled *The Periods of Human Life,* followed by *Studies on the Basis of Psychology.* These books postulated a 23-day physical cycle in all human beings and a 28-day emotional cycle (distinct from, though sometimes coinciding with, women's menstrual cycle). Swoboda was a methodical man. His final work, *The Year of Seven,* tried to prove his theories mathematically, which gained him an honorary degree.

Less fortunate was Wilhelm Fliess, born in 1859, a nose and throat specialist who observed for himself the 23- and 28-day cycles. He first suspected the existence of biorhythms when he noticed the variation in resistance to diseases among his patients on 23- and 28-day cycles. Fliess sought for a reason behind these cycles and turned to the basic hermaphroditic cell. Influenced by Freud, he reasoned that human beings, just like their cells, are profoundly bisexual. To the female element in the human body, Fliess ascribed the 28-day emotional cycle, to the male the 23-day physical rhythm. Fliess explained the fact that men undergo a 28-day emotional cycle by this elemental bisexuality.

Freud took up Fliess' theories in Vienna but, despite becoming President of the German Academy of Sciences, Fliess faced scepticism in his own country. It was another Austrian, Alfred Teltscher, a doctor at Innsbruck University, who noticed that his students' intellectual powers seemed to wax and wane in a 33-day cycle. This was accepted by Fliess and Swoboda who suggested that this cycle might be regulated by secretions of the pineal and thyroid glands. Since

then, research has confirmed their hypothesis, but for a long time it remained little more than that. It offended the "scientific" views of many in the medical world, although support came from the quite independent findings of Rexford Hersey and Michael John Bennett at Pennsylvania University, who had also discovered a 33-day intellectual cycle in the early 1930s. A comparative study by Hans Schwing, of the Swiss Federal Institute in Zurich, of accidents and accidental deaths, linked them clearly to the biorhythms of the individuals concerned, and it was in Switzerland that doctors and surgeons began to use biorhythms to determine the best time for operations.

Few people who check the pattern of their biorhythms fail to find the results useful when planning their lives: Triple critical, or even double critical days should be especially noted. There is plenty of empirical evidence that the strains of such days can affect the judgement. Of 204 accidents to

The theory of biorhythms

The theory is simple. All three cycles start at birth from a neutral baseline and continue their individual courses throughout life, ceasing only at death. The first half of each cycle is the "plus", ascending, progressive period, during which we are full of vigour and enthusiasm, be it physical, mental or emotional. This reaches a peak halfway through the positive phase, then starts to decline, through the baseline, into the negative or rejuvenatory period (comparable to a recuperative period after an operation). Halfway through this, the rhythm concerned will hit its nadir and start to climb again. All humans have these rhythms and all are affected by them, to a greater or lesser extent.

The days when each cycle moves from one phase to another (crossing the baseline) are called critical days. These critical days have been shown to attract far higher rates of accidents to the individuals concerned, and have therefore received much publicity. The most famous and tragic case was probably the warning given by George Thomnen on a radio interview on November 11, 1960, to Clark Gable, the actor, then in hospital recovering from a heart attack he had

suffered six days earlier while filming *The Misfits*. November 16 would be a critical day in Gable's physical rhythm, warned Thomnen; he was right, for Gable died of another heart attack that day. "Critical day" is something of a misnomer, however, both because the phase can last up to 48 hours and – more importantly – because it does *not* mean that accidents will definitely happen. Rather it serves as a warning that this is a time of exceptional vulnerability and the person should take special care.

There are at least six critical days each month, sometimes eight, in each person's biorhythms. This means that you are in the critical phase of at least one biorhythm for at least 20 percent of the time. But there are numerous days when a person may be in a double critical phase – when two of the rhythms are critical at the same time. These can be times to try to avoid over-exertion or special stress. And once in everyone's life comes the Grand Triple Critical Day, when all three rhythms reach the same stage as at birth and start again. This triple critical occurs 21, 252 days (or 58.2 years) after birth. (See p.188 for the exact calculations).

187

The three cycles

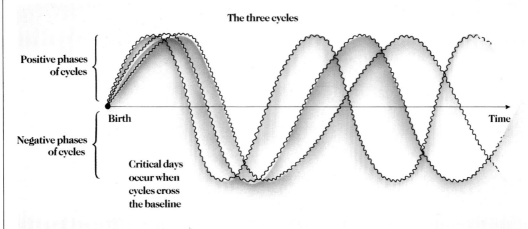

Positive phases of cycles

Birth

Time

Negative phases of cycles

Critical days occur when cycles cross the baseline

Calculating your own biorhythms

It is possible to buy gadgets such as personal calculators, computers or books of charts on which biorhythms can be automatically calculated. In the US, biorhythms have become so widely accepted that predictions can be obtained for a few cents from vending machines. In Europe, however, although some firms will provide a computer print-out showing critical days, it is still necesary to work out your own biorhythm charts but fortunatley the method is very straightforward.

1. Take your age at your next birthday
and multiply it by 365, the number of days in a year,
e.g. if you will be 50 next birthday .... *50 × 365 = 18,250*

2. Add the number of leap years you have lived through from your birth to your next birthday.
if this is 13 .... *18,250 + 13 = 18,263*

3. The emotional cycle is obtained by dividing by total by 28.
e.g. .... *18,263 ÷ 28 = 652 (remainder 7)*

4. The physical cycle is obtained by dividing the total by 23
e.g. .... *18,263 ÷ 23 = 794 (remainder 1)*

5. The intellectual cycle is obtained by dividing the total by 33
e.g. .... *18,263 ÷ 33 = 553 (remainder 14)*

6. The number of days you have left over in each case will be the number of days previous to your birthday on which each cycle crosses from negative to positive. So, in the case of the 50-year-old in our example whose next birthday is on, say, May 15, the emotional rhythm will go into positive on May 8, the physical rhythm will go into positive on May 14, and the intellectual rhythm will go into positive on May 1.

When you have calculated these three dates, you can work out your biorhythms for the rest of the year by simply counting the requisite number of days for each cycle backwards or forwards.

If you are using a calculator for the above calculations, you will probably find several figures appearing after the decimal point in the results. Ignore these – they are actually the "days left over" expressed as a fraction. To work out the actual number of days left over, work back through the calculation. For example, taking the intellectual cycle from our calculations above:

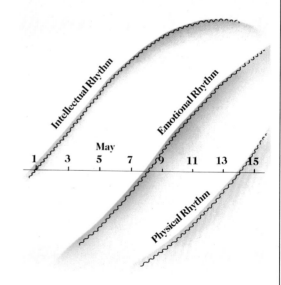

Using a calculator .... *18,263 ÷ 33 = 553.42424*

Delete numbers after decimal point .... *= 553*

Multiply by number of days in cycle .... *553 × 33 = 18,249*

Subtract new total from old .... *18,263 − 18,249 = 14*

So there are 14 days left over.

planes in the Swiss Air fleet which were studied by Dr Friedrich Pirchner, 70 per cent were found to have occurred when the pilot was experiencing a critical day. Professor Reinhold Bochow of Humboldt University, studying accidents involving agricultural machinery, concluded that such accidents were more than 171 times more likely to occur on critical than non-critical days.

Some official bodies now check the biorhythms of their employees: Swissair will not permit two pilots to share the same cockpit on days when the biorhythms of both are critical; the Zurich Municipal Transit Company cut the accident rate of its drivers by 50 per cent after applying a study of their biorhythms to the scheduling of routes.

In Japan, the Ohmi Railway Company, which administers a fleet of taxis and buses in Osaka and Kyoto, studied all accidents experienced by its drivers over five years, and found that between 59 and 61 percent had occurred when drivers' biorhythms were critical. The company issued all drivers with cards indicating their biorhythm patterns, and within a year the accident rate was cut by half, and continued to fall against an overall trend showing a rising general accident rate.

The medical profession is slow to accept theories of this kind; but just as the most conventional doctors are now forced to accept the use of acupuncture as an anaesthetic, so many are paying attention to biorhythms as a means of predicting the course of illnesses, and in suggesting when there may be a particular susceptibility to infection.

Neil Armstrong (*above* and *top, left*) became the first man ever to land on the Moon on July 20 1969, after piloting the capsule down himself. Then, on the 24th, he experienced the immense strain of earth re-entry. On both those days his mental and emotional rhythms were in peak form for balanced, lucid judgement, as he was born August 5 1930. His physical rhythm, however, was in a negative phase but in that low or no gravity environment physical strength was less important. Interestingly, July 16, the day of blast off, had been a physically critical day for him and he had experienced a triple mini-critical on July 22 – luckily while merely travelling to the Moon.

Runes

The Runic alphabet was an early form of Germanic writing, and was in use throughout the whole North European world, including Scandinavia and Anglo-Saxon England. But runes have also always possessed a magical and divinatory significance. Traditionally the property of the one-eyed god Odin, lord of death and rebirth, they were used by shamanic rune-masters to cast spells, heal sick people, protect sacred sites, and call up the dead. They were also essential for foretelling the future.

From the first, each of the 24 runes in the alphabet had its own special name. Almost as soon as the alphabet was written down (and the oldest runic writing we know of dates from the middle of the third century), people began to use its letters for magical purposes, such as casting spells, healing the sick and in particular for divining the future – a purpose for which they have been used ever since. Although the phrase "casting the runes" has always remained familiar, it is only in the last few years that this method of prediction has once more become popular.

Runes appear originally to have been used by the rune-masters as a means of interpreting omens of the northern pagan gods – in particular, Woden or Odin (the counterpart of Mercury). When Bishop Ulphilas (Wulfila), the apostle of the Goths, translated the Bible in the 4th century and came to St Mark's allusion to "the mystery of the Kingdom of God", he used the word *runa* for mystery.

The legend told by the Rune masters connects the runes with Odin: one of his personae was as shaman or wandering wise man (though he was also warrior, lawgiver and lover of Jovian proportions). His myth paints him in cloak and broad-brimmed hat, one-eyed and carrying his blackthorn staff. One of the legends of his life relates how for nine days and nights he hung upside down from Yggdrasil, the "world tree", until he perceived some runestones on the ground beneath him. Stretching painfully, he picked them up – and was immediately set free by their magic.

The rune-masters and mistresses were figures of power and authority, casting spells to assure good weather, to affirm love and to bring good or ill fortune to individuals. An anonymous thirteenth century writer has described one:

Her cloak was studded with precious stones around its hem, and upon her head was a hood made from the fur of white cats. In her hand she bore a gnarled staff and about her waist a belt, gathering her cloak about her and bearing a purse of charms (runes). . .

The rune-masters apparently made their own runes, carving them from stone, wood or leather and staining them with magical preparations (sometimes said to include blood). Consulted upon a coming event, they would scatter the runes on the ground and then make their predictions, "reading" only those which landed with the lettered sides uppermost.

Runes today

The original magical symbolism of the separate runes has been lost. The American anthropologist and linguist Ralph Blum, perhaps the best known practitioner, freely admits in his *The Book of Runes* that his interpretation of the significance of each letter is simply his own: he sat looking at each rune, "meditating on it, copying down what came to me". This was an entirely proper way of going about providing a set of modern interpretations, for the runes, like all oracles, work in this way: they bring out the unconscious meaning of things, expressed to most people only through half-forgotten dreams.

In the following pages, however, we offer our own interpretation of the runes, linked to many predictive techniques, including astrology, numerology and the *I Ching*. Just as with the coins by which the *I Ching* hexagrams are chosen or the cards of the Tarot, there is no magic in the stones or wooden blocks which bear the rune symbols. As Mr Blum puts it, the runes "bring people to themselves – connect them with their intuitive process". Many psychologists use the runes as a tool in analysis and counselling, as others use the *I Ching*.

Making your own runes

If you find it difficult to obtain a set of runes, by all means make your own – from a set of similar-sized stones or pebbles on which you can scratch or paint the symbols, or from wooden blocks. Many specialists suggest that runes made by the person who intends to use them work best of all.

The Runes Interpreted

The Runes have both Old English and Old German names: *Feoh* in Old English becomes *Fehu* in Germanic, *Fyd* becomes *Naupiz*. We have chosen to use the Old English names, in the traditional order of *Futhark* (the name comes from the first five letters of the alphabet). We have for convenience used a modern transliteration of ancient letters when printing the names of the runes.

There are 24 runes and one blank one, called *Wyrd* or fate.

1. Feoh – *Harmony, fertility*
The rune associated with good luck and the good things of life, and particularly with property and possessions – chiefly cattle originally, and there is a strong association with the astrological sign of Taurus. Though promising material gain, it warns against self-indulgence and stagnation. *Feoh* encourages creativity, underlines reciprocal love and offers fulfilment.

2. Ur – *Power, energy*
Ur is the symbol of a wild ox whose immense energy and power must be tamed if it is to be used positively and constructively. *Ur* suggests that the querant is entering a period of change, growth and greater self-awareness. Opportunities may arise out of setbacks and even tension and strain. It also suggests sexual passions.

3. Thorn – *Strength, good news*
A restraining rune which encourages the careful consideration of any situation – temporary inaction, a pause for thought, whether in everyday matters or in psychological development. However much we have achieved, we must now for a time be circumspect. The rune is sometimes called "the gateway" – we must pass through it, but should first consider what lies on this side. The gate may lead to confrontation with an unknown danger.

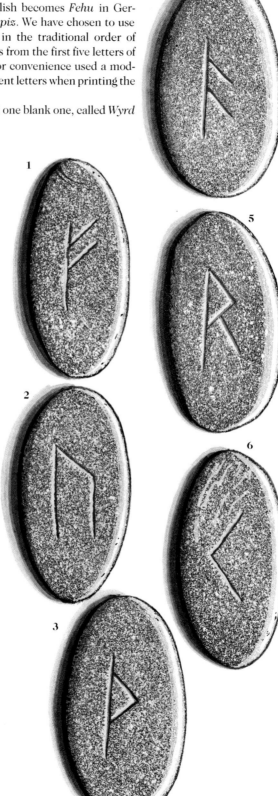

4. Os – *Odin, wisdom*
This is the rune of the spoken word and communication, linked to Mercury, traditionally the communicator with divine powers. It also relates to Odin, the god who had so painfully acquired wisdom through hanging on Yggdrasil. It suggests wisdom and help from someone older. Improved communication, possibly of a magical or psychic nature, perhaps with colleagues, is also indicated, but beware of tricksters. Woden's day, Wednesday, is the same day as Mercury's in the Romance languages.

5. Rad – *Wheels, journeying*
This rune signifies long journeys – traditionally on horseback – particularly pleasant ones. (*Rad* itself means wheel in German.) This journey may be either spiritual – in the sense of someone's personal development, or even the last journey of the soul to Valhalla, home of the gods – or it can mean that a message is being sent or received. It can also refer to the lessons a querant must learn. Again, there is a link to Mercury, the messenger god.

6. Cen – *Creative fire, light*
This, the rune of light and fire, enables the querant to see the current situation more clearly. The accent also is on fieriness and fertility – and on the clearing away of obstacles and the attainment of objectives through enthusiasm and optimism. *Cen* has all the fiery energy and force of the planet Mars – it is the torchbearer of the runic family – and also passion and sensual desire. If blocked, this can impede a person's progress.

7. Gyfu – *Gifts, generosity*
Gyfu literally means "gift offered to the gods" and is, appropriately, the sign of gifts and giving. Here is friendship, generosity and simple joy. It is also the rune of partnership, and a splendid one to draw if about to become engaged or married or start a business partnership. All partnerships require a certain degree of sacrifice and this should not be underestimated: selfishness can ruin all types of sharing. There is also a warning against laziness and indecision, but it is a generally positive rune.

8. Wyn – *Joy, happiness*
A rune which suggests joy, strength and fruition. The querant – perhaps frustrated by excessive self-criticism – is encouraged to recognize and enjoy a well-deserved change for the better. There is also a slightly equivocal element of sexuality: though physical enjoyment is emphasized, there is a suggestion of deception. While the individual's experience of love and life may be broadened, it may be at some expense. Possible complications and difficulties should not be ignored.

9. Hoegl – *Hail, setbacks*
This rune suggests a frustrating and difficult time with unexpected problems and setbacks or illness. The querant must be encouraged not to allow a philosophical approach to problems to degenerate into hopelessness, or to permit frustration to boil over into rashness. There is a strong possibility that changes are in the offing which will affect the long-term future. There may be a certain amount of hardship and some struggle, but additional effort will lead to increased prestige.

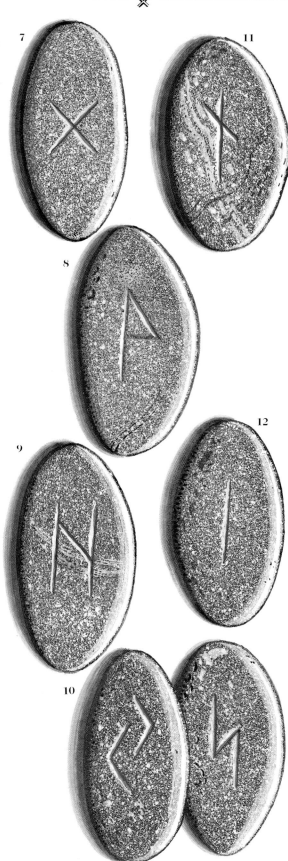

10. Nyd – *Need, necessity*
This important rune emphasizes the need for patience, so encourage the querant to consider every action carefully before taking it, as well as the motives behind the actions. He or she may be his or her own worst enemy. Greed or desire can easily prove destructive. Emotional, material and spiritual riches are not far away but attainment depends on a softly-softly approach. If we are dissatisfied with our lot in life, even if with good reason, it is *we* who must do something about it.

11. Is – *Ice, coldness*
Frustration and obstacles are the keynote of this rune and patience is needed to face them. There is an association with the idea of ice, of coldness between people, especially in family relationships. The querant may be in a situation in which manoeuvre seems impossible – or perhaps he or she lacks awareness of what is really going on. For the present, the querant should sit tight until the sun breaks through and the thaw comes, when new emotions and outlooks may emerge.

12. Ger – *Year, natural cycle*
This represents the annual cycle of the seasons, especially the time of harvest, and when it is drawn or cast it relates to work in progress, encouraging the individual to persevere and drive on towards ultimate success. Short cuts will be disastrous: the natural process of sowing, tending and finally reaping the crop must be allowed to go forward. Allow patience to govern the free flow of physical and mental energies.

13. Eoh – *Yew tree, journeys of the dead*

The yew tree was sacred to Odin in particular, who gathered the souls of the dead for their journey to the underworld. This rune therefore denotes the importance of death in human life, or else a change in the querant's life and the passing of old ways and habits. It need not be a negative rune, for it can mean the querant is approaching the goal successfully, depending on the other runes.

14. Peorth – *Hearth, mystery*

This is one of the more enigmatic runes, about which there has been no real agreement. It suggests something mysterious and also refers to the home and hearth. A gift or legacy may be coming but it should be examined with care. The emphasis is on secrecy, linking up with the occult, even with psychic initiation.

15. Eolh – *Defence, protection*

A very positive rune which suggests that the querant is not only in a strong and successful position but is living through a period of life which should be enjoyed to the full. There is a probability that new and exciting challenges and opportunities will keep presenting themselves. It is important to be reminded by *Eolh* that emotions should be kept under control, that the strength of the current position should be used positively. Be careful if involved with people who tend to use others, and take no risks with health.

16. Sigel – *The Sun, good health*

This is the rune of success and happiness; the querant's natural abilities should come to the fore and be positively employed, real

potential being fully developed. It indicates success and the creative will. Sometimes *Sigel* can enquire whether we are not perhaps doing too much at once, and should not reduce our activities. It also warns against showing off or being over-dramatic, encouraging positive creativity.

17. Tir – *War, courage*

In some way this rune, symbolizing courage and dedication, displays the powerful, masculine energy of the sun, with passion bringing happiness. But it also recommends patience, and reminds us that there are rules which must be adhered to. We are encouraged to stand on our own feet and be self-reliant. If we take positive action and are steadfast, we gain others' respect. Mythologically, there is an influence from the Germanic god Tir, somewhat related to Mars.

18. Beorc – *Birth, new beginnings*

There is an allusion both to fertility and to regeneration and healing. *Beorc* encourages us to atone for past misdeeds and to break bad habits, especially those with negative effects on our health, such as smoking or drinking. It also offers encouragement to women trying to conceive, as it is the birth sign. There is a connection with the Moon, both in astrology and as a symbol of the Great Mother, the goddess of fertility. If some project is in doubt, *Beorc* suggests we should review the whole matter.

19. Eoh – *Horse, change*

This rune is traditionally related to travel and change. A querant involved in a business project should be encouraged but emotional relationships may need restructuring or revitalizing. There is an accent on spiritual journeys. The

194

overall emphasis of this reassuring rune is on progress, and it suggests that we should make a special effort to complete tasks if we want to ensure inner fulfilment.

20. Man – *Intelligence, culture*
This rune represents the querant and is strongly influenced by the runes surrounding it. It stands for the best in all of us – culture, memory, intelligence and other distinctively human characteristics. We should be broad in our judgments, and our own lives should be in balance, our emotions under control, our energy conserved and our bodies respected. Our opinions and attitudes should be flexible but positive. Man usually offers advice, sometimes impartial. If it is cast during a difficult period of life, he should be reminded that problems often arise out of our own actions. The solution lies in ourselves.

21. Lagu – *Water, the unconscious*
Lagu, related to flowing water, is thus linked to our emotions and intuitions. We should get in touch with our intuition and emotions, allowing them free (but controlled) rein. Deep-rooted instincts should not be permitted to overwhelm or get the better of us, nor make us overemotional. Psychic awareness should be encouraged, along with hidden creativity. Self-transformation is a theme, with increased happiness a result.

22. Ing – *Fertility, completion*
This is an almost completely felicitous rune, suggesting the successful completion or accomplishment of a project or an idea, or in the sense of someone developing fully their greatest potential. Linked to it there is a sense of relief, indicating

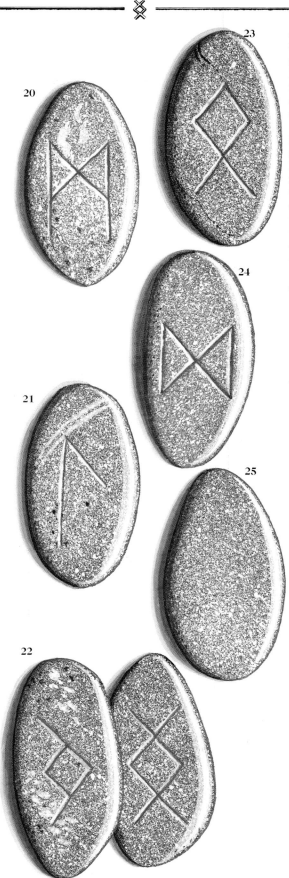

a mind set free from worries, though this need not come from completing something. It is a highly significant rune, often signalling the arrival of a turning point in a querant's life.

23. Epel – *Ancestral property*
Beginnings and endings; family traditions and inheritance – but often in the context of a severance of old influences and perhaps relationships. Any such changes will have long-term effects and be important to the person concerned. Although these could be difficult under the influence of *Epel*, serious mistakes are unlikely. There is an affinity with *Hoegl*, above.

24. Daeg – *Day, awakening*
Daeg seems to represent the culmination of all things and can symbolize spiritual development. There might well be some kind of transition, one which will be very beneficial to the querant. At its most positive, this rune states boldly that darkness is over and light, achievements and prosperity ensured. If this is too fatalistic, *Daeg* certainly encourages seizing the opportunity and acting on it if it is not to be missed. The warning is to avoid recklessness and encourage at least some quiet meditation.

25. Odin's Rune – *Fate (Wyrd)*
This completely blank rune, though ignored by some writers, seems to represent to us both ends and beginnings – the transformation of death (but not actual physical death for the querant or anyone else). It can symbolize something a person cannot know, a step into the unknown. One implication is of personal development, and a new phase of life or a quirk of fate may eventually decide the issue.

195

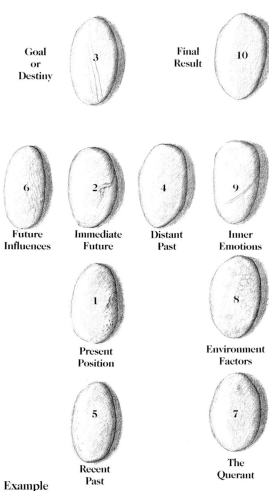

Goal or Destiny — 3
Final Result — 10
6 — Future Influences
2 — Immediate Future
4 — Distant Past
9 — Inner Emotions
1 — Present Position
8 — Environment Factors
5 — Recent Past
7 — The Querant

Inverted Runes

Some textbooks give a very full interpretation of what runes mean when inverted, as opposed to their meaning when upright. We are inclined to take the same view of inverted runes as of inversion in the Tarot (or to the retrograde motion of planets in astrology). We therefore suggest that an inverted rune will probably indicate nothing more disastrous than a slowing down of the influence concerned, but of course the presence of an inversion can be considered to strengthen an already negative indication.

Casting the Runes

For a simple yes/no reply to a question, the "points spread" suggested in the Tarot section (p.67) can be used, but when interpreting it, be careful to study the runic symbols, some of which look much the same whether upright or inverted.

Perhaps the most useful runic spread is the 10-rune casting (*right*) which adheres to the rules for the 10-card Tarot spread. For a more detailed reading, 12 runes can be set out in a circle, starting with the first in the 9 o'clock position and progressing anticlockwise around the circle (*below*). The runes will then represent the 12 houses of the zodiac; if you wish to learn what each house represents, you can add another dimension to your reading.

There are cross-references to astrology and the Tarot in one or two of the interpretations that follow. Occasionally, more than one rune shares a relationship with a particular planet, because the planetary range of influences is broad; a rune will relate to some areas of planetary influence, another to others.

196

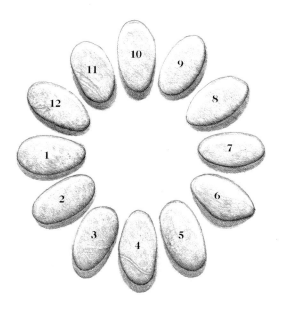

Example

The question was asked on behalf of a young mother who developed an extremely powerful premonition of disaster connected with a flight to South Africa with her family, to visit her elderly parents-in-law for Christmas. Her concern was at first for the outward flight, but then concentrated on the return flight. She eventually concluded that only she was at risk, and could not decide whether to go or not. Julia consulted the runes on her behalf (if the querant is not present during a reading, the seer must concentrate on the question in the querant's mind.)

Conclusion

After the runes were cast and before Julia knew of her pregnancy, the querant announced that she would definitely make the journey to avoid disappointing so many people. Although there is a shadow over her trip, cast by the inverted rune of *Rad*, other runes are firmly supportive. *Gyfu* is especially encouraging for her relationships, while *Man* suggests that the problem may lie with the querant herself. The final and important place of *Cen* sheds a protective light over her. Probably the querant realized that the answer to her problem lay in her own psyche, perhaps stemming from unconscious apprehension of her pregnancy.

Position 1: Rune 15 – *Eohl*
In a position representing the present, it suggested that, at the moment of reading, the mother had her emotions under control but should resist the temptation to take the easy way forward and take no risks with her health. The current situation should be carefully evaluated.

Position 2: Rune 23 – *Epel*
This, in the position of immediate influences, obviously relates to family tradition and influence. Not only was the journey taken in order to visit elderly parents, but within a few hours of casting this spread Julia learned that the querant was again pregnant. This illustrates a clear link with the rune's emphasis on inheritance.

Position 3: Rune 5 – *Rad*
This rune, which was inverted, suggested that the querant should realize the possibility of delays or difficulties in her journey, perhaps in a spiritual or psychological sense. Being inverted and in an important position in the spread, both the interpretation and the warning offered were clearly important.

Position 4: Rune 17 – *Tir*
This relates to the past and tradition. It suggests that courage and energy, especially in family dealings, will bring happiness and rewards, and it emphasizes self-reliance.

Position 5: Rune 12 – *Ger*
This suggests that something fruitful, from the cycles of life, will come through effort. One aspect of *Ger* suggests patience and a free flow of mental and physical energy, and it is possible that this may relate to her recent conception and the natural cycle to be fulfilled with the birth of the new child.

Position 6: Rune 21 – *Lagu*
Lagu provides a strong focus on powerful intuition and emotion; there is a warning that while these should not be stifled, she should not be overcome by them. This is related to the Moon and therefore to fertility. Control of emotion is emphasized.

Position 7: Rune 20 – *Man* (*inverted*)
This is strongly influenced by surrounding runes. Both *Man* itself and the seventh position represent the querant. The previous rune warns that emotion should be controlled and also insists that problems arise very often because of our own actions. *Man's* inversion emphasizes that its warnings *must* be observed.

Position 8: Rune 8 – *Wyn* (*inverted*)
Wyn underlines the fact that, while the querant is very eager for more children, both the household finances and living space will be under pressure. A warning particularly connected with the journey.

Position 9: Rune 7 – *Gyfu*
This offers a happy, compensatory and positive message. It does point out that every relationship is in some way related to sacrifice. In this case, for the sake of her husband and his parents, the querant must sacrifice her feelings. But this is the rune of people coming together and of deepening relationships.

Position 10: *Rune 6 – Cen*
This is strongly placed. *Cen* is the rune of creative light and fire, and also passion. As *Cen* represents the superior partner in any relationship – here between the querant and her parents-in-law – it suggests some unexpected gift or offer. *Cen* also signifies the protective element of fire.

Crystals

Crystals have always been mysterious: strange, dull pieces of rock which, when cut and polished, shine with a brilliance and life of their own. Until the 17th century it was believed that they were made of water, frozen to an astonishing hardness by intense cold, and unable to regain their fluid state.

Although crystallography has now explained much, crystals still retain their mystery, and mankind has discerned in them healing qualities, and possibilities for divination. The "crystal ball" of the traditional fortune-teller was used as a means of focusing the psychic's powers, most potent when using them rather than some other symbol or method.

Prediction and healing

Healers have related particular crystals to particular illnesses, and assert that wearing a crystal can speed healing and protect against illness. In this way amber has been used for healing sore throats and emeralds for curing depression.

Crystals have also been used for prediction, and in the past two or three years there has been a strong revival of this practice. Modern crystal-readers underline the association with astrology but stress also the psychokinetic element.

Crystals are surprisingly inexpensive and can often be obtained by mail as well as from specialist shops. It is easy to build up a collection of them for both healing and predictive purposes. One authority on crystals recommends the following range of minerals for crystal divination: agate geode, labradorite, Botswana agate, aquamarine, iron pyrite, amethystine agate, tiger's eye, petrified wood, quartz crystal, tektite, dendritic agate, fluorite octahedron, serpentine, ruby, purple agate, red or green jasper, amethyst, light green jasper, turquoise, white and amber agate, moss agate, rutilated quartz, agate with fossils, rose quartz, citrine quartz, blue lace agate, agate quartz, bloodstone, pink/grey jasper and turritella agate.

As with other aids to prediction, make your crystals your own. They should first be washed in pure water, then kept near to you for some time and often taken out and studied. Make sure you can identify each crystal immediately. Though hard, crystals are susceptible to damage so take special care of them. Ideally, each should be wrapped in its own piece of soft cloth; they should never be dumped, unwrapped, in the same bag or box.

The stones and their meanings

Agate geode. Note whether the stone is placed with its rough exterior uppermost, or showing its bright interior. If the latter, the querant has a strong intuition; if the former, a more practical approach is suggested. In either case, the querant should consider whether either intuition or the blocking of intuition is not contributing to the problem, by false suggestion or by refusal to recognize the truth because no positive proof is available. Especially with its glamorous side uppermost, it represents the female principle, or a particular woman.

Labradorite. Distance is suggested by this stone; either physically – as in an overseas country – or psychologically – as in an inability to get close to a friend or a problem. It also stands for romance.

Botswana agate. This stone is usually taken to mean the unexpected – the unforeseen or even unforeseeable event or action. Most crystallographers also feel it to be a "fortunate" stone, usually a positive one.

Aquamarine. Logic and common sense are emphasized by this stone, and these should be applied to the problem. It has strong masculine implications, and may refer to a particular man, or problems related to a man.

Iron pyrite. This negative stone indicates folly or deception. According to its position, it could be suggesting deceit by someone else, or deceit contemplated by the querant. Hesitation in choosing this stone could indicate that the querant is contemplating deceit but reluctantly, or that he or she is loathe to recognize deceit in someone close to them. Neighbouring stones are very important in deciding the true relevance of iron pyrite.

Amethystine agate. This stone suggests change, often physical change – moving job, house or school. The move can be the querant's, or someone else's (consult the stone nearest to it). Having several amethystine agates of various sizes will indicate a timescale – the largest representing a move some time away, a smaller one suggesting a more immediate change.

Tiger's eye. There is a hint of loneliness about this stone perhaps indicating promotion to a position of lonely authority, or the possible break-up of a partnership. But this is a positive stone, and it is a strong indicator of independence.

Petrified wood. An extemely down-to-earth and practical stone, connected with official actions, with authority in the form of the civil service or the law, and very often with official documents.

Quartz crystal. A positive stone indicative of good will, good health and happy outcomes, this stone also has something ruthless and "sharp" about it; it can suggest self-interest, putting one's own happiness first.

Tektite. No doubt because of its blackness, this stone is regarded as a negative influence, suggesting despair, something wrong somewhere, in the querant's life or that of someone close. The nearby stones are most important in discovering the source of the trouble, and suggesting ways of overcoming it.

Dendritic agate. A splendid stone with its bright yellow glow and all the positive attributes of a Leo personality; it is ruled by the Sun, and represents pleasure as well as positivity, simple enjoyment as well as a successful outcome.

Fluorite octahedron. Another yellow stone which, again, like the Zodiac sign Leo, is much concerned with creativity in all forms. Leonine preoccupation with high standards is emphasized – so is a possible authoritarianism and an overbearing domineering manner.

Serpentine. A down-to-earth rather stubborn stone which emphasizes practicality and authority; it also indicates age – an elderly relative or friend, perhaps – and the middle of the year.

Ruby. Here is the representation of perfection, or of aspiration to perfection. If it has a dark side, it is because it suggests relentlessness and perhaps overwork.

Purple agate. The stone representing the emotions. The suggestion is of a dreamy, unrealistic attitude to life. It has been linked with spirituality, but of a kind often connected with rather offbeat religious cults rather than with traditional religions. The stone also symbolizes water, and therefore both the unconscious and the principle of motherhood.

Red or green jasper. A negative stone, with a feeling of deception about it – that things are too good to be true, of too much "smoothness". Red jasper can, deceptively, mask very strong feelings, often of anger or jealousy connected with sex. Green jasper suggests rejection in some form or another – perhaps because an overt display of emotion has resulted in reaction.

Amethyst. There is an Aquarian coolness here, and a suggestion of the spiritual – but unlike the purple agate, with a possibility of a true religious vocation, or convictions strongly but sensitively held.

Light green jasper. A calming, joyful, positive influence when there are problems or difficulties, for it insists that a calm assessment of the situation will suggest the right solution.

Turquoise. A feeling of calm and content pervades this stone, which has strong

199

Cancerian associations with the home and with parenthood. It promises final resolution of problems.

White and amber agate. An equivocal stone, suggesting that there are two sides to every question. The stone is strongly associated with Gemini, and thus with communication and the media. It can also indicate study.

Moss agate. Unlike the white and amber agate, the moss agate has an air of rest and quiet about it, although it does carry a tinge of excitement – more often an intellectual rather than a physical stimulation like the excitement of the reader discovering an interesting

author, or a student finding a new subject for study. In terms of human relationships it suggests friendship rather than sensual love.

Rutilated quartz. Here is another Leonine stone, full of positivity and creativity; in this case, however, with indications of frustration. Real determination is needed to force talent through to success.

Agate with fossils. "Hidden rewards" is one of the messages of this stone, indicating that the querant is not making the best of his or her accomplishments, or of a particular situation. The stone also represents increased money.

Rose quartz. A healing stone, which suggests that the querant needs to concentrate on putting something right – healing a quarrel, looking after someone with an illness, or healing him or herself.

Citrine quartz. Like the rose quartz, healing is suggested, but here there is a strong emphasis on the physical, so this may be a warning of physical strain or overwork. It can represent a new venture, but one which may involve much strain.

Blue lace agate. Traditionally, this stone represents a girl, and also has strong, emotionally calming associations.

Agate quartz. This stone traditionally represents a young man, or a son with whom there may have been a quarrel.

Bloodstone. The stone which above all is associated with the physical, and usually with a physical ailment of some kind – either the querant's or someone else's. It is traditionally "negative".

Pink or grey jasper. An older person, perhaps a parent, who is going to affect the querant in some way.

Turritella agate. Perhaps because of its speckled surface, this stone is associated with change.

The stones as healers

The use of crystals for healing falls outside the scope of this book; but when reading the stones remember that *agates* are energizing stones, supporting quick physical action; *aquamarines* encourage good eyesight, coolness of mind and the capacity to weigh up situations; *pyrites* encourage the circulation of the blood; *amethysts* encourage our knowledge and understanding of the unconscious; *tiger's eyes* reduce headaches and promote calm understanding; *quartz crystals* encourage depth of thought, meditation and

assimilation of food; *serpentines* promote restraint and calm; *rubies* are energizers and prevent schizophrenia; *amethysts* underline spirituality and also encourage revelatory dreaming; *green jaspers* are antidepressants and combat ulcers, *turquoises* (sacred to the Amerindians) are protectors against physical ill; *rose quartzes* stimulate the intellect and encourage the imagination; *citrines* help restrain undue emotion; *bloodstones* fight depression and stimulate blood circulation.

How to do it

As with so many other means of divination, the querant must make the choice of crystals to comment on a situation or question, or reveal future trends. This can be done in one of two ways: either "blind" – that is, by allowing the querant to select the stones with eyes shut – or, more commonly by consciously choosing the stones. The latter course cannot be taken if the querant knows the properties and meaning of the different stones, for the selection will probably be affected, consciously or not, by this knowledge.

Before the sitting, spread a dark cloth on a flat surface, and place the crystals on it, in no particular order, but close together at one end of the table. The lighting, while not disturbingly bright, should show the crystals off well; a low-powered spotlight is the best.

When the querant is comfortably seated, invite him or her to choose a number of crystals. There seems to be no particular favoured number, although some suggest seven, others twelve. If you are learning the art of interpreting the stones, use a fairly small number at first. Then the querant should select the stones and

place them on the cloth.

Note how the stones are chosen and placed. The stone taken first relates to the querant's main problem and the stones immediately following will comment upon it. The way in which they are picked up, too, is revealing: if the querant quickly gathers all the stones, then there is one special problem above all; hesitation and uncertainty in choosing the stones indicate a more worried state of mind.

Similarly, the way in which the stones are placed is revealing. If thrown down haphazardly the querant may have despaired of finding a solution to his problem; if placed carefully, much thought has been expended, but presumably without result. Slow, unsure placing of the stones shows confusion about the problem, and a lack of confidence.

The stones rejected are also important for they represent qualities which the querant rightly or not, has discarded as irrelevant. Any picked up but then rejected have a special importance; they probably relate to solutions considered but for some reason not "taken up".

In starting to interpret the crystals, look at how the

stones have been placed. Are there several of one colour or type? If so, this may indicate a determination to approach a problem in one way only. Are there two groups of stones very different from each other? Then two problems or ideas are in question, and the contents of each group will tell its own story. The relative distance between different stones speaks of the strength or weakness of the influences concerned.

Crystallography is not as free with its revelations as astrology or palmistry. There is no heritage of textbooks showing how to "read" the crystals (though there have been several in the past few years, when the subject has begun to be popular.) To read the crystals well one has to be more clairvoyant than the astrologer or graphologist needs to be. Only practice will reveal whether you have a particular feeling for this art.

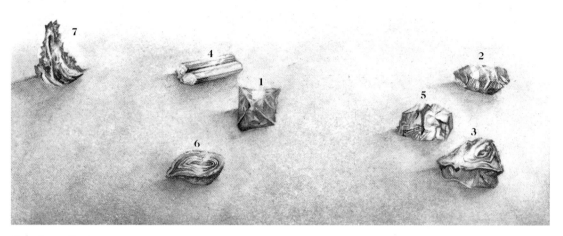

Sample reading

The crystals were chosen and placed in the following way:

1. Fluorite octahedron was placed centrally, suggesting the querant's immediate recognition that he himself dominated the situation.

2. Amethystine agate was selected next and placed some distance away, reflecting change, past, present or future.

3. Turritella agate was the third stone chosen, and it was placed separately from the others. This again suggests change.

4. Aquamarine was placed equidistantly from the other two, bringing common sense and rationality to bear on the situation.

5. Iron pyrite, placed close to the turritella agate, hinted that one of the querant's choices would have negative results and deceit was involved.

6. A white and amber agate was placed near the fluorite octahedron, underlining the need for impartiality.

7. A citrine quartz was placed nearest to, but at a distance from, aquamarine – a warning of a lack of spirituality.

The querant, seeing this laid out before him, realized he was being warned that his self-satisfied vision of himself as the dominant person in the situation must be adjusted. His last gesture said that this was a position irreconcilable with a really moral view and he must discuss it with his wife. The change indicated by the turritella agate seemed to have already occurred – the alteration in his behaviour responsible for the problem. Setting it next to the iron pyrite confirmed that view, for it indicated deceit and negativity – which he had already recognized.

The amethystine agate now represented the change which he must contemplate to set the situation right: the stone often indicates physical change and suggests an alteration in the actual pattern of his life – that is, a decision to spend time at home rather than away from it. The fact that stones 1 and 6, the fluorite octahedron and the white and amber agate, are the only two in close proximity stresses the necessity for openness and discussion. The absence of any divinatory stones suggests that the result of any decision made depended on the way the subject was approached: a future reading, carried out after a decision had been made and put into action, might reveal more.

Tea Leaves & Coffee Grounds

Reading tea leaves or coffee grounds, properly known as tasseography, is a traditional means of prediction, especially popular in the 19th and early 20th centuries, when tea and coffee drinking had become universal. Long before then, the Romans had sought out the shape of things to come in the lees of their wine; later, the Chinese began reading tea leaves, probably before tea first reached the West in the 17th century.

Although the technique for reading tea leaves is simple (exactly the same method applies to coffee grounds throughout this chapter) interpretation takes some practice. The diviner must first recognize the images formed, then interpret the meanings of each, and finally combine the different symbols into a coherent message. Each emblem requires the predictor to discern a particular shape in the leaves, for which both imagination and intuition are needed. It is not really possible to lay down the exact procedure, but the following guidelines are recommended and very generally practised.

The cups used should be white or plain on the inside. The querant should drink the tea (or coffee) holding the cup in the left hand and swirling the liquid three times clockwise. Then, inverting the cup into the saucer, allow the liquid to drain away while counting seven. Next, turn the cup the right way up, keeping the handle facing the reader of leaves, and start the reading.

Many leaves in the cup imply a rich, full life; smaller amounts mean a tidy disciplined mind. Many specific images may imply several issues important to the querant. The handle of the cup is usually taken to represent the querant, and symbols on the right of the cup sometimes are thought to show things to come – the future – and those on the left, the past. More usually, the cup is divided vertically, signs near the bottom referring to the past, those towards the top to the near future or present. Often, signs at the bottom are thought unlucky, those near the top lucky. Also, the following general markings are widely thought to have specific meanings: *dots* signify financial affairs, *wavy* lines show disturbed or unsettled conditions, *straight* lines signify a straight course.

It is important to take into account the relative size, positions proportions and clarity of the symbols. Do not read them in isolation but together, allowing the mind to range freely and the images to stimulate your imagination. Do not worry if the signs at first appear indistinct; with practice, clear pictures may soon begin to emerge. Clairvoyance – which tasseography approaches – cannot be taught and, in the light of modern thinking, it might be easier to use the symbols in the same way as dream symbols. In other words, the querant rather than the reader discerns the images in the cup and their meanings, the interpreter only assisting.

Below we give a list of symbols and their traditional meanings. Remember that they *are* only traditional and not fixed for ever, although some (such as a letter indicating news, bells pointing to a wedding) are obvious. Keep a notebook of your findings and add to this necessarily limited list.

The Symbols

Acorn: At the top of the cup, success, with money; at the middle, good health.

Acrobat: Tenseness and danger; greater security must be found.

Aircraft: A journey; if broken, risk of an accident.

Anchor: At top of the cup, success, constancy; if clouded, expect difficulties.

Angel: Good news; this can mean the guardian angel.

Apple: Business achievement, the fruits of success.

Arrow: Unpleasant or disturbing news: if with dots near it, connected with money.

Axe: Difficulties, but if near top of the cup they will be overcome.

Baby: Possibly a baby or a series of small worries; if near the cup's bottom, trouble through careless talk.

Bag: A trap ahead: if it is open, you can escape, if it is shut, you will be caught.

Balloon: Possible short-term troubles.

Bell: Unexpected news, generally good; if at the bottom, sad news; if there are several bells, a wedding.

Bed: Inertia or something finished i.e. put to bed.

Bird: Generally good news; if birds of passage, connected with divination.

Boat: A visit from a friend, safe protection.

Book: A symbol of wisdom. If open, expect good news, if closed, delays and the need for troublesome and perhaps lengthy inquiries.

Boot: Protection, especially from pain.

Box: If open, romantic troubles are solved; if closed, things lost will be found.

Cabbage: Jealousy; if dotted, at work.

Car: Good fortune with things moving ahead.

Cat: Treachery or deceit, false friends.

Circle: Success, completion; with a dot, a baby.

Clouds: Troubles ahead; if with dots, money problems.

Coin: Money coming, debts repaid.

Crossroads: Decision making, a crossroads in life.

Dagger: Dangers ahead, beware of recklessness.

Dog: Good and faithful friends; if at the cup bottom, a friend in need.

Egg: Prosperity, success, the more the better.

Eyes: Caution and care needed, especially in business.

Fire: Achievements; danger in haste.

Fish: Very good fortune all round.

Flag: Danger ahead.

Flower: Wishes coming true, unless at the bottom of the cup when sinister

meanings can be intended.

Football: Attaining a goal.

Fork: False friends, flattery.

Fruit: Prosperity.

Gate: In a new phase of life, opportunity and success.

Glass: Integrity.

Goat: Beware of enemies.

Grapes: Happiness, love gratified.

Gun: Trouble, anger, if near the cup top, discord in love; if at the bottom, slander; for a military person, a call to arms.

Hammer: Hard work and ruthlessness required.

Hand: If open, friendship; if closed, and argument.

Handbag: Security, secretiveness.

Harp: Romance, harmony in love.

Hat: Changes; at the bottom of the cup, rivalry; at the top, harmony and improvements.

Head: New intellectual opportunities.

Heart: Pleasure, love, marriage, friendship.

Hill: Obstacles and setbacks.

Horn: Abundance, inheritance; if with dots, money through marriage.

House: Security, success.

Human figures: To be interpreted according to what they are and their context.

Iceberg: Danger ahead.

Ladder: Promotion, a rise.

Leaf: Prosperity, success; if at bottom, late in life.

Letters: News; near dots, news about money.

Mask: Insincerity, excitement, insecurity.

Moon: Romance, sadness; surrounded by dots, marriage for money.

Palm tree: Success, honour.

Pig: Prosperity, possibly greed.

Ring: At the top of the cup, marriage; at the bottom, a long engagement; if broken, an engagement broken off.

Scales: Lawsuits; if balanced, justice; if unbalanced, injustice.

Ship: Successful or worthwhile journey.

Snake: An enemy, but also wisdom.

Spade: Hard work, success.

Star: Hope and health.

Sword: Arguments.

Table: Social gathering; if dotted, a financial conference.

Toy: Childhood, security nostalgia.

Train: Readiness to move forward.

Tree: Changes for the better, improvements.

Triangle: Something unexpected.

Umbrella: Annoyances; if open, shelter from them, if shut, shelter refused.

Volcano: Emotions out of control.

Waterfall: Prosperity.

Wheel: If complete, good fortune; if broken, disappointment; if near rim of cup, unexpected money.

Whip: Aggression, sexual energy.

Wings: Messages, good or bad depending on position in tea cup.

Witch: Unpleasantness in women.

Wolf: Jealousy, selfishness.

Woman: Pleasure, fertility, wealth; if several women, scandal.

These are only a selection of symbols with their most commonly accepted meanings. Many more symbols may suggest themselves in the shapes made by tea leaves. Buy a good dictionary of symbols (see our Bibliography p. 221); this will give you many ideas on possible interpretations.

Bringing it all Together

The Techniques Compared

It is comparatively rare to find someone interested in one of the occult disciplines who is not also interested in the others. But it seldom happens that several disciplines are used at the same time by those seeking advice or attempting to consult the future. As we shall see, such an approach can provide very interesting results.

No one who has studied a number of these subjects can be unaware that some of them share interesting links. This is partly because they are expressed in terms of the oldest and most profound symbols of human life; for example, runes, astrology and the Tarot are connected with ancient myths and legends, and deal with the most basic human desires, hopes and fears. Perhaps it is not surprising that correspondences can be found between them.

On the other hand, the disciplines themselves are often so different in their origins and approaches that one might expect no correspondences at all. To put the matter to the test, we decided to invite one person to consult a variety of prediction techniques as to what lay ahead, and to compare the results. We found as we studied them that even those predictive techniques which have become associated mainly with fun usually have something to say to the open mind. The most profound and ancient methods have moved with the times – or perhaps the times have moved around them! – and will be as meaningful to someone in the year 2000 as they were in the year 1000. Human problems remain much the same; and good advice remains good advice.

Perhaps the most profound of the techniques we have examined are the *I Ching,* the runes, the Tarot, astrology and palmistry. These are universal advisers; their wisdom is timeless; without being fatalistic, they offer a vision of the future which enables the querant to deal with ambition, lethargy, apprehension, joy or even despair. They do not present a freeze-frame snapshot of next Wednesday, next June, next year; nor do they tell anyone what they *should* do. They present the world of possibilities, offer guidance and leave the querant to act.

Freedom of action is an essential ingredient of a free life, and most practitioners of "futurology" agree that it is vital to allow the querant space, not to hem him or her in by laying down sets of tracks along which they must travel. And so it is that the main characteristic of a good astrologer, Tarot-reader or palmist is not necessarily the ability to study the technique but a deep interest in people which enables them to present the message in a sympathetic way, adding and subtracting nothing from it. That is an important qualification: the palmist or Tarot-reader who pre-faces remarks with the words "I see . . ." is perhaps always to be mistrusted. Talented clairvoyants have their own methods, but these cannot be learned from a book – maybe they cannot be learned at all. The techniques outlined here are empirical; nothing a rune-master, astrologer or palmist says comes out of the air. Intuition is an important ingredient, of course, but it is the cards, the stones, the palms, the planetary positions, which are the arbiters.

The next few pages are unique, an extension of the many inter-relations you will have found throughout the book. We have taken astrology, perhaps the most complex and ancient of disciplines, as the basis of comparison. Each "family" has as its founder-member a Zodiac sign or a solar system planet, and within it dwell some of the runes and crystals and some of the characteristics of graphology and palmistry. There are, of course, some gaps where disciplines have taken their own lines of inference and reasoning, and have not followed the characteristics of others.

This section can be constructively used. When practising one of the disciplines it is often possible to broaden your understanding of a symbol by examining the comments another member of the same "family" has to offer; a greater breadth and depth of interpretation will then be possible.

The great thing to remember is to be selective, in much the way we have already several times suggested. If a statement ultimately does not seem to apply, discard it – though not immediately; often a symbol must be worked at before it reveals its meaning. Frequently if it is not apposite the first time, it will recur, and on its second appearance will have much to say to you.

The *I Ching* hexagrams find no place in the following pages. That ancient system has such a vast, panoramic spread, and its symbols are at once so universal and so capable of specific application that it seems irrational to cramp it by trying to confine it to our comparative groups.

For the rest, we have used a range of disciplines when answering our guest querant's question. And there is every reason for the reader to construct his or her own pantheon, and study the way each method of constructing a pattern of the future relates to the others.

207

Inter-relations between techniques

The astrological houses have no significant part to play in this section of the book. But it is interesting to note that the Tarot Hanged Man and the runes *Thorn* and *Daeg* are very strongly associated with the Twelfth House – that which deals with the unconscious, self-sacrifice, service to others, and negatively with escapism, often through drugs.

The World and the Midheaven

The Tarot card, the World, is associated with that area of the fully calculated astrological birth-chart known as the Midheaven – the point of the sky directly overhead at the precise time and place of birth. Astrologically, this represents our ambitions, aspirations, achievements, careers and worldly standing.

Crystals

Placing the crystals within the zodiac family, we have not taken into account the traditional astrological rulership of the stones, but have placed them according to their interpretation. Some of these placings relate to the traditional associations; others do not.

The Aries family

Positive traits: A pioneering, adventurous spirit, enterprise and courage, high energy, a love of freedom and hatred of restriction.

Negative traits: Selfishness, lack of subtlety, impulsiveness, pugnacity, quickness of temper, dogmatism, impatience.

Palmistry: The spatulate hand (shared with Sagittarius).
The Tarot: The King of Swords; The Fool (the straightforward, simple, Arian motivation and the element of Everyman match well with Aries); at best, endearing and positive, at worst negative and primitive.
The Runes: *Man* (though the relationship between Aries and *Man* is somewhat tenuous, its advice is particularly relevant to Arians.)
Crystals: Quartz crystal.
Graphology: The often small writing will usually be well-spaced, but the lines will perhaps ascend to the right – as will the t-bars. Many letters will be only half-formed; initial strokes will be missing.

The Taurus family

Positive traits: Practicality and reliability, good business sense, endurance, good sense of values (especially in the arts), enjoyment of comfort and good food, determination, persistence, affection, warm-heartedness, trustworthiness, a faithful friend.

Negative traits: Possessiveness, laziness, self-indulgence, fixity of opinions, greediness, stubbornness, resentfulness, obsessive routine.

Palmistry: The square hand and fingers.
Tarot: The King of Coins (though Taureans are unlikely gamblers).
Runes: *Feoh.*
Graphology: Neat, uniform writing with no margin; careful punctuation; the small letters close together and all the same size; rather old-fashioned capitals and letter forms, sometimes with unnecessary initial strokes.

The Gemini family

Positive traits: Versatility and adaptability, intellect, wit and logic, spontaneity, liveliness, a flair for communication.

Negative traits: Restlessness, cunning, vagueness, inconsistency, inquisitiveness, superficiality, gossip.

Palmistry: The conic hand; the line of Mercury.
Tarot: The Knight of Wands.
Runes: *Eoh.*
Crystals: Moss agate.
Graphology: The usually small writing will have letters of various sizes, and often a forward slant; the t-crossings will be strong and the lower loops of the letters long. Terminals will ascend to the right.

The Cancer family

Positive traits: Kindness, sensitivity, sympathy, imagination, well-developed maternal or paternal instinct, protectiveness, caution, tenacity, shrewdness, thrift.

Negative traits: Overemotionalism, hypersensitivity, touchiness, moodiness, self-pity, instability, untidiness, susceptibility to flattery.

Palmistry: The square hand.
Tarot: The Queen of Cups.
Runes: *Peorth.*
Crystals: Turquoise, rose quartz, purple agate.
Graphology: Well-spaced vertical or forward-slanting writing with small letters of variable sizes will have is carelessly dotted, gs and ys with full loops, and looped stems on the ds and ts.

The Leo family

Positive traits: Magnanimity, generosity, creativity, enthusiasm, organizational ability, expansiveness, confidence.

Negative traits: Dogmatism, pomposity, snobbishness, intolerance, fixity of opinion, condescension, preoccupation with power, conceit.

Palmistry: The Line of Apollo.
Tarot: King and Queen of Batons.
Runes: *Ing.*
Crystals: Fluorite octahedron, rutilated quartz.
Graphology: The small letters of words will gradually increase in size; the writing will otherwise be uniform, down-strokes concave. Lines and words will be well-spaced, and the words sometimes connected by sweeping dashes. The small fs will frequently have strokes instead of loops, and the ts will be heavily crossed.

The Virgo family

Positive traits: Discrimination, good powers of analysis, meticulousness, modesty, tidiness.

Negative traits: Worry, hypercriticism, overfastidiousness, exceptional conventionality.

Palmistry: The square-hand; the Mercury line in its relationship to health; lines on finger tips.
The Tarot: The Popess; Temperance; Queen of Swords.
Runes: *Ger.*
Crystals: Ruby.
Graphology: Careful, precise writing, with words as well as letters connected; looped *t*-stems will often have the bar ascending, and there will be closed *a*s and *o*s. The numerals 7 and 9 will have long, graceful tails.

The Libra family

Positive traits: Charm, harmoniousness, tolerance, romanticism, diplomacy, idealism, refinement.

Negative traits: Indecisiveness, resentfulness, frivolousness, changeability, flirtatiousness, gullibility.

Palmistry: The conic hand.
Tarot: Justice.
Runes: *Gyfu.*
Crystal: Light green jasper.
Graphology: The small letters of words will often decrease in size towards the end, the first small letter being the biggest; *a* and *o* will be open, capitals simple, a high stem to the *d*. The left-hand margin will be straight.

The Scorpio family

Positive traits: Powerful emotion, purposefulness, high imagination, discernment, subtlety, shrewdness, determination.

Negative traits: Jealousy, resentfulness, obstinacy and intractability, sharpness, secretiveness, suspicion.

Palmistry: No single indication in palmistry seems to fit the typical Scorpio.
Tarot: The Devil.
Runes: *Peorth.*
Crystal: Red or green jasper.
Graphology: Right-sloped, rounded writing will have letters with long lower loops and long terminal strokes turned up to the right. Letters will often be disconnected, but words and lines well and often widely spaced. Capital letters may be idiosyncratic.

The Sagittarius family

Positive traits: Joviality, optimism, open-mindedness, adaptability, love of freedom, sincerity, dependability, scrupulousness.

Negative traits: Extreme reactions, tactlessness, restlessness, carelessness, blind optimism, boisterousness, irresponsibility, capriciousness.

Palmistry: The spatulate hand.
Tarot: The Chariot.
Runes: *Cen.*
Graphology: Badly-spaced forward-sloping writing with wide margins often getting

wider towards the bottom of the page. Small letters will be variously sized, lower loops extended, and the writing will often be rather large.

The Capricorn family

Positive traits: Reliability, determination, ambition, prudence, sense of humour, self-discipline, patience, perseverance.

Negative traits: Rigidity of outlook, mistrustfulness, pessimism, conventionality, meanness.

Palmistry: The fate line.
Tarot: Knight of Coins.
Runes: *Daeg.*
Crystals: Aquamarine, which emphasizes logic and practicality; petrified wood.
Graphology: Careful punctuation, well-spaced lines, rather compressed, small writing with the letters crowded together; there will be short lower loops and decided hooks at the end of strokes.

The Aquarius family

Positive traits: Independence, friendliness, progressiveness, originality, inventiveness, loyalty, idealism, intellect.

Negative traits: Unpredictability, eccentricity, rebelliousness, contrariness, tactlessness, perversity.

Palmistry: The conic hand.
Tarot: The Wheel of Fortune (underlining many of the qualities for which Aquarians should aim).
Crystals: Amethyst, labradorite.

Runes: *Thorn.*
Graphology: Often rather square writing will strike recipients as unusual; the final strokes of the *d*s and *t*s will fall below the line, and bars will be heavy and downward-pointing. Capitals will be simple, but there may be consciously round *i*-dots.

The Pisces family

Positive traits: Humility, compassion, sympathy, unworldliness, sensitivity, adaptability, intuition, receptivity.

Negative traits: Vagueness, carelessness, confusion, indecision, dreariness.

Palmistry: The psychic hand; the *Via Lascivia.*
Tarot: The Star.
Crystal: The purple agate.
Runes: *Ger.*
Graphology: Carelessness may be a characteristic – letters omitted in words, *t*s left uncrossed and *i*s undotted; but the writing will often have grace and charm. What *t*-bars there are will be above the stem at the right of the letter, and short. Spacing will be erratic.

THE PLANETS

The Sun's family

Positive traits: Creativity, generosity, joie de vivre, organizational ability, love of children, affection, magnanimity, dignity.

Negative traits: Pomposity, domination, extravagance, condescension, bombast.

Palmistry: The life line; the Apollo finger and mount.
Tarot: The Sun (the astrological solar qualities are perfectly mirrored in this card).
Runes: *Sigel.*
Crystals: Dendritic agate.

The Moon's family

Positive traits: Patience, passivity, tenaciousness, imagination, sensitivity, receptivity, sympathy, shrewdness, good memory.

Negative traits: Moodiness, clannishness, changeability, weak reasoning, unreliability, gullibility.

Palmistry: The mount of Luna (which also has a relationship to Venus).
Tarot: The Moon (this is a traditional association, but many of its warnings apply to the negative influences of Neptune.)
Runes: *Beorc, Lagu, Ing.*
Crystals: Agate geode, amethystine agate, turritella agate.

Mercury's family

Positive traits: Perception, reasoning power, versatility, good apprehension of reasoning in argument, intellect.

210

Negative traits: Inconsistency, hypercriticism, inquisitiveness, argumentativeness, cynicism.

Palmistry: The Mercury finger and mount.
Tarot: The Magician.
Runes: *Os.*
Crystals: White amber agate (also associated with Gemini; Mercury is the Geminian planet).

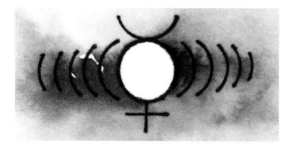

Venus' family

Positive traits: Kindness, friendliness, tact, adeptness in love, adaptability, placidity, refinement.

Negative traits: Laziness, indecision, romanticism, carelessness, impracticality, dependence on others.

Palmistry: The mount of Venus, the heart line.
Tarot: The Empress, the Lovers.
Runes: *Feoh.*
Crystals: Blue lace agate; agate with fossils.

Mars' family

Positive traits: Decisiveness, directness, strong sexuality, positivity and liveliness.

Negative traits: Aggression, irascibility, brutality, foolhardiness, selfishness, quarrelsomeness, overhastiness.

Palmistry: Upper and Lower Mars, the Plain of Mars.
Tarot: The Emperor, the Tower (see also Uranus), Force (suggesting the best possible use of Martian energy).
Runes: *Cen, Tir* (see also Jupiter).
Crystals: Citrine quartz; agate quartz.

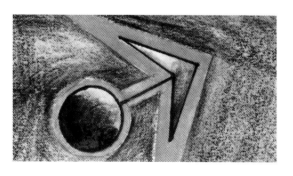

Jupiter's family

Positive traits: Optimism, generosity, loyalty, joviality, compassion, breadth of vision.

Negative traits: Blind optimism, extremism, waste, self-indulgence, extravagance, lawlessness, conceit.

Palmistry: The Jupiter finger and mount; the head line and branches sweeping upward from it.
Tarot: The Pope.
Runes: *Eolh, Tir* (see also Mars), *Ing* (with the Moon), *Wyn* (see also Neptune).
Crystal: Agate with fossils (see also Mars).

Saturn's family

Positive traits: Practicality, caution, responsibility, patience, ambition, thriftiness, solidity, reliability, trustworthiness, self-discipline.

Negative traits: Meanness, selfishness, despondency, narrow-mindedness, aloofness, pessimism, dogmatism, heartlessness.

Palmistry: The Saturn finger and mount. Islands on major lines are similar to the square and oppositions of Saturn; breaks in the fate line similar to the trine and conjunction of Saturn.
Runes: *Hoegl, Is* (see also Uranus), *Epel*.
Crystals: Tiger's eye, serpentine, pink or grey jasper, turritella agate.

Uranus' family

Positive traits: Humanitarianism, friendliness, kindness, independence, originality, inventiveness, versatility.

Negative traits: Crankiness, eccentricity, perversity, abnormality, rebelliousness, unpredictability.

Palmistry: Stars on a major line.
Tarot: The Tower (see also Mars).
Runes: *Ur, Is* to some extent.
Crystals: Botswana agate, tiger's eye (see also Saturn), turritella agate.

211

Neptune's family

Positive traits: Idealism, spirituality, imagination, sensitivity, subtlety, artistic creativity.

Negative traits: Deceit, carelessness, sentimentality, indecision, self-deceit, impracticality, worry.

Palmistry: The mount of Neptune.
Tarot: The Moon (see also the Moon, above).
Runes: *Nyd, Wyn* (with Jupiter).

Pluto's family

Positive traits: Business flair, financial security, analytical mind.

Negative traits: Underhandedness, overcritical tendencies, cruelty, even sadism.

Palmistry: Bars across a major line are comparable to the specific influences of Pluto (see p. 118).

Tarot: Death, Judgement ("transformation", the key word for this card, is also strongly related to Pluto, especially when Plutonic influences are positive).
Runes: *Rad. Eoh. Odin's Rune* also has some Plutonic overtones.
Crystal: Tektite.

Combining the disciplines

We invited our young friend Ann to consult all the disciplines outlined in this book. In interpreting what astrology, the Tarot, the runes and the others have to say, we should underline the fact that we *only* used the information set out in these pages.

Ann is in her twenties, and is carving a very successful career as a beauty therapist. Born in Plymouth, in southwest England, she now lives and works in London. Tragically, her father died very suddenly when she was 14½; but she has an excellent relationship with her mother and stepfather, who remain in Plymouth.

She began work in London just before her 20th birthday. She has no permanent emotional relationship. At the time of the readings, she and three friends had just been given notice to leave the flat they had shared for some years. Her friends were, in any event, about to go their separate ways, so she felt somewhat uncertain about the future. Her question was: "How will my life work out over the next three years?"

The readings were completed in January, 1988, and look forward to the end of 1990.

As you read the following, you may find it useful to refer back to the main interpretive text of each discipline in turn; this will help you build your knowledge of how the techniques are used; and you will also be able to make comparisons and enlarge on certain areas which, for reasons of space, we are unable to explore fully here. We begin with graphology, to show how a character sketch of the subject can emerge from his or her handwriting.

Graphology

Ann's writing is of average size, and the spacing, both vertically and horizontally, is well balanced, which shows that she herself is to all intents a poised and confident young woman with a well-organized mind. Short upward initial strokes denote self-confidence, and the narrow left-hand margin indicates a degree of caution and good management in everyday affairs. Well-connected writing and short *l*-loops show rationality; perhaps her imagination needs stimulating.

A slightly less confident note is struck by the fact that the loops slope vary slightly in different directions, and this normally shows emotional uncertainty. The *very* low *t*-bars are usually a sign of self-doubt in one area or another – but in Ann's case more probably indicate caution in every area of life; the relatively small capitals underline this. The assertive *I* seems to show confidence again; but once more slopes slightly backwards, which suggests that she welcomes support from others. Ann's signature is of normal size, but again has a slight backward tilt, perhaps indicating a degree of repression. There is a backward-slanting emphasis throughout which indicates that she is cool and collected. The emphasis on the lower zone shows a normal sexuality, but also a materialistic streak – and the short terminals suggest that she is careful and practical in financial matters.

The *i*-dots are high, and there is a very slight overall upward tilt to the lines of writing, so Ann has a generally optimistic attitude to life; with self-confidence and rationality she should be able to face the future positively.

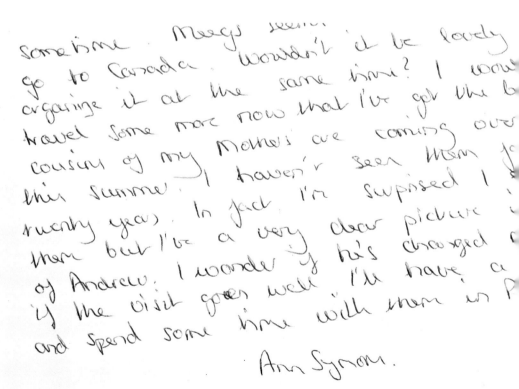

Tarot

The pyramid spread seemed most apt for assessing future trends and the pattern of life for a specific period; the Rider/Waites pack was used.

Of the 21 cards drawn, nine were Batons, suggesting an emphasis on enterpise and growth and an accent on hard work, which would probably be very much at the centre of Ann's life between the time of the reading and the end of 1990. Twelve cards were inverted, warning her not to expect everything to fall into place overnight; she should anticipate delays, and all-round progress would be rather slow.

1. Queen of Wands. A few weeks previously, Ann had been abroad attending the wedding of a close friend, whose personality the card entirely matched.

2 & 3. Three of Wands, Three of Coins, which followed, described her attitude: a practical one, centred on career development (she had turned down a proposal of marriage which would have made her a very wealthy young woman). She was ready to be assertive.

5. Justice. (The first keycard): Ann was experiencing a particularly important period, and heeded the advice of this card (see p. 51).

6. Three of Swords seemed to refer to a meeting (later on the day of the reading) with a new friend, with a view to flat-sharing.

7. Knight of Wands suggested an imminent change of address (or travel).

8. Page of Wands hinted at important news, soon.

9. Knight of Cups (key-card 2) seemed to promise new opportunities (possibly during February, when Jupiter's specific influence would be working for Ann, see later).

10. Ace of Wands, following offered a positive start, though its inversion suggested delay; perhaps a new job?

11. The Chariot emphasized hard work in the near future, and another indication of travel (maybe this time because of work?)

12. Death related to the previous cards and underlined the fact that changes were afoot.

13. Queen of Swords, the third key-card, represented Ann's mother, who was perhaps to be involved in the next turn of events.

14 & 15. Ten and eight of Wands, following showed respectively additional responsibility and prestige, and promotion as a result of hard work, careful planning and caution.

16. The Tower, a somewhat drastic card, marked a breakthrough, but also suggested an unexpected element.

17. King of Cups, key-card 4, represented the distant future – an older man,

perhaps a business partnership.

18 & 19. Eight of Cups and the Hierophant (Pope) followed this up with a warning that Ann should not become too materialistic in outlook, but should develop spiritually and intellectually.

20. The Lovers showed her faced with a choice towards the end of the three-year period: an emotional relationship seemed probable.

21. The four of Wands, keycard 5, suggesting the eventual outcome, summed the spread up positively, suggesting that Ann would win through and, with care, peace, prosperity and happiness would surround her as she enjoyed the fruits of her hard work.

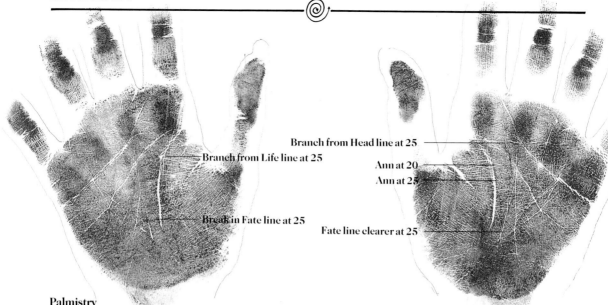

Branch from Head line at 25

Branch from Life line at 25

Ann at 20

Ann at 25

Branch from Life line at 25

Break in Fate line at 25

Fate line clearer at 25

Palmistry

We examined Ann's palm prints – she is right-handed – looking in detail at the three lines from which an assessment of future trends can be made.

Ann's 25th year – which covers the period between December 1988 and December 1989 – showed many interesting indications. There was a bar across the right-hand life line, and a branch on the left-hand one, a small branch from the right-hand head line, and a break in the left-hand fate line (clearer than that on the right hand).

From this it seemed likely that Ann would have to cope with some obstacles (because of the barred life line), but the branch from her head line (towards the Jupiter finger) suggested that she could achieve some success. Her fate line was strongly emphasized during that period of her life: it became considerably clearer on the right hand after about her 25th birthday. It seemed that from that time forward her life would become much more settled, and she would see the way ahead more clearly. Her emotional life seemed likely to fall into focus, for there was a branch on her left-hand life line which – with the decided break in the fate line, again on the left hand – pointed to the development of an emotional relationship.

Crystals

Ann drew the crystals slowly but rhythmically, without hesitation or indecision until the end of the draw, when she announced that she had finished – but then, after a moment or two, took two more stones. She laid them out in a very orderly, almost geometrical pattern (see above).

Three white stones (3, 9 and 11) showed clarity of mind and happiness – and 11, one of the two "afterthoughts", a young man. The tektite (7), preceded by light green jasper (6) and followed by labradorite (8), indicated her practicality and ability to distance herself from problems, assessing them coolly and rationally. Labradorite has a bearing on love life, and denotes a possibly rather distant attitude; it indicated that Ann realizes that she has a somewhat cool attitude towards men, and

is giving it some thought; the spread represented a three-year pattern, and the problem seemed likely to be resolved during that period. One of the "afterthought" stones (11) had its place here, and the last stone drawn (fluorite octahedron, 12), focused on her independence and need to be in control, and was also revealing.

The first stone she drew (blue lace agate) suggested a young girl: it may be that this represented Ann herself – but see the first card of her Tarot draw, especially as there is a certain sentimental, emotional feeling to blue lace agate!

Overall, her independence (financial and emotional) and practical approach to life were at the centre of this draw, the strong final stone suggesting firmly that whatever happens, Ann will remain in control.

214

Tea leaves

We used for the consultation of tea leaves a fairly large cup and medium-sized leaf tea. The clearest symbol by far was a large flag flying on top of a hill. A flag represents danger, either obvious or hidden, present or to come, and as we saw another, less marked flag, the message was obvious – Ann must take care. A box near this second flag suggested that the danger – or problems – might involve romantic trouble. But the appearance of the emblem of a boot signified protection, especially from any pain, while the fish sign near it is one of the luckiest of all symbols, indicating good luck in all aspects of life. Danger will therefore be overcome.

3. Cen

10. Peorth

6. Ger

2. Man

4. Daeg

9. Eolh

215

Runes

The runes were arranged in the same pattern as has been described on p. 196, putting the first three in the centre and arranging the others around them.

Odin (rune 1) is very significant in the centre, representing new beginnings and endings, also the step into the unknown. *Thorn*, immediately beneath it, suggests good news and protection, as well as a gateway. Above the central rune, *Man* emphasizes the human qualities of intelligence and culture Ann will need, while *Cen* at the very top throws a creative fire and light over the whole pattern. *Ger*, to the left, suggests that the natural cycle of the year may influence Ann more than she perhaps realizes.

1. Odin

5. Thorn

Daeg, in the middle by itself, represents the culmination of all things and can symbolize spiritual awakening and development – a very promising rune. The other four symbols modify these – *Peorth*, the rune of mystery, *Eolh* suggests protection and defence (including self-defence), *Beorc* birth and regeneration. Only *Hoegl*, at the bottom right, suggests unexpected problems or setbacks but – with the other runes all so positive – Ann has a generally hopeful and encouraging message from this reading.

(This is not the only way to read the runes, of course; there are several others but we chose this way to be consistent with our main example).

8. Beorc

7. Hoegl

Cards

We consulted the Great Star spread for Ann, who chose the Queen of Hearts to represent herself.

There was an immediate suggestion (8 Clubs) of a dark lover who would bring Ann happiness – though at the same time there was the implication of some loss of financial independence (7 Clubs reversed). In the past there seemed to have been an element of boredom in her romantic life (7 Hearts) which gradually increased (7 Spades). The situation may have been affected by an element of flirtatiousness (Queen Diamonds) which perhaps led to a temporary setback in her love life – but the future seemed, cheeringly, to offer sexual happiness and financial stability.

A friendly older woman (Queen Spades) might help towards good fortune in love or career, but the Knaves of Hearts and Spades, both reversed, showed that deceit on someone's part could result in dissatisfaction – a friendly critic (7 Diamonds) might help expose such deceit (King Diamonds reversed). An older man (King Spades) might in the past have placed an obstacle in the way of happiness; a parting (10 Clubs) from a true lover (Knave Clubs) was suggested. Love and the longing for a permanent relationship seemed connected in some way with a minor health difficulty. Finally, a friendly, dark woman (perhaps Ann's mother?) presided over the whole thing, offering support.

Dice, biorhythms

Making a single throw of the dice, Ann came up with a double two, which supported the advice of the more complex disciplines (see p. 90). She will need to approach the next few years with caution, and this throw also relates potently to her attitude to her emotional life.

We also worked out her biorhythms, warning her about triple critical days on which she should take special care when doing anything with an element of chance (such days do not occur every year).

Ann's Astrology: specific influences

On three occasions during 1988 the two powerful planets Saturn and Uranus meet on Ann's Sun degree (27° Sagittarius), and these strong influences will dominate her year. In addition, Pluto makes a minor semi-square twice in 1988 and once in 1989. Jupiter makes a marvellously positive trine to Ann's Sun during February 1988, and a square aspect in July; and the influence returns in February 1989. Jupiter then goes on to make an opposition to the Sun between June and September. The planets are less active for Ann during 1990.

1988

January: ♄ + ♅ = 27° ♐ = ☌

January – end of March: ♇ = 12° ♏ = ∠

February: ♃ 27° ♈ = △

July: ♄ + ♅ = 27° ♐ = ☌
♃ = 27° ♉ = □

October – November: ♄ + ♅ = 27° ♐ = ☌
♇ = 12° ♏ = ∠

1988: New Moons (all make aspects to Ann's Sun)

January 19th: ♑ = ⊻

February 17th: ♒ = ✱

March 18th: ♓ = □

April 16th: ♈ = △

1989

March – May: ♄ + ♆ = 12° ♑ = ∠

June – September: ♇ = 12° ♏ = ∠
♃ = 27° ♊ = ☍

1990

July – August: ♆ = 12° ♑ = ∠

August: ♃ = 27° ♋ = ⚻

October – November: ♆ = 12° ♑ = ∠

Astrology

Ann was born on December 19, when the Sun was on 27° Sagittarius. We looked at the specific astrological influences which would be working for her between January 1988 and the end of 1990, using only the relationships made by the major or slow-moving planets – i.e., Jupiter, Saturn, Uranus, Neptune and Pluto (see box above). We also looked to see if there were any New Moons aspecting the position of the Sun on the day of Ann's birth (Remember that when interpreting trends in this way, only the Sun's natal position is used – and do stress to your querant that the planetary picture is far from complete!)

We concluded that 1988/9 would be an eventful period for her. There was a strong possibility that she would accept new responsibilities which would add to her prestige, and unexpected new developments would probably occur. Interestingly, the matter of her domestic upheaval and change of residence was quite clear – during the first four months of 1988 the New Moon made a series of aspects which often have a bearing on domestic changes.

February seemed likely to be a specially good month for her, since Jupiter – the planet which rules her Sun-sign, Sagittarius – would make a really excellent trine aspect. She should not on any account let good opportunities slip at that time, but should be assertive, making sure that those who could help her (especially in her career) know her full capabilities. The less positive influences of Jupiter indicated times when she should be careful not to lose her sense of perspective, or overdramatize things.

The minor influence of Pluto was not strong, but she should accept the fact that there would be frustrations – especially in 1988, when the influence ran in tandem with other strong trends.

Looking at 1990 we could see some respite: she would be more settled, and perhaps the changes made during 1988/9 would have left her in a more prestigious and satisfactory position. Mild influences from Neptune and Jupiter colouring that year suggested that her emotional life might be emphasized.

Conclusion

The reader will decide, on reading the various comments on Ann's question, to what extent the various disciplines have the same sort of thing to say; the conclusion may be that there is a remarkable similarity between many of them (this becomes more apparent if you follow the indications through in the separate sections on interpretation, rather than merely reading our short summaries, above). Of course, many of the comments are general; but advice *can* only be general if directed towards a general situation. Ask for comments on a particular question, and you may well be even more surprised at the unanimity of the advice offered.

Glossary

Aeromancy Divination from cloud shapes and the winds
Angularity One of the four types of connection noted in graphology showing spiky, firm, assertive characteristics
Arcades One of the four types of connection noted in graphology showing artistic, formal, pretentious characteristics
Archetype One of the recurring or inherited mental images suggested by Jung as emanating from the collective unconscious
Ascendant The planet that is rising in the eastern sky at the time of a horoscope's casting
Aspects The angle formed between two planets as seen from earth
Astragalomancy Divination by casting sheep's anklebones or vertebrae
Batons One of the four suits of the minor arcana in the Tarot
Bellomancy Divination by casting bundles of arrows
Birth chart See *horoscope*
Cartomancy Divination by playing cards
Chariot, The (Tarot) major arcana card indicating vitality
Combination Hands Those that in palmistry combine different hand and palm types
Conic One of the four shapes of hand or finger recognized in palmistry
Conjunction A powerful astrological aspect and a focal point in the birth chart, laying positive or negative stress
Critical days Days on which one of the three biorhythm traces passes from negative into positive, or vice versa
Crystallography In the modern version, the colour, form and placing of crystals chosen by a querant to comment on questions or problems under consideration
Cusp The starting point of a new astrological sign or house
Death (Tarot) major arcana card indicating change
Devil, The (Tarot) major arcana card indicating self-awareness
Elements The four influences (fire, earth, air, water) governing each astrological sign
Emotional cycle The 28-day cycle governing emotions in biorhythms
Emperor, The (Tarot) major arcana card indicating action
Empress, The (Tarot) major arcana card indicating security
Ephemeris Astronomical tables giving precise daily positions of the Sun, Moon and planets
Extravert Jung's terms for a person orientated outward to

people and events
Fool, The (Tarot) major arcana card indicating Everyman
Force or Strength (Tarot) major arcana card indicating equilibrium
Garlands One of the four types of connection noted in graphology showing an easy-going, sympathetic, friendly character
Geomancy Divination by the earth – usually meaning sand or dust
Hanged Man, The (Tarot) major arcana card indicating transition
Haruspicy Divination by the entrails of sacrificed animals
Head Line One of the three principal lines on the hand, used in palmistry, relating to the mind
Heart Line One of the three principal lines on the hand used in palmistry, relating to love and marriage
Hemisphere One of the two sides of the brain, especially in palmistry
Hepatoscopy Divination by the liver of slaughtered animals
Hermit, The (Tarot) major arcana card indicating truth, knowledge, prudence
Hexagram Six-lined figure formed from broken and unbroken lines to give one of 64 in the *I Ching*
High Priestess, The (Tarot) major arcana card indicating discrimination
Horoscope or birth chart A chart of the heavens drawn up for the time and place of a person's birth
House In astrology, one of 12 sections of the horoscope, each relating to a sphere of everyday human life
Hydromancy Divination by water
Intellectual cycle The 33-day cycle in biorhythms governing mental powers
Introvert Jung's term for people turned inward into themselves.
Inverted In runes or the Tarot, a sign that is upside down and therefore with a different emphasis, often strengthened if negative
Island In palmistry, a mark on a line indicating a blockage in the subject's life
Justice (Tarot) major arcana card indicating balance
Kaballah Ancient Jewish mystical tradition based on magic of letters and numbers derived from Old Testament, sometimes linked to alchemy
Key word Used in astrology and

other disciplines to summarize a psychological characteristic (e.g. harmoniously)
Life Line One of the three principal lines used in palmistry, relating to health, vitality and illness
Lover, The (Tarot) major arcana card indicating love, harmony or choices
Lower Zone One of the three zones used in graphology
Magician, The (Tarot) major arcana card indicating skill, adaptability
Major Arcana (Tarot) Deck of 22 picture cards
Metoposcopy Divination and study of character from foreheads
Middle Zone One of the three zones used in graphology
Minor Arcana (Tarot) Deck of 56 number and court cards
Moleoscopy Divination or character-reading by moles on the body
Negative influence In astrology, the influence of a planet or aspect that accentuates negative, decreases positive, effects, but can add inner strength
Oneiromancy Divination by dreams
Opposition Astrological aspect accentuating polarities in a birth chart
Palm prints Prints made from the palms for palmistry purposes
Pentacles One of the four suits of the Tarot
Phalanges The bands, 3 on the fingers, 2 on the thumbs, used in palmistry
Physical cycle The 23-day physical cycle in biorhythms governing the body
PK (psychokinesis) Moving or affecting a physically distant object solely by mental power
Pope, The (Tarot) major arcana card indicating enlightenment
Psephomancy Divination by casting pebbles
Psychic One of the four shapes of finger or hand recognized in palmistry
Pyromancy Divination by fire
Quadruplicities Sometimes called the *qualities,* these are three groupings of the Zodiac signs, which are defined as either *cardinal* (outgoing), *fixed* (resisting change) or *mutable* (changeable)
Quincunx An aspect in astrology, unpredictable and difficult to interpret
Retrograde motion The apparent reverse motion (seen from earth) of a planet
Scrying Divining through a

crystal
Semi-sextile A minor *aspect* in astrology, suggesting tension
Semi-square A rather weak astrological *aspect* indicating tension
Sesquare An astrological aspect indicating strain
Sextile An aspect in astrology. Under this influence, two planets work harmoniously for the individual
Sidereal Time The actual time of the earth's rotation on its axis – 23 hours 56 minutes 4.09 seconds – not the conventional 24 hours
Sortilege Divination by casting lots
Spatulate One of the four shapes of hand or finger recognized in palmistry
Square 1. A negative astrological *aspect* which can give drive and strength to a character
2. One of the four shapes of hand or finger in palmistry
Taoism The ancient, often mystical, philosophy of China whose concepts of Yin and Yang, harmony, and man's place in the universe underly much of the *I Ching*
Tasseography Divination by tea leaves or coffee grounds
Temperance (Tarot) One of the major arcana cards indicating moderation
Thread One of the four types of connection noted in graphology, showing intelligence, versatility, deceitfulness
Tower, The (Tarot) major arcana card indicating risk, breakthrough
Transit The present movement of a planet in the sky which brings it into relationship with another planet as placed in the birth chart
Trigram Three-line character forming part of the *I Ching's hexagram*
Trine A positive aspect that helps strong characters but may weaken shallow people
Triple Critical Days upon which all three biorhythm traces pass at once from negative to positive, or the reverse
Triplicity See *element*
Upper Zone One of the three zones noted in graphology
Wands One of the four suits of the Tarot cards
Yarrow Stalks Stalks used traditionally in consulting the *I Ching*
Zodiac The imaginary belt of sky which contains the 12 zodiacal constellations and within which the Moon and planets appear to move

Bibliography

GENERAL READING
Beloff, John, *New Directions in Parapsychology* (London 1974)
Carington, W., *Telepathy* (London 1954)
Christopher, M., *Seers, Psychics and ESP* (London 1971)
Davies, Rodney, *The ESP Workbook* (Wellingborough 1988)
Dodds, E.R., *The Greeks and the Irrational* (London 1951)
Douglas, Alfred, *Extra Sensory Powers* (London 1976)
Farnell, L.R., *Cults of the Greek States* (London 1937)
Feller, W., *An Introduction to Probability Theory and its Application* (New York 1968)
Fenton, Sasha, *The Aquarian Book of Fortune-Telling* (Wellingborough 1988)
Fortune, Dion, *The Mystical Qabbala* (Wellingborough 1987)
Graves, Tom, *The Diviner's Handbook* (Wellingborough 1987)
Greenhouse, Herbert B., *Premonitions – a Leap into the Future* (London 1972)
Heywood, Rosalind, *The Sixth Sense* (London 1966)
Holroyd, Stuart, *PSI and the Consciousness Explosion* (Middlesex, England 1957)
Journal of Parapsychology (London 1936 ff)
Journal of the Society for Psychical Research (London)
Jung, C.G., *Synchronicity: An Acausal Connecting Principle* (London 1955)
Le Shan, Lawrence, *The Science of the Paranormal* (Wellingborough 1987)
Lethbridge, T.C., *ESP: Beyond Time and Distance* (London 1967)
Mathers, S.L., *The Kaballah Revealed* (London 1951)
Moss, Thelma, *The Probability of the Impossible* (New York 1974)
Ostrander, Sheila and Schroeder, Lynn, *PSI: Psychic Discoveries Behind the Iron Curtain* (London 1973)
Perry, Michael, *Psychic Studies: A Christian's View* (Wellingborough 1987)
Playfair, Guy Lyon, *The Indefinite Boundary* (London 1976)
Pollack, Rachel, *A Practical Guide to Fortune-Telling* (London 1986)
Randall, John L., *Parapsychology and the Nature of Life* (London 1975)
Rhine, J.B., *Extrasensory Perception* (Boston 1934)
Smith, Susy, *The Enigma of Out-of-Body Travel* (New York 1965)
Temple, Robert K.G., *Conversation with Eternity* (London 1984)
Thorndyke, Lynn, *The History of Magic and Experimental Science* (London 1941)
Van Dusen, Wilson, *The Presence of Other Worlds* (New York 1974)
Vaughan, Alan, *Patterns of Prophesy* (London 1974)

ASTROLOGY
Capp, Bernard, *Astrology and the Popular Press* (London 1979)
Crummere, Maria Elise, *Sun Sign Revelations* (New York 1974)
Eysenck, H.J. and Nias, D.B.K., *Astrology: Science or Superstition* (London 1982)
Garin, E., *Astrology in the Renaissance* (London 1983)
Gauquelin, M., *The Cosmic Clocks: From Astrology to Modern Science* (London 1969)
Cosmic Influences on Human Behaviour (London 1976)
Lilly, W., *Christian Astrology* (facsimile) (London 1985)
Lindsay, Jack, *The Origins of Astrology* (London 1971)
Parker, Derek and Julia, *Life Signs* (London 1986)
The New Compleat Astrologer (London 1985)
The Zodiac Family (Wellingborough 1988)
Parker, Julia, *The Astrologer's Handbook* (London 1985)
Thomas, Keith, *Religion and the Decline of Magic* (London 1971)
Thorndike, Lynn, *The History of Magic and Experimental Science* (New York 1983)

BIORHYTHMS
Gittelson, Bernard, *Biorhythms* (London 1978)
West, Peter, *Biorhythms: Your Daily Guide to Achieving Peak Potential* (Wellingborough 1986)

CARDS
Dee, Nerys, *Fortune-telling by Playing Cards* (London 1972)
Thorpe, C., *Card Fortune-Telling* (London 1972)

CRYSTALS
Markham, Ursula, *Fortune-Telling by Crystals* (Wellingborough 1986)
The Crystal Workbook (Wellingborough 1987)
Melville, John, *Crystal-Gazing and Clairvoyance* (Wellingborough 1987)

DICE
Line, David and Julia, *Fortune-Telling by Dice* (Wellingborough 1988)

DREAMS
Brook, Stephen, *Oxford Book of Dreams* (Oxford 1983)
Coxhead, David and Susan Hiller, *Dreams: Visions of the Night* (London 1976)
Faraday, Ann, *Dream Power* (London 1974)
Jung, C.G., *Memories, Dreams, Reflections* (London 1963)
Murray, E., *Sleep, Dreams and Arousal* (New York 1965)
Parker, Derek and Julia, *Dreaming* (London 1985)

GRAPHOLOGY
Holder, Robert, *You Can Analyse Handwriting* (New York 1958)
Marcuse, Irene, *Guide to Personality through your Handwriting* (New York 1974)
Marley, John, *Graphology* (London 1967)

I CHING
Blofeld, John, *The Book of Change* (New York 1966)
Douglas, Alfred, *The Oracle of Change: How to Consult the I Ching* (London 1971)
Needham, Joseph, *Science and Civilization in China* Vol II (Cambridge 1956)
Wilhelm, Richard (trans), *The I Ching* (London 1951)

PALMISTRY
Altman, Nathaniel, *Palmistry Workbook* (Wellingborough 1988)
Cheiro, *Book of Fate and Fortune* (London 1985)
Language of the Hand (London 1968)
Hutchinson, Beryl, *Your Life in Your Hands* (London 1977)
Luxon, Bettina and Goolden, Jill, *Your Hand: Simple Palmistry for Everyone* (London 1983)
Reid, Lori, *The Female Hand* (Wellingborough 1986)
How to Read Hands (Wellingborough 1986)

PHRENOLOGY AND PHYSIOGNOMY
Lavater, J.K., *Essays on Physiognomy* (4 vols) (London 1804)
Paterson, D.G., *Physique and Intellect* (New York 1930)
Pearson, K., *Relationship of Intelligence to Size and Shape of Head* (London 1906)

RUNES
Blum, Ralph, *Book of Runes* (London 1985)
Cooper, D. Jason, *Using the Runes* (London 1987)
Howard, Michael A., *The Magic of the Runes* (Wellingborough 1980)
Willis, Tony, *Understanding and Using the Power of the Runes* (Wellingborough 1986)

TAROT
Doane, Doris Chase and Keyes, King, *How to Read Tarot Cards* (New York 1984)
Gray, Eden, *The Tarot Revealed* (New York 1960)
Kaplan, Stuart R., *Tarot Classic* (New York 1972)
Lind, Frank, *How to Understand the Tarot* (Wellingborough 1986)
Papus, *The Tarot of the Bohemians* (London 1975)
Pollack, Rachel, *Arcana and Readings* (Wellingborough 1980)
The Open Labyrinth (Wellingborough 1986)
Pushong, C.A., *The Tarot of the Magi* (London 1970)
Walker, Barbara G., *Secrets of the Tarot: Origins, History and Symbolism* (New York 1985)

TEA LEAVES
Fenton, Sasha *Fortune-Telling by Tea Leaves* (Wellingborough 1988)

Index

Acknowledgments

PICTURE CREDITS
p. 7: Michael Holford;
9: Gene Cox;
12: Werner Forman Archive;
13T: E. T. Archive;
13B: Mary Evans Picture Library;
14: BBC Hulton Picture Library;
15: Robert Harding Picture
Library;
16L: BBC Hulton Picture Library;
16R: Sonia Halliday Photographs;
17: E. T. Archive;
20/21: Jean-Loup Charmet;
22L: E. T. Archive;
22R: Michael Holford;
23: BBC Hulton Picture Library;
24: Bridgeman Art Library;
25: Pat Hodgson Library;
26: Werner Forman Archive;
27L: Mansell Collection;
27R: E. T. Archive;
28: Mansell Collection
29L/R: E. T. Archive;
30T/B: Jean-Loup Charmet;
31L/R: Michael Holford;
32: Mansell Collection;
33: Jean-Loup Charmet;
34: BBC Hulton Picture Library;
35: Jean-Loup Charmet;
36: E. T. Archive;
37: Imperial War Museum;
38: Bettmann Archive/BBC Hulton
Picture Library;
39: Jean-Loup Charmet;
42T: Mary Evans Picture Library;
42B: Robert Harding Picture
Library;
43TL: Society for Psychical
Research/Mary Evans Picture
Library;
43TR: Robert Harding Picture
Library;
43B: Werner Forman Archive;
44T: Jean-Loup Charmet;
44B: Camera Press;
94/5: Robert Harding Picture
Library;
96-101: Bodleian Library, Oxford;
110: Bibliothèque Nationale, Paris;
118/9: Lowell Observatory;
173T: Pat Hodgson Library;
189T/B: Science Photo Library.

Frances Broomfield painted the
full-colour illustrations appearing
on the following pages: 2, 10, 18,
40, 46, 72, 88, 92, 128, 132, 170
(and cover), 176, 182, 186, 190,
198, 202, 206.

Other illustrations provided by:
Samantha Lawrence 187, 188,
210-11
Iona Mackenzie 178-181, 201, 204
Julia Parker 106
Graham Patten 89-91, 175, 184-5,
213, 215T
Patten and Stroud 74-79, 81-84,
90-91, 208, 209, 214B, 216
Jonathan Weiss 64, 66, 68, 168,
192, 197, 215B
Christine Thery 135-167, 169
Mark Bullen 85, 102-108, 110,
111-118

The Tarot cards on pages 9, 45,
48/9, 50-63, 65-67, 69, 70, 71 and
205 were reproduced with kind
permission of France Cartes-
Grimaud.